THE IMPOSSIBLE DREAM

Barry J Whyte is an award-winning journalist and author. He is currently Chief Feature Writer for the *Business Post*.

THE IMPOSSIBLE DREAM

THE SPECTACULAR RISE AND FALL OF STEORN, THE CELTIC TIGER'S MOST AUDACIOUS START-UP

BARRY J WHYTE

Gill Books

Gill Books
Hume Avenue
Park West
Dublin 12
www.gillbooks.ie

Gill Books is an imprint of M.H. Gill and Co.

978 07171 88048

Edited by Ruairí Ó Brógáin
Proofread by Kristin Jensen
Printed by CPI Group (UK) Ltd, Croydon, CR0 4YY

The paper used in this book comes from the wood pulp of managed forests. For every tree felled, at least one tree is planted, thereby renewing natural resources.

A CIP catalogue record for this book is available from the British Library.

5 4 3 2 1

For Gillian, Grace and Conor, with love.

The history of perpetual motion is a history of the fool-hardiness of either half-learned, or totally ignorant persons.
– Henry Dircks, Perpetuum Mobile: Or, A History of the Search for Self-Motive *(1861)*

Let's be straight about this: I accept there were failures in the political system; I accept that I have to take responsibility as a member of the governing party during that period for what happened. But let's be fair about it: we all partied.
– Brian Lenihan, Jr, Minister for Finance, on RTÉ Television, 24 November 2010

ACKNOWLEDGEMENTS

First, a note on sources and references. This book was based on hours of interviews with dozens of people involved in Steorn and people who had observed or studied it, as well as thousands of documents, whether statutory filings with the Companies Registration Office or internal company documents. Where possible, I have named the source of the information within the text of the book, whether it is a person I've interviewed, a document I've read, or a contemporary media report. In some instances, it has not been possible to explicitly name a person by virtue of their having asked for anonymity. In those instances, I've endeavoured to give enough information to establish their credentials without breaching their confidentiality. Some crucial people – for example, Pat Corbett and Mazhar Bari – declined to be interviewed or simply couldn't be reached. In those cases, I have noted this in the text.

Similarly, over the course of more than five years of reporting on Steorn, I have personally contacted – by email or phone – more than two hundred people who invested in Steorn or were associated with the company. A great many of them either declined to respond to my emails or replied and apologised, briefly giving their reasons for not wanting to talk about it. For the most part, they were feeling hurt or embarrassment and sincerely wanted to move on. I understand this, and I am sorry for having revived an unpleasant memory.

All of which means I am even more grateful to the people who did agree to speak, many of whom gave enormous chunks of their time and effort to tell me their stories, how they came to be involved in Steorn, and more.

Primarily, I am grateful to Shaun McCarthy. More than most, he was held up as the embodiment of Steorn, and it's not excessive to say that he was defamed repeatedly and vividly over those years as a scam artist or a crook when he was neither. He spent years of his life in the company before it went into liquidation and lost plenty of his own money, but perhaps his biggest loss was his reputation. Speaking to me as openly as he did was not in his interests, but I'm thankful that he did.

I also had several interviews with Mike Daly, McCarthy's co-founder. He too was open and obliging, helping to fill in parts of the story that McCarthy had forgotten or was not there for (such as the final months of HephaHeat). As with McCarthy, he had no reason to speak to me and every reason not to: I'm very appreciative that he agreed to talk.

Among the investors who did choose to speak, I want to thank James Murphy, Edward Sheehan, Folke Rohrssen, Robert Seale and Alan Wallace. Wallace, in particular, was diligent and careful in keeping so many notes and documents related to the company. All of these men shared their perspectives openly and unguardedly, and a journalist cannot ask for more than that.

Also, thanks to Tom Byrne, who certainly didn't need me bothering him repeatedly.

On the jury, Ian MacDonald was invaluable for his insights into the work of the jury and the thinking behind its eventual decision. He was also instrumental in putting me in touch with his fellow jury member Guido Stockhausen, who himself had put in hundreds of hours of research into and analysis of the company's 'finding' and was very gracious in sharing his conclusions and – more than that – explaining them in terms that a non-scientist could understand. In relation to the science of the matter, Michael Coey, Plamen Stamenov, and Phil Watson provided very important insights. If I've mistranslated, the error is mine rather than theirs.

Special thanks to my agent, Faith O'Grady, who took a chance on the book when I had almost given up on it.

I am indebted to the team at Gill Books – commissioning editor Conor Nagle for his enthusiasm, my editor Aoibheann Molumby, who put up with my many wobbles and my inability to use Track Changes, and Teresa Daly and Avril Cannon. Thanks also to copy-editor Ruairí Ó Brógáin, proofreader Kristin Jensen and lawyer Kieran Kelly.

I would like to also thank Richie Oakley and Susan Mitchell at the Business Post, who agreed to let me have a month off to write the first draft of the book.

But most of all I'd like to thank my family: my wife Gillian and my children Gracie and Conor. Their love and support were utterly vital during the latter half of 2019 and the early portion of 2020 – the months leading up to publication when most writers indulge in a kind of temporary, ego-driven madness. Their patience was the key element in this book getting this far. I once read that Stephen King described his wife, Tabitha, as his Ideal Reader (the capitalisations are his) and how he would sit, impatiently, watching her read first drafts, desperately trying to read her facial expressions and judge where she was in the book. Under such pressure, she would chide him for being so needy. I didn't understand at the time what he meant. But in the last decade, Gillian has become my Ideal Reader and nothing I write – nothing of any substance anyway – leaves my desk without her imprimatur. And, like Tabitha King, she has better things to do with her time than placate my insecurities. Finally, I am eagerly looking forward to Gracie and Conor being able to read the book themselves, so they can finally see what all the fuss was about.

CONTENTS

1. INTRODUCING SHAUN McCARTHY

Shaun McCarthy in His Own Words

Steorn was the kind of thing that, if you're in any way interested in technology, and if you've seen the shit I've seen – and I know that sounds kind of like, 'Hey, I've seen aliens, dude' – you know that the technology was really important. And that's not something we're ever going to walk away from.

I put a quarter of a million of my own money into it, which is small beer compared with the rest of the investors, but then I didn't have millions to spend.

That's the nature of being a founder or proponent of these things. Nobody would've won as much as me if I'd pulled it off – and I still think one day I'll pull it off – but that's the nature of capitalism, ultimately.

We risked more. I know that the people who wrote very large cheques don't see it that way, but we did risk more than just money. That became very apparent. Just use Google. That's just the nature of trying to be aggressive with a start-up business. When it all works out, you're a legend; when it doesn't, you're a scumbag.

We love a failure, Barry, you know that.

Maybe if we hadn't gone out and raised so much money and put ourselves in this position … I mean, I'm not trying to avoid responsibility, but we put ourselves in a situation which resulted in where it resulted, whereas, in hindsight, the project should've been done a completely different way.

I have to measure it by a different yardstick now in hindsight. What we're doing now with the technology is so completely different in its approach.

If you don't learn the lessons of your life, the lessons aren't lessons.

———————

In November 2016, I sat down in a noisy coffee shop near Trinity College, Dublin, with Shaun McCarthy. McCarthy is an eminently likeable character. Roguish, rumpled, wearing a permanent uniform of T-shirt and jeans, and almost perpetually wreathed in cigarette smoke, he revels in an anti-establishment outlook and never resists an opportunity to deprecate himself, an apparent effort to puncture any sense that his ambition might be mistaken for pomposity.

Yet that morning he was despondent. His shoulders were slumped and his face, usually impish and smiling, was slack and looked exhausted. His usual stream-of-consciousness style of near monologue had slowed to a crawl and he preceded a great many of his answers with short, rueful sighs. He had some justification: his life's work – the creation of what he claimed was perpetual energy – had come to a juddering halt. His company, Steorn, originally founded as a consultancy firm and named for an old Irish word meaning 'to guide or to manage prudently', was being liquidated. Its failure was not just the loss of more than a decade's work by him, and the loss of €23 million invested by his shareholders, but also the loss of his reputation.

He knew that he had confirmed the prejudices of thousands of sceptics and cynics who had declared his company a fraud.

'If I was looking at this from the outside, I'm either an idiot or a scam artist. There's no middle ground. The laws are immutable,' he told me that day. 'And after 15 years, the possibility for a scam is reduced to near zero, which means you're just wrong, which means you must be an idiot.'

He was playing online poker to pay the bills, he told me, aware that a decade spent as chief executive of Steorn did not look great on his CV. 'I wouldn't get a job as a taxi driver in this town. I knew from the moment I said "I think we should make this public" that this was – in poker terminology – an all-in play. I don't get to pull my chips back now.'

But of more concern to McCarthy than his reputation was his awareness that plenty of his investors were angry about the outcome. 'We took their money. We raised their expectations, and it fell flat on its fucking face. They've a right to be angry about that.'

To understand why, you have to remember that, a decade before, Ireland had been at the apex of a period of collective madness. It was rich, and it wasn't handling it particularly well. In its defence, it had never been rich before – it was used to being the poorest of the rich countries, with no industry of its own and no financial centre, just fields, and its biggest export had always been its young men and women – but that summer it had reached the peak of a bizarre time known as the Celtic Tiger, during which time it often seemed like Ireland was drunk on money.

Over the course of the preceding decade, Irish people had come to possess that most heady of combinations: confidence and cash. It was an incredible, unprecedented, unrepeatable time, and it wrought an abiding change in the country, its people and its habits. Instead of emigrating to New York to work in bars, as they had always done, Irish people were flying there for the weekend to do their Christmas shopping. Instead of bringing ham sandwiches wrapped in tinfoil to watch two local Gaelic football teams slog it out in some winter league match, they were flying to Rome in the spring to watch Ireland's rugby team beat the much weaker Italian team, boasting 'Veni, vidi, VISA' as they did so. It was a motto for a spendthrift age. Prudence and caution were gone, relics of a bygone era. The old rules no longer applied.

The summer of 2006 was also when Ireland learned about Steorn and Shaun McCarthy. The company took an advertisement in the *Economist* to announce that it had discovered a machine that could create energy from nothing. Imagine never having to recharge your phone, it asked. Imagine never having to refuel your car. It channelled George Bernard Shaw: all great truths begin as blasphemies.

The advertisement was bold and brash, and it irritated a great many people in that new and confident Ireland. After all, we were rich now, no longer peasants, no longer to be looked down on. Why were these characters trying to embarrass us on the world stage?

For others, it wasn't embarrassing: it was exhilarating. Oil prices were surging. A house in Longford, Cork or Mayo was worth as much as a house in London or New York. And prices were still rising, never to fall again. Why couldn't it be true that the old rules no longer applied? Maybe this Steorn thing wasn't just blasphemy. Maybe.

On such fertile ground, Steorn was born. If the price of a house could go up forever, why was it impossible that someone could create energy from nothing? It was a feverish and intoxicating time and, as we know now, utterly wrongheaded. More than that, it was out of character. After centuries of near poverty, Irish people had, within a few years, shed their caution and frugality and apparently decided that our wealth would simply continue to create itself. From where? It didn't matter, just so long as we continued to spend and invest.

More than four hundred people did precisely that in Steorn, and they weren't just the gullible and unsophisticated investors one might expect would invest in a company promoting perpetual energy. Steorn's share register was a veritable who's who of high society during the Celtic Tiger years. There were high-profile figures from virtually all of Dublin's best-known brokerages and financial institutions. There were barristers, solicitors and bankers as well as small- and medium-sized business owners from every part of Ireland. There were doctors and consultants, academics and accountants, pensions advisors and business consultants. You may conclude that an investment in Steorn was stupid, but its investors were not.

Take Michael, a house-builder. That isn't his real name; he doesn't want people to know that he was an investor in Steorn. He agreed to speak, off the record, only because he wanted people to know *why* he invested.

> I put it down to greed now. It was a form of gambling. It was the culture of the time: the Celtic Tiger. I was in construction. I still am. It was flying. There was money everywhere. I had sold about 40 houses at the time and made a substantial profit, so €50,000 was very small change for me.
>
> It was money you could afford to lose. It was something that didn't affect your mortgage payments or where you shopped or where you went on your holidays. It was just surplus cash. It was something you could take a gamble on. Truthfully, €50,000 was probably what €500 is now. That's the extent the country was awash with money.

Michael invested with four friends, each putting in €50,000. On a chance of an everlasting battery, a promise of free energy, a dream of perpetual motion, they put in a quarter of a million euro. No big deal. They didn't even bother to get receipts.

The guys I hang around with are incredibly successful motor dealers. They have numerous garages; they're savvy people. I was out with them one night, and one of the lads said there's an exciting opportunity coming up. They showed me a video of a pump out in a desert running [which had been purportedly built by Steorn] and it was three or four years in production. It didn't need electricity and it didn't need to be recharged. This is what pulled us in. They were my peers and I trusted their opinion.

I think peak oil was close to happening and this was the new alternative to oil, we were told.

Michael and his friends attended meetings of shareholders in regional towns around the country. The average age at one of the meetings was 70 – a lot of bachelor farmers with money in the mattress. Still had their Communion money, as the old joke goes. Suddenly, though, they were spending. That's how it was during the Celtic Tiger: even the thriftiest were being convinced to spend. Greed, Michael said. 'We all wanted to make a quick buck.'

Michael visited the Steorn lab – lots of people in white coats milling around, looking busy. Today, he thinks it may have been a show put on to impress investors. Students, perhaps, drafted in for the day.

I realised the money wasn't coming back when he [McCarthy] came look-ing for more. And we realised the shares had been diluted and the level of shareholding we had.

For the next two or three years, they'd come back and try to get another €50,000 here or €100,000 there, and I suppose some people gave it to them. It was always just about to happen, three weeks away or six weeks away; he always had a story attached. He always said it was going to come back tenfold, twentyfold – phenomenal figures. At one stage, he said the company was go-ing to be worth €5 billion. But I think it was just for their wages at times. How foolish we were. There is no such thing as endless energy. ... I've no bitterness about making bad business decisions, but what happened after that was disgraceful.

Michael is angry with himself for the lost money, but he was angry with McCarthy too. McCarthy, the most prominent face of Steorn, seemed to be the embodiment of the Celtic Tiger economy: brash, confident, maybe a little boorish. Money with an Irish accent in a T-shirt and jeans and driving an expensive car. He was an engineer but could have been a builder; just like Michael, he had money where he hadn't had any before.

As soon as he took that ad in the *Economist*, McCarthy was pegged as a scam artist, a fraud, a conman. How else could he have raised so much money? But he wasn't the man people thought he was. He wasn't a conman or a chancer or a wide boy: he was a zealot and a true believer, and maybe that's worse.

Steorn is a parable of the country that got rich and didn't know what to do with its money.

To understand Celtic Tiger Ireland, you need to understand Steorn; and to understand Steorn, you need to understand Shaun McCarthy.

Shaun McCarthy: From Birmingham to Baku

I grew up in Birmingham in the United Kingdom, and we moved to Ireland in the 1970s because of that whole Birmingham pub bombing carry-on by the IRA. We had an Irish name in an English town, and I can remember coming home [one day] and there was red paint on the front of the house. So my parents – my mother's English and my father's a Paddy – decided to come here.

I wasn't living in hardcore Birmingham or anything – it was a leafy suburb – and then my parents ended up buying a house out in Meath and I hated every single fucking moment. I ended up hating the Irish for a long time. Again, you talk of the context of the time – the Troubles – and I would've considered myself English. Then you move out to shithole Dunshaughlin, Meath, and it's not the leafy suburbs of Shakespeare country.

I battered my way through school – or was I battered through? – because I was the only English kid in the village. To be honest, I probably wouldn't have helped myself. I'd be fairly libertarian. I only own one poster: Sid Vicious.

I ended up going to college in Bolton Street in Dublin, doing engineering for two years, then production engineering. I graduated in 1988, then I fell off the roof of a pub and smashed my back up and I was in hospital for a while. I was the only kid out of my college that year who hadn't gotten a job. As usual,

80 per cent of them were jobs in the States, the UK or Germany. The college must've felt some sympathy for me, so they set me up with an interview with a company called Combustion Engineering in Dundalk, which, considering my political leanings at the time – in 1988 – was a bit … y'know …

So, anyway, I went up, did an interview and they were looking for people to write software for automating paper machines. I loved that. I was mad into software. Took a job doing that in '88. A year later, we were bought out by a company called ABB, which was a massive Swiss–Swedish–German conglomerate, and I stayed with them all over the world doing different jobs through to 1999.

In '99 I was managing the Colombian market – which sounds a bit shady – but the context was that I had got a position managing the sales of their tech into the Middle East based out of Bahrain in '94, something like that. We did really well there. A Swedish–Swiss–German company is not particularly good at entering these kind of markets: they're very American-dominated, in particular after the first Gulf War. So, the Americans and Brits were getting money thrown at them, and this poor Swedish–Swiss company, which would've been comparable in size to GE, was sitting there saying, 'Where's our cut?'

I was really successful there after three years – grew it from $927,000 turnover to just over $2 billion, so they obviously thought I knew something. (I'm not sure I did.)

That's where Colombia came in. At the time, Colombia Ecopetrol, the state oil company, was opening up to allow the bigger oil companies to move in. I got involved. I was based in Houston, Texas, but the business was in Colombia, and again we did really well there. I loved it.

Then the Caspian Sea was opening. So, it was a 'Go east, young man!' sort of thing in terms of markets to be cracked out in Azerbaijan and those kinds of places. So, I said to my then missus – after our first kid was born in Bahrain and our second kid in Texas – I said, 'Look, let's go to Baku, because that's where the action is.' She said, 'You can go to Baku. I'm going to Dublin.'

2. NOUVEAU RICHE

The Ireland to which Shaun McCarthy brought his children in 2000 was very different from the one to which he had arrived in the 1970s. The biggest difference was not hard to discern: money.

In 1980, when McCarthy was 13, Charles Haughey, today one of Ireland's most notorious Taoiseachs, gave a television address, providing a downbeat assessment of the country's finances. Fixing the audience – and, by extension, the country, since there was only one Irish television channel – with the kind of grave look a doctor would give a dying alcoholic, Haughey, with a long, sharp nose that gave his face a fierce, lupine quality, enhanced by a pair of calculating eyes and a fading mane of hair swept back and away from his high forehead, told the country that it was broke. In his trademark nasal Dublin accent, he addressed his audience.

> I wish to talk to you this evening about the state of the nation's affairs, and the picture I have to paint is not, unfortunately, a very cheerful one. The figures which are just now becoming available to us show one thing very clearly: as a community, we are living a way beyond our means. I don't mean that everyone in the community is living too well: clearly many are not and have barely enough to get by. But, taking us all together, we have been living at a rate which is simply not justified by the amount of goods and services we are producing. To make up the difference, we have been borrowing enormous amounts of money – borrowing at a rate which just cannot continue.

To convey the scale of the problem, Haughey presented some figures.

> At home, the government's current income from taxes and all other sources in 1979 fell short of what was needed to pay the running costs of the state by about £520 million. To meet this and our capital programme, we had to borrow in 1979 over £1,000 million. That amount is equal to one-seventh of our entire national output.

The remedy was cuts in spending, Haughey said, and a plan to 'reorganise government spending so that we can only undertake the things which we can afford'. Many things would 'just have to be curtailed or postponed, until such time as we can get the financial situation right'.

Then there were the strikes, go-slows, work-to-rules and stoppages in key industries and essential services, Haughey said, which 'caused suffering and hardship; at times it looked as if we were becoming one of those countries where basic services could not be relied upon to operate as part of normal life'.

Twenty years later, in 2000, when McCarthy brought his family to Ireland, people were living far more like Haughey – whose personal finances were conspicuously spendthrift, vulgar and almost entirely based on unsustainable debt – than like their parents and grandparents, who had watched Haughey give that address.

With hindsight, it is easy to understand how the accelerator could have been pressed down so swiftly. The parsimony and financial caution of previous generations had been imposed rather than innate; the difference between making a penny stretch when you're naturally thrifty and making one stretch because you have only one penny only becomes clear when you get several pennies at once. You might not be inclined to stretch. What the Celtic Tiger illustrated dramatically was that Irish people hadn't learned good financial habits: they had simply learned to hate being poor.

When money began to trickle into the economy and into household budgets, and when that trickle became a torrent, the money flowed out as quickly as it had come in. Why not? After all, the old days were gone, never to return.

The sense that we were in a new era of wealth and prosperity was reflected not just in bank balances and house valuations, but in even more fundamental changes to the global economy. The railways made Britain powerful; the car made America an empire; and the internet was making Ireland rich. The reign of the mobile phone began so recently that it's easy to forget that there was a time when we didn't have this slim, wallet-sized device that contains the sum of human knowledge available at the swipe of a finger, along with the entire works of William Shakespeare and Charles Dickens, the music of the Beatles and Bach, with room for thousands of family photos and our entire financial history, along with the ability to call a sister in Australia to tell her that the blackberries are in season.

In the new world of technology, the country's population felt a million years separated from its forebears and their gruelling, impoverished lives. Things had changed, and they'd never change back. And now Shaun McCarthy was home.

Shaun McCarthy: Consultant to Tech Developer

How I ended up back in Dublin was that there was a guy called Graham O'Donnell – you may remember Graham: he was one of these dotcom billionaires and he owned a company called Microsol, which did substation control systems controlling electrical utilities. They had a lot of stuff out in the Middle East, which is where I met him.

One hungover Sunday morning, sitting at my kitchen table, he said, 'Well, why don't you come back to Dublin? I've got this dotcom thing going, and you can get involved with us.'

I said, 'I'll do it for a year.'

I set up Steorn without a plan … Myself and a couple of the lads from Microsol set it up [in 2000] and then decided to figure out what to do later. Basically, what we were trying to sell was the project-management skills the lads had.

There was always a risk. I was damn well-paid for what I did over the years. Used to be that when I got on a plane, I didn't realise how long the plane was because there was always a curtain there behind me. I know that's fucking terrible, but that's the way it was.

It was fascinating setting up a company. I only realised just how fascinating the day I walked into the office for the first time and had to open the front door for myself. In the 12 years I was out in the world, I had never had to unlock the front door of the office myself. Then you begin to hire people, so there's that responsibility.

The first thing we got was the World of Fruit banana-trading project from Fyffes. It was just a gold rush: if you weren't doing web, you didn't exist. So, a banana import–export business needs to invest millions in e-commerce. They probably did need to invest, but it was driven, in my opinion, by all of these companies driving their share price up by doing something on the web rather than by any real business cases.

There was a capital appreciation involved. If you look at the day that World of Fruit was announced, there were hundreds of millions added to their share value for committing to spend the money. That's not a criticism of them; that's just the way it was: everyone had to play the game. Everyone was doing it, and if you didn't do it you were getting a beating in the market.

I don't want to pick on Fyffes; if you look back now, it seems kind of funny to be trading bananas online, but it's a big fucking business.

I didn't know the McCanns that well. I met the old boy, Neily [Neil McCann, former Fyffes chairman and chief executive], one time in the old building and he fascinated me because he literally had this office with a phone, a desk – right beside the canteen where he used to make himself toast and tea – and no chair. … I thought he was an incredible fella. You could see how, with that mentality, he had grown that business and how some of the legend had built up around him because, basically, here's a guy from the border counties importing bananas. I loved it. I had huge respect for him.

We got involved because, from their side, they had lots of contractors, but they had no real technical project-management experience to be able to pull this all together and try to get some value for money.

Then we did stuff for Bank of Ireland. They set up this entity called BOI-E out in Sandyford and they hired a building, and it was all e-commercey, and that kind of slipped away.

We weren't setting the financial pages on fire, but we were doing okay. Then there was the dotcom crash. I don't care what anyone says: it was 9/11. That was just an opportunity for anyone to say, 'If you've got a shit internet project, drop it now.'

So, we wound up after a year sitting there going, 'There's no fucking market,' because people had realised that they didn't all need to be involved in web and the tech had matured to such an extent that you didn't need to throw hundreds of millions at building websites.

Then we met a start-up company who was doing anti-fraud tech. We said we can kind of pull that off technically; we have the skills – or at least we've access to the skills. The company was called Fraudhalt, and they'd this idea that credit card fraud is big, and on this credit card there's this hologram, which is very difficult to counterfeit. If you can determine whether the hologram is counterfeit, you can determine whether the card is real. So, it's a very simple idea from a technical point of view, and it's really cool, because there's optics and vision-recognition technology and software electronics. So, we went, 'Yeah, we'll do that.'

It was during that period we also started to do kind of opportunistic stuff, because there was no plan. The plan was, 'Let's have a job.'

We weren't making a killing in any way. We were struggling along, but we were loving what we were doing. That was the funny thing. At a time when most people's salaries were going through the roof, we were probably earning half of what we would've done in our old lives. But we were loving it.

3. THE FIRST ROUND

S haun McCarthy may not have been making the kind of money that put him in business-class airline seats, but there was certainly plenty of money around and some of it was beginning to flow towards him and Steorn.

Within a year of having founded the company – and with his reputation in Dublin growing – McCarthy took a call from someone in the accountancy firm BDO. They had run a €7 million business-expansion fund, which raises a pot of money for investment in domestic companies, usually with some form of structured tax break for the investor. It was being run in conjunction with Davy stockbrokers, the biggest brokerage in the country. The fund had €61,000 left over and had to give it all away – part of the terms of the fundraising – so McCarthy was asked if he would take it. He did, but he would later reflect on whether he had actually spent more in fees trying to complete the transaction.

Then he got an even better call, from the head of corporate finance at Davy, Tom Byrne. For the previous 13 years, Byrne had held one of the highest-profile positions in Ireland, at the biggest brokerage in the country. Between 1987 and 2001 he was in effect one of the most important and influential people in Irish corporate finance circles, bringing companies to market, helping them raise finance and advising them on floating their shares on the stock exchange.

Byrne had worked with companies like Xtra-vision – the chain of video-rental shops that was huge in the 1980s and '90s – and had been watching closely as the economy had changed in that period, driven largely by the sale of increasingly expensive tracts of land as well as by billions in debt taken on by borrowers against the value of that newly valuable land.

What Byrne could see most acutely, though, was that the newly wealthy investor was not particularly sophisticated. During the 1990s, Byrne's colleagues in Davy would often have to take aside some new customer, just in off the street and with a big lump sum of newly acquired money, and talk them through the basics of investing, tempering their expectations and instilling in them a sense of prudence.

Byrne was also watching his own wealth grow in the same period and was making personal investments. One of these investments was in Steorn, which appeared on his radar when his friend Francis Hackett – a director at Steorn and McCarthy's brother-in-law – told him about the company.

It seemed a reasonable bet to Byrne. The dotcom bubble was rapidly deflating and most investors were wary of direct internet investments. For Byrne, Steorn seemed to be a good compromise: it was positively exposed to dotcom and would benefit from any rise in activity in that sector. After all, although the dotcom crash had resulted in the evaporation of hundreds of well-funded companies, plenty survived and thrived in the newly cleared forest. Companies like Amazon and eBay survived and later flourished, while the likes of Facebook and Google hit their stride in the period after the bubble burst. Byrne knew that the dotcom fad had been driven by incautious financial speculation, but he also knew that the premise – that the internet would become an ever-greater driver of global trade – was solid. A company like Steorn, offering consultancy, advice and technical skills, could still trade on that while diversifying into other areas.

By the same token, it wasn't a pure dotcom play: the Steorn lads could find business in other sectors, if necessary, and had also built up a decent reputation. Their work for Fraudhalt had led to work with An Garda Síochána, the PSNI, the Metropolitan Police Service and Europol on credit card and financial security, so the company had sufficient insulation from the volatile years of the early internet economy. Byrne knew by this stage that the Steorn team had done the World of Fruit project for Fyffes – a multi-million-euro investment by the company in an online fruit-trading platform – and that they were selling themselves to similarly high-profile potential customers, all of which impressed Byrne.

Moreover, and perhaps most importantly, Byrne took an immediate liking to McCarthy, who had made a presentation in Davy's offices, impressing Byrne with his grasp of his industry. It seemed to Byrne that

McCarthy was looking forward to what dotcom companies were doing. McCarthy's CV gave Byrne a great deal of confidence too, particularly his years spent with ABB. As far as Byrne was aware, ABB was not an easy company in which to rise through the ranks; McCarthy's doing so showed skill and talent. On a personal level, McCarthy was straightforward and plain-speaking, neither underselling the company's capacity nor promising multi-millions.

By the time of Byrne's investment in Steorn in January 2001, the Celtic Tiger had begun to hit its dangerous stride and there were gentle warnings. In 2002, future Central Bank governor Patrick Honohan and fellow economist Brendan Walsh described the economy, in similarly zoological terms, as the Irish Hare. Since the 1980s and '90s, they argued, Ireland had been trying to catch up with the rest of the world economically. Now, by inference, it risked over-running the rest of the world.

People living in Dublin's affluent suburbs – in essence, living in old houses in a second-tier European city with poor public infrastructure – were beginning to conflate the market value of their houses with their personal wealth. They would greedily watch the house price – a paper figure that would materialise only if the house was sold – rise and would chatter to each other that they were a lot wealthier than they had been two months before.

During this period, Byrne had to chastise a nephew who was considering an investment in an apartment in Bulgaria – and not in the capital city, Sofia, but in a rural area his nephew couldn't find on a map when he was challenged to do so. Fortunately for him, he took Byrne's advice and didn't go through with it.

Byrne had run the rule over Steorn and precluded it as an investment for any of Davy's clients; but, given his experience, he decided to take it on himself, convincing two colleagues, Barry Nangle and Hugh McCutcheon, to join him. Byrne put in €50,000 and they each put in €25,000, for a total investment of €100,000.

Even when the dotcom bubble finally burst, laying waste to stock markets from New York to London to Tokyo, Byrne kept faith in Steorn. It would be going too far to say that he believed his money was safe, but he watched the Steorn team as they took the difficult decisions to make employees redundant and redouble their efforts to win new customers, and was heartened.

From McCarthy's perspective, the investment came as something of a surprise. After all, consultancy firms tend not to raise money in the early years. Unless a firm is looking to hire people fast, quick money isn't usually required.

Steorn didn't need the money, but McCarthy and Byrne hit it off immediately, McCarthy being struck by Byrne's sincere interest and the sense that he seemed to care about the business and the team. In particular, Byrne gave McCarthy two pieces of advice that stuck with him. The first was, 'Don't let me ever see you driving in a Jag.' The second was, 'You're going to develop your own technology.'

Shaun McCarthy: Skunkworks

He was right. We had a real interest in actual technology versus just making a margin on advising or managing for others. So, we were playing around and we would've developed a few in-house projects which, mostly, we kept in-house. They weren't all software projects: they were combined physical and software.

So, in our little skunkworks [a small, informal lab for developing new products within a company], we were looking for problems that we had the skills to solve. And we had discounted lots of them. We'd say, 'Okay, we'll have a few beers, come up with an idea, kick it around, probably discount 99 per cent of them within a week.' Then some of them we pushed fairly far.

There was an idea called Smartplate, which was a car registration plate, and if your tax ran out it would change colour. It was a cute idea – that you'd have any of the regulatory things you need on your car, and if they run out, the number plate changes. The idea behind it was that you're unlikely to park this car in your front garden and let your neighbours see your number plate is red or whatever.

We thought it was a really cool idea, by the way, so we developed it and we spoke to the Department of Whoever Deals with It, and they were enthusiastic, but we thought, 'Jeez, we're dealing with government departments here.' … We went away and spoke to a few other players and thought, 'Y'know, we'd be here forever trying to get this to market,' and we moved on.

One of the other ones we were looking at was, instead of having a password to log in, why not – because everyone types in a unique way – look at the typing pattern? You'll type your password in a distinct way, so, in many ways, the speed and the way you touch the keyboard or the screen is a kind of biometric. We did a bit of analysis on that, and, again, it was a really good idea; but it was software only, and we didn't really like software. We should've patented that, because it would've been a fucking winner. I forget what we called that.

We had a couple of jokey ones. We set up WhatsMyExcuse.com. It was an online excuse exchange. So, you post up your problem, and people post excuses for your issue in real time. It was a bit of a joke, but we actually did do it. 'I'm driving home and I forgot the chicken. What's my excuse?'

Then we were looking at CCTV systems and emergency stations for things like DART lines that you could automatically detect in real time. Problem with CCTV is you can have a hundred cameras, but they're great for after something happens. Or you've got an operator looking at something, but he can only realistically monitor four screens. We said there are specific actions we could take from someone that we could deem to be aggressive and that could flash up that specific action to an operator, and he could decide to intervene or not.

We had built up an expertise in vision-recognition systems, as in when it's pointing a digital camera at something and trying to package how a forensic expert would look at it. So, you need to analyse, and so we had some fairly smart software and optics guys who would develop software algorithms, look at an image, etc. That's old hat now, but back in the day it was fairly sophisticated.

We were still working with Fraudhalt and they had developed ATM TV, an anti-fraud system to prevent skimming on ATMs. It was a kind of advertising hoarding that goes around the ATM; it's got cameras looking at the ATM, loads of them, and it detects a shape change on the ATM. If you put a skimmer on the ATM, you can detect that in real time using visuals in real time and also catch the guy or girl who did it.

The micro wind turbines were the death of us.

4. ORBO

The principle behind a wind turbine is pretty simple: you erect a series of wind-catching blades on top of a pole, and they begin to spin. That spinning generates mechanical energy, which turns a shaft attached to the rotors. That shaft is attached to a generator that converts – using magnets and copper wire – the mechanical energy into voltage, thus turning wind energy into electricity, which is stored and transmitted to whatever purpose it is needed for. From a towering 10-storey turbine in an off-shore windfarm to a tiny whizzing generator that takes advantage of small currents of air to drive some mini engine, they all operate on the same principle.

But – and this is crucial – they only generate as much energy as the wind gives them, and in truth the drop-off from what the wind provides to what the transformer can absorb is usually fairly high.

Shaun McCarthy knew this. He wasn't a physicist, but such elementary scientific knowledge was certainly lodged in his brain – as it was in the brains of all the other engineers in Steorn – when they took the ATM job from Fraudhalt to devise a tiny engine for the CCTV camera.

For McCarthy, the key was battery life. Such a device would be useless if it ran out of battery on Saturday morning at 2 a.m. when the residents of a rural town were all drawing money for their nights out on the town. A dead ATM skimmer detector would be worse than useless: it would be an invitation for scammers to take advantage of lowered inhibitions, impaired perception and exuberant ATM withdrawals.

The Steorn engineers were tinkering with the generator's internal magnets to improve efficiency when they discovered that the generator appeared to be putting out more energy than it was taking in. The device was simple, using wind to pass a magnet over a coil, which in turn generated electricity. It was supposed to work according to the laws of physics, converting one form of energy – heat or light or wind or something else in the atmosphere – into a usable source of power. That, very reductively, is how the law of the conservation of energy is supposed to work.

Except, to the Steorn engineers, the turbine was throwing up an anomalous result: instead of producing less energy, as they had expected (because, of course, the energy was going towards powering the ATM camera), the generator was producing more.

'During that process, we said, "Hang on, there's something fucking strange here," McCarthy recalls. 'That's how it started, and we just kind of left it there, because it was just too weird. So, in its weirdness, we put it aside.'

At first, it seemed a mistake to McCarthy; there was no come-to-Jesus moment, and there were certainly no high fives and no eurekas. In fact, McCarthy was grumpy at first that someone had broken the system. 'We're a little company, and we'd spent money on expensive sensors, and the biggest concern at the time was who broke the sensor, you know? Not that we'd discovered a world-changing technology, just which asshole has broken this thing, because it can't be reading right.' And yet, the anomaly wouldn't go away.

Mike Daly is a short, stocky, guarded man, with sleepy eyes and the demeanour of a small bear ready for hibernation; in conversation he is laconic and droll, but extremely guarded. In many ways, he is the cold splash of realism to Shaun McCarthy's enthusiastic fervour, though he is no less firm in his conviction that Steorn had stumbled on the find of the century.

Daly met McCarthy when McCarthy returned to Ireland in 2000, but they didn't immediately hit it off. Daly thought he was smarmy and condescending; moreover, McCarthy was being parachuted in over Daly's head in Microsol to oversee some of his projects. Any reservations swiftly passed – the pair worked it out over a pint in the local pub, where McCarthy's charm began to win over the extremely sceptical Daly, even convincing him to later leave Microsol and join Steorn.

Daly has a slightly different recollection of how what would become the Orbo phenomenon first revealed itself. (Daly's version is borne out in a presentation Steorn would later give on the discovery of the anomaly.) Instead of occurring during work for a CCTV system for a mounted ATM, it occurred during work on a security system for the DART train system in Dublin. The proposal from Córas Iompair Éireann (CIÉ), which operates the DART, was to use renewable energy to run the security cameras.

The project had plenty of false starts. Initially, Daly designed a camera system to sit atop a pole in Pearse Street Station – one of the busiest in the country – but it looked like 'an ugly lamp-post with a fucking mushroom on top'. Worse, it wobbled and vibrated when a train thundered into the station; and, worse again, the station is almost entirely roofed, with very little natural light coming through, meaning its solar panels didn't work particularly well.

Steorn tried at first to harness the motion of the trains as kinetic energy, a source of energy that has been used to power some wristwatches, but they eventually settled on wind turbines because the DART line, being a coastal line, is subject to plenty of coastal breezes. To make the blades less intimidating to the commuting public, they took a few wind turbines apart to see how they would take the arrangement of blades and wires and bearings and magnets and make them more efficient and, thus, smaller and less obtrusive.

Whether it was an ATM CCTV or a security camera on the DART is, in truth, irrelevant, because where it matters, Daly's and McCarthy's story synchronise: using various housings, mounting methods and arrangements of magnets, they started to get anomalous results.

However, before they could delve into it, CIÉ shelved the project and Steorn was left with this anomalous test system that had repeatedly thrown up inexplicable results, but that wasn't going to pay the bills and it wasn't part of an ongoing contract. So, the system and its anomaly sat in the corner, neglected when they had paying work and tinkered with when they had downtime, remaining a little quirk that was at that point more a hobby than anything else. And, of course, there was no way it could be what it seemed to be. Of that, Daly was sure.

Mike Daly and Shaun McCarthy remained guarded. There were many potential explanations for the anomaly that were well within the bounds of conventional physics, they thought, measurement error not being the least of them.

Yes, they concluded, it was clearly a measurement error. After all, a company run by engineers and business consultants doesn't stumble on scientifically ground-breaking findings by accident. It can only be a mistake. Yet the more they turned it over and tested it and ran it through its paces, the more confident they got that they were on to something.

McCarthy started to do research, not just on testing systems and the physics of energy, but also on

what other whack-bots had been claiming – because we're neither the first nor the last to claim something like this. … Anyway, we kept looking at it, and one morning, as we often do, we had a coffee and said, 'Could there possibly be something there?'

Like McCarthy, Daly agreed that it left them with a conundrum. The only way to solve it was to focus entirely on it, neglecting new work and wrapping up old work as quickly as possible. That left them with a money problem: if they weren't earning, they would need some other source of funding.

That wasn't a small decision. The dotcom crash had begun to lose some of its severity, and people had stopped complaining that the crash was proof that the internet was a bubble. Money was beginning to trickle back into those types of consultancy jobs that had previously dried up, and these seemed more stable and predictable, since companies were behaving more prudently than they had been a few years prior.

Then there was the construction boom, which looked like it had plenty of room left to develop and was throwing off plenty of money. A company like Steorn – with its record of working with some of the biggest companies in the country, like Fyffes, and with several police forces – could easily hire project managers with construction experience and bid for work on the surge in construction both in houses and in commercial buildings. It was far simpler than tech consulting and it was highly lucrative.

Daly knew that there was money in construction and in tech consulting and that Steorn and the team had the skills and experience necessary to make a lot of money from them, but he didn't find the prospect alluring. It was well paid, certainly, but he was bored by the prospect of sitting down with Irish tech firms to explain to non-engineers why a certain project had been delayed by a week or why a particular machine part was late and by the prospect of having to walk someone through the rudiments of a job.

Like McCarthy, and even allowing for his more temperate approach, Daly saw an opportunity. They wanted to be their own bosses instead of constantly flogging themselves to other people, and this thing – whatever it was – was beginning to look like a money-making idea. To Daly, it was a free roll of the dice: if it worked, they'd be rich; if it didn't, they could go back to that well-paid consultancy work, or at the very least they could get jobs as engineers in a big company and earn a reliable salary until they retired. At least they'd have tried it.

They were not physicists, though, so they would need experts to look at the idea first. But anyone McCarthy commissioned to examine the findings came away scratching their head. That's when they decided to ask a grown-up.

5. SEEKING VALIDATION

For centuries, magnets have held a nearly mystical allure. The way they draw certain things and repel others makes them seem almost conscious, almost alive. These rare pieces of stone hewn from the earth, which can push or pull, or point and direct, are commonplace now, and our knowledge of them is full and well founded. We understand the invisible fields that dictate their behaviour and the different materials that exert these powers and their relative strengths. We even know how to take materials that have no magnetic power and give it to them by the application of electricity.

Humans have been using magnetised needles as a compass for direction since the turn of the first century, and they have continued to draw the attention of even the greatest minds. Albert Einstein noted in his autobiography that, when he was four or five, his father showed him a magnet.

> That this needle behaved in such a determined way did not at all fit into the nature of events which could find a place in the unconscious world of concepts … I can still remember – or at least believe I can remember – that this experience made a deep and lasting impression upon me. Something deeply hidden had to be behind things.

Magnets are more than a curiosity, however, and more than just a way of finding true north or affixing a note to the fridge door. In the past two centuries, magnets have become central to the advancement of a perhaps surprising number of technological developments, from recording music to storing data on hard drives to creating images on television and computer monitors to constructing giant superconductors.

And, of course, they are central to batteries and electricity generators, which is where Steorn and Shaun McCarthy stumbled on them.

———————

So, just what was Steorn claiming to have found? How did its supposed discovery work? According to the law of the conservation of energy, in an isolated system, energy cannot be created or destroyed. Therefore, an engine, for example, will produce only as much energy as the fuel that drives it will allow. It cannot produce more energy than the fuel will allow, and – because of the inefficiencies of even the best-built engines – it will produce a lot less than the fuel will allow, since a good proportion of that fuel energy will dissipate in heat or other forms of energy.

That's no mere scientific hypothesis: the law of conservation has been found over and over through the centuries to be true based on thousands of experiments, deliberate and unintentional, that have shown that energy only decreases in such a system.

The Steorn team, emboldened by their research on the topic, said that they were not necessarily trying to overturn the law of conservation of energy but rather an associated theorem by the German mathematician Emmy Noether, who argued that such laws were time invariant. What Steorn and McCarthy were claiming was that they had stumbled on an exception that overturned Noether's theorems, which had been a bedrock of particle physics for almost a century. Orbo, as Steorn termed its new technology, was described on the company's website as being

> based upon time variant magnetic interactions, i.e. magnetic interactions whose efficiency varies as a function of transaction timeframes. It is this variation of energy exchanged as a function of transaction time frame that lies at the heart of Orbo technology, and its ability to contravene the principle of the conservation of energy. Why? Conservation of energy requires that the total energy exchanged using interactions are invariant in time. This principle of time invariance is enshrined in Noether's Theorem.

Steorn was, they said, using two basic techniques.

> The first … utilises a method of controlling the response time of magnetic materials to make them time variant … The second … decouples the Counter

Electromotive Force (CEMF) from torque for electromagnetic interactions. This decoupling of CEMF allows time variant magnetic interactions in electromagnetic systems.

Steorn was claiming that its specific arrangement of magnets around a large rotating wheel wasn't necessarily pushing one magnet forward and then giving it a kick on the way past to generate momentum. It was, the company claimed, doing something much more complex: delaying the magnetic field so that on one side the magnetic field was weak, and the other was strong – an imbalance that somehow created a momentum that pushed the spinning wheel and registered on the oscilloscope as a gain of energy.

If that doesn't make sense, McCarthy had a typically folksy explanation.

Shaun McCarthy: Time Machines

Okay, well, what we had created here was a time machine … Not in the H.G. Wells 'Let's travel to 1870' sort of way, but conservation of energy has one fundamental requirement: that the length of time it takes something to happen doesn't affect the amount of energy exchange. In simple terms, if I push a glass a metre across the desk, and if I do that in one second or a millisecond, the energy exchanged is exactly the same. You can think logically about why that is: because if you believe in the conservation of energy, if I lift a ball quickly and let it drop, and I lift it slowly and let it drop, there should be some conservation of energy. Time can have no part in it, yeah?

Believe it or not, the conservation of energy – thou shalt not create or destroy energy – is not a commandment. It's based on a theorem from Emmy Noether. And it's very simple: the laws of physics can't change in time – that's a no-no – otherwise, energy just can't be preserved. The amount of time that's involved in an energy reaction cannot change the amount of energy produced; otherwise, conservation of energy doesn't hold.

But, actually, what Noether's theorem says is that the reason the conservation of energy exists is that the laws of physics don't change in time, and the energy interactions are time invariant.

What we discovered – or rather what we discovered that we'd discovered – was that we had these magnetic interactions that exchange different energy in different time frames. Therefore, by just changing the amount of time between the push and pull – by walking up the hill slowly and running down, in Orbo terms – we got a net non-zero result and the permanent magnet version, the electromagnetic version and, ultimately, the solid-state version [of the Orbo device] all worked on this principle. Once we understood what was really happening, we could engineer it in difficult physical formats.

What we claimed to have discovered was a magnetic interaction that was time variable rather than time invariant. When you boil it all down fundamentally, the logical process after that is that you're creating or destroying energy.

Even to this day, I'm slightly embarrassed by the claim. I'm a professional engineer. I've done this shit for 30 years. I enter any conversation about Orbo with the premise that people clearly must think I'm an asshole. That's not me expressing a lack of confidence in Orbo or what we've developed: it's me thinking how I would feel if someone came and told me they have this magical magnetic machine with spinning magnets that can produce energy forever.

It's the audacity of the claim that we've broken the fundamental law of physics. It is controversial, and, ultimately, it's very difficult to put any kind of a scientific wrap around it. But then science itself is, as anyone who's looked at quantum mechanics knows, a very strange area. There are a lot of rational explanations that are still a huge stretch – explanations with respect to dark energy and energy conversion from unknown sources. When we were talking to these people, we weren't talking about how a bunch of Irish lads had disproved the laws of physics. We said, 'Look, we have something here; we've filed a patent; we have validation. It needs a lot of work, and we have a market to go for.'

By now, McCarthy had brought a handful of engineers through the Steorn offices to test the system and try to find a flaw, either in how they had built the wheel or how they were interpreting the data. So far, no one had. But McCarthy knew that this wouldn't be good enough: extraordinary claims need extraordinary proof, and the inability of a random selection of engineers invited by the company to disprove the concept was not going to be considered evidence.

So, McCarthy went to his alma mater, the Bolton Street college of Dublin Institute of Technology, and asked someone in the engineering department to look at the system. An engineering student, supervised by a lecturer at the college, designed a test system and came back to Steorn in early 2005.

The report, signed off by the student's supervisor, outlined his efforts to replicate Steorn's experiment. The main purpose of the experiment was 'not to prove or disprove the basic physic laws but only to show some strange and unusual results concerning the principle of the conservation of energy'. It seemed to confirm that Steorn had stumbled upon an anomaly that merited further study and examination. Not everyone concluded that they had found something, though. One lecturer at the School of Engineering at University College, Dublin, had been invited to see the Steorn device by a friend who was considering investing in the company. The lecturer came to their offices in the Liberties area of Dublin – which is where they were before they moved their offices to East Wall Road – only to find that the machine wasn't working that day because they were making modifications to it. He came away deeply sceptical of the whole affair.

Soon after, McCarthy invited a highly regarded English physics professor to Dublin to test the system. This professor has asked not be named – he signed a non-disclosure agreement and doesn't want to breach it, even after all that has happened since – but he said McCarthy met him on his arrival in Dublin and brought him to the offices through the Port Tunnel, McCarthy explaining along the way that its ceiling had been built too low, which entertained the professor greatly. When they arrived, McCarthy left him in the offices to do the test. Immediately, the professor noticed that the experiment was flawed: McCarthy, he said, was making some elementary (to a seasoned magnetician, anyway) measurement errors.

He explained this to McCarthy, who agreed to recalibrate the experiment and try again; but the experiments were still flawed. Eventually, the professor took McCarthy aside and explained that even if the numbers were correct, it was not a useful finding: the figures McCarthy was producing were simply too small to be of any practical application. Even if you scale it, he told McCarthy, your battery would be providing fractions of what an ordinary battery of the same size would provide.

McCarthy didn't seem to get the polite message that the system was fundamentally flawed. The professor concluded that McCarthy – despite his evident engineering skills and commitment to the scientific process – was never going to give up. This anomaly had become his crusade, and it was blinding him to the message he was getting: this simply wasn't going to work.

Eventually, the professor wrote a report for Steorn, for which he was paid and in which he tried, as politely as possible, to point out that the experiment was flawed and that, even if it hadn't been, the finding was not worth delving more deeply into. He compared the energy output of the Steorn system to that of a random battery, and the energy output of the Steorn battery was orders of magnitude lower. To this professor's mind, McCarthy was a well-meaning amateur who had become intoxicated by the idea that he had found something science couldn't explain.

———————

That's when McCarthy decided to go directly to the doyen of magnetism in Ireland: Prof. Michael Coey, whose office sits snugly in the back of Trinity College, Dublin, in its School of Physics. His office is a square box filled from floor to ceiling with bookshelves, sheaves of paper, bulging filing cabinets and a desk that's barely visible under exam papers. Not infrequently, he balances his laptop on his knees so as to be able to do any work.

Coey is among the pre-eminent experts in magnetism and spin electronics in Europe, and few people in Ireland understand as well as he does the breadth of uses to which magnets are put. He also knows the thrill they've given the human imagination for centuries – and the many ways in which we have overestimated their powers, believing that they can create energy from nothing.

Coey also knows that to the uninitiated, magnets can seem fundamentally weird and that their faintly mysterious dance can convince even the smartest people that this energy can be harnessed simply by experimentation and tinkering. Put enough magnets in a room, arrange them just right, spin them once and, presto, they can surely get each other whipping around independently like a never-ending chain of playing cards, each tipping the next and charging up some notional battery.

As well as his day job in the physics department, Coey has taught and written a great deal about the myriad ways in which magnets can gull the untrained and the non-scientist into believing that they are on the brink of a major discovery. As Coey has written in *Magnetism and Magnetic Materials* (2010), the magnet's

> ability to attract ferrous objects by remote control, acting at a distance, has captivated countless curious spirits over two millennia … To demonstrate a force field that can be manipulated at will, you only need two chunks of permanent magnet or one chunk of permanent magnet and a piece of temporary magnet such as iron … When we come to the middle ages, virtues and superstitions had accreted to the lodestone like iron filings. Some were associated with its name. People dreamt of perpetual motion and magnetic levitation.

Coey also notes the many historical examples of magnetism's being misunderstood, including Petrus Peregrinus's description of a perpetual-motion device in his *Epistola de Magnete* (1269). A copy of the manuscript sits in Trinity College Library, and the first part of it is a sober, scientific account of the properties of magnets. The second part, however, runs through potential applications, including a spinning gear wheel that would spin past a magnet, moving by being drawn at one side and then repelled and pushed forward at the other.

This was a basic misunderstanding that would be repeated hundreds, perhaps thousands, of times in the following eight centuries – that magnets, properly arranged, could generate motion independent of any other source of energy. Even the formulation of the laws of thermodynamics in the late nineteenth century – laws which expressly state that such a reaction can never take place – has not dissuaded a great many amateur tinkerers from declaring that they have done just that.

The scientific method, of course, demands that even its most sacred truths be open to scrutiny and testing, and it requires that should they be found wanting, they be overturned and replaced. But the law of conservation of energy has held fast for centuries in the face of countless claims to the contrary.

Quite apart from the expectation that so many gifted amateurs working towards this goal would, if it were possible, have produced by now something close to a working over-unity device (that is, one that produces more energy than it receives as input), the flipside of the law of conservation of energy is not simply that the evidence shows us that energy cannot be created or destroyed, but also that logic tells us that if it could be, it would be happening all around us constantly and destabilising the universe.

Yet perpetual-motion machines remain an obsession for those amateur scientists who believe in Nikola Tesla's oft-repeated idea that

> throughout space there is energy. Is this energy static or kinetic? If static our hopes are in vain; if kinetic – and this we know it is, for certain – then it is a mere question of time when men will succeed in attaching their machinery to the very wheelwork of nature.

It's a beguiling idea, to be sitting in a shed in one's back garden, tinkering at a machine built of pieces of equipment that can be bought for a few euro in any hardware store, eventually developing a machine that can generate even a small amount of energy.

It's beguiling because – as Coey knows – magnets can indeed be employed by private industry to develop new and more efficient ways of, say, making sure that pesticide is sprayed more efficiently. However, as he has warned,

> one lesson from a study of the history of magnetism is that fundamental understanding of the science may not be a prerequisite for technological progress. Yet fundamental understanding helps … Much progress in science is made empirically, without recourse to basic theory.

That's a far more generous and forgiving characterisation of the kind of amateur approach to magnetism than most scientists would give. In fact, physicists tend to have as much regard for perpetual-motion propositions as doctors have for anti-vaccine campaigners. And Coey's characterisation was far more generous and forgiving than he would be when Steorn came to his door.

———

Actually, Steorn and McCarthy did not go directly to Prof. Coey but to one of his PhD students, Mazhar Bari, a Dubliner whose family owned several businesses in the city, including the franchise for Häagen-Dazs ice cream and some fashion boutiques.

Bari had the perfect combination of scientific training and commercial instinct, having studied at Trinity College, Dublin, where he also spent a few years as a researcher and lecturer before moving to the University of Birmingham, where he was a research fellow. He had earned his PhD at Cambridge before returning home to get an MA in UCD's Michael Smurfit Graduate Business School. All the while, he had served as a director and held shares in several of his family's companies.

All this meant that when he returned to Trinity in 2001, his keen commercial mind made him the ideal candidate for a project entitled 'Conception and Implementation of Nanoscale Spin Electronics', which had a budget of €6.5 million, funded by the state-backed research organisation Science Foundation Ireland.

Bari's job was to 'commercialise' the research innovations his fellow scientists were working on and to build a revenue stream by exploiting those developments. It was an ideal job: he could help his colleagues develop their abilities to take an idea from the page to the balance sheet and he could also use the job to build serious commercial contacts with executives all over Europe.

So, when Steorn approached Bari, he must have spotted yet another chance to 'commercialise' a piece of research. He was a more than competent scientist – after all, he had graduated from Trinity and then been rehired, which would be unlikely if he was inclined to be duped by hucksters and conmen – so he put a small team together, with some funding of around €50,000 from Steorn, to interrogate this anomalous finding, and they, too, came back with an anomalous result.

Plamen Stamenov, first a student and later a lecturer at the Department of Physics at Trinity, knew Bari well and respected him.

Stamenov had come to Ireland from Bulgaria in 2002 and was immediately struck by the buzz in the country. Just a year before, Ireland had adopted the euro and there had been inflation in the price of food and ordinary consumer products. Even if most people in Ireland didn't see it – the currency difference and the general sense of extra money in everyone's pockets made up for it – Stamenov certainly did. Prices in shops, he felt, were ridiculous: groceries were hugely expensive and rent was exorbitant.

But there was also an intoxicating excitement in the country: jobs were being created everywhere and people were flying in from all over the EU, giving Ireland a cosmopolitan and sophisticated vibrancy.

In 2005, Bari asked Stamenov to meet the guys from Steorn, but Stamenov cut him short: he would not meet them if they were claiming to have overturned the laws of physics. Bari would not be entirely unsuccessful, though. He eventually convinced two of his fellow Trinity postgrads – Dr Fernando Rhen and Dr Venki Munuswamy – to examine Steorn's claim. In two reports, the scientists examined the anomaly and concluded that there were certainly grounds for further study. For Steorn, Bari's reports were not only academic validation but also commercial validation from one of the main business brains in what is regarded as the pre-eminent physics department in the country. Shaun McCarthy could have been forgiven for getting just a wee bit excited.

However, for Prof. Coey, the whole thing was an embarrassment. The first embarrassment was that Steorn could be given the room and space to posit theories that were so clearly impossible; the second was that they had in effect gone behind his back to hire one of his PhD students to test this system. It was all too much. When McCarthy and Bari came into his office to talk about the report Bari wrote in late 2005, Coey lost his temper and 'swept a bunch of papers off his desk. I shit you not. He totally lost it,' according to McCarthy. (Coey does not recall sweeping anything off his desk but admits he was dismayed and probably angry that anyone in his research group could have endorsed such a scheme.)

It was a shock for McCarthy. Up to that point, he hadn't been sitting around the offices thinking everyone in Steorn was going to become a trillionaire. He merely thought that this finding, this anomaly, was interesting and merited further study. Coey, he felt, was surely the ideal person to ask.

Whatever his original intention, and whatever Coey's reasons for being so grumpy about it all, the nature of Coey's reaction was indicative of the response of the scientific community generally. It was also precisely the response that was likely to embolden McCarthy to dig his heels in and harden his conviction that he had something that was not only real, but which also challenged the crusty dogmas of professional science. Right or wrong, rational or not, the scepticism he met with in those early engagements was a vital part of the fuel that drove Steorn in those early years. As McCarthy would later reflect, 'What convinced me in part was Coey's response. Maybe it's just a Shaun thing: you push me, and I'll push back.'

So, the Steorn team began to work in earnest to hone their testing. In McCarthy's words, 'we began to develop – which is always a dangerous thing for a bunch of engineers – a working theory as to what was happening'.

Eventually, he boiled the possibilities down to just three. One was that they'd violated the laws of physics – 'which is clearly a lynching offence'. The second is what McCarthy describes as the 'dark energy argument', which is that the machine was draining energy from some unknown energy source. The third, in his words, was 'that we haven't a fucking clue how to measure something'.

This third point is where it started to get pricey for Steorn. Testing equipment is expensive, and the best testing equipment – the kind they would need to eliminate any suggestion of measurement error and any lingering suggestions that they had simply done it wrong – would cost anything from hundreds of thousands to millions of euro.

It left McCarthy with a decision to make. Despite his self-deprecating claims that the business was struggling, Steorn was doing quite well, and McCarthy had built a reputation as a go-to man if a company needed technical analysis done on a fraud case. If a skimming machine was found in Ireland, Steorn could take the skimmer, scan it, discover how many card names were on it and stand in court and give reliable testimony to that effect. It was a word-of-mouth business, and their reputation was good. Moreover, people weren't going to stop coming up with innovative ways to steal money electronically, so Steorn could rely on human nature to provide it with a steady stream of business. It wouldn't make the Steorn team billionaires, but it was a comfortable business in a small industry – one that rivals would struggle to break into.

Many would have seen the risk as too great. But not McCarthy. 'When you've got this thing with serious potential, you have to make a decision. The decision is: if we're going to pursue this, we have to drop the day-to-day forensic stuff.'

It was not an easy decision to make. Steorn was then a respectable, reputable business with contacts in the Gardaí and in Europol. When the police needed someone to scan a skimming device, Steorn was among the few companies they went to. That kind of reputation is hard won and it's worth real money. It also leads to more contacts and more business. Fraudhalt, for example, was working with Microsoft to develop anti-counterfeiting systems for CDs and Steorn was involved in that too.

To McCarthy's ambitious mind, though, this was merely a lifestyle business – a company that could earn him and his colleagues a solid living but that was going nowhere. It wasn't going to make them fortunes.

And then there was the nagging question about this thing – this finding, this anomaly, this measurement error, whatever it was. It was bugging McCarthy and bugging Daly, and they were trapped in limbo. They couldn't let it go without testing it, but they couldn't test it further without the kind of money and time that would alter the nature of Steorn. McCarthy reflects that

> as an engineer, the discussion isn't even necessary. Curious engineers just don't walk away from something like this. You can't do it as a hobby. There was never going to be a moment where we said, 'Ah, fuck it, forget about it.' We told ourselves to shit or get off the pot. If you live the Orbo dream for a minute and say, 'This is real,' then there isn't anything that stops you doing it.

At another time in Ireland's history, the option may not have been there. But this was the Celtic Tiger: anything was possible.

If this was 1998, maybe not. But it was 2004, and while maybe everyone didn't have an apartment block in Bulgaria yet, people had risk capital and they were starting to get ballsy – and with all their investments, not just us. People were starting to throw money into tech start-ups and obscure property investments.

To test the system, the Steorn team needed more than just small investments from canny old operators like Tom Byrne of Davy stockbrokers or the tail end of tax-break funds; they needed more than just a few hundred grand in accidental investment.

Shaun McCarthy: Raising Funds

At that stage, we had a couple of Trinity College postgrads who had written up a report, and we had [a report from] DIT, which would have been written by engineers rather than scientists.

So, we had to change the direction of the business. We were effectively the technical department of an Irish company called Fraudhalt. The guys who were working on the Fraudhalt project, we identified a chief technical engineer for them, and we took the guys and said, basically, 'It's time to fly the nest and leave us to our own strange little world.' And we let the forensic stuff wind down. I was still doing court cases five years down the road, but we weren't taking on any new business.

Then we hired an engineer who could design tests systems and an engineer who had done an awful lot of data analytics on high-end physics products. Basically, someone who's really good at Excel spreadsheets.

This was different from any other project we'd been involved in. If you asked us what it takes to build a corporate, business-to-business website, we could map out the project with a high degree of certainty and, plus or minus a little bit, we'd be right. This was a different world, and there was no real road map to follow.

So, we stuck our finger in the air and came up with a number. Now, we did an awful lot of justification of sticking our finger in the air with respect to time frames and costs, but we were in an area where, in reality, you can't really call this stuff.

We identified €20 million – which seems a very round number – but that's what we came up with, and it's probably about right in terms of maturing the tech, inasmuch as we got a chance to do it.

The guy doing the corporate finance work for us in the UK – because, again, we were initially doing this through venture capital – was called Michael Moriarty, from a firm called Dawnay Day, and he began to ram some real discipline into us.

The raising of the money didn't happen from just meeting a few lads in a pub to say, 'Give us €20 million.' We went through multiple layers of due diligence and all this stuff that, when you're dealing with large sums of money, you need to do very carefully. And we still had some skill sets from the old Steorn that were very good in terms of putting together plans and everything that goes into raising money.

Mike [Moriarty] is a corporate finance guy. He basically beats you into a pulp to make sure that your plans are realistic, and a whole world of things in terms of market validation and tech validation – plans that everyone said in the information memorandum (we were told to call it that for legal reasons, rather than a prospectus) we had to have validated by lawyers. So, when I say, 'I'm Shaun McCarthy, and I worked for ABB,' someone has to go off and check all of that.

So, it was done to a standard, and a lot of that was us as well, saying, 'We're not idiots: we're coming out and asking people to invest in what has got to be viewed by a lot of people as a clear scam.' So, we went to the nth degree in terms of everything we did with these placing documents.

And in the end, nobody actually read the fucking things. Or, at least, very few people did.

So, the original plan was to go down the venture capital route, and Mike was making those introductions for us. At the time, our reputations hadn't been sullied, so I think anyone who checked me said, 'This kid has a bit of real-world experience.' We met them, they went through us. At that time, we did have that documented validation from a couple of guys with PhDs, so it wasn't thrown out immediately, and we sat down with these people.

There was no 'Are you fucking idiots?' moment. They may have said that when they read the document. I've done that myself, where you're sitting in the office and some ludicrous thing comes in and you say, 'Jesus, I've got to meet these people.' But, certainly, they didn't give that impression when we were talking to them.

We were in fact discussing with a big Canadian VC [venture capital] who we had progressed furthest with when the money started to flow from the less institutional side.

You couldn't live in Dublin in the tech scene and not see that every asshole was raising money. So, while we were working away with Dawnay Day, one of my neighbours – which, again, was a very Irish thing – was bringing a corporate finance guy back and forth, and he was looking for projects. We had met him on a couple of projects on opposite sides of the table, and we asked him would he come and sit in our camp and walk us through the process of raising money.

It was all very institutional, all VCs, all again probably in hindsight what we should've done; but, again, at the time, this country had convinced itself that we were all rich, buying apartment blocks off plans in places they'd never heard of and never would see.

So, there was an appetite, and you could call that good luck or bad luck for us. In retrospect, it was bad luck; at the time, it was definitely good luck.

But, Ireland being Ireland, we met a guy who said, 'I'll get you the fucking money.' And he did.

6. INTRODUCING PAT CORBETT

Mr Whyte, Pat Corbett coming back to you. I really wouldn't have any interest in contributing towards your book. I might have an idea what it's about, but I wouldn't have any interest. I've had a life-threatening operation in the last couple of months, and the cardiologist has told me not to put myself in the way of anything that would potentially jeopardise my condition, which is to stay alive. So, I would choose not to comment in any way. I wish you the very, very best. Good luck. Goodbye. – Voice message from Pat Corbett, 18 September 2019

Pat Corbett, born in 1963, started out as an accountant in the early 1980s. His career was interrupted very early on when tragedy intervened. He had been working his apprenticeship in a Dublin accountant firm – one of the small ones, but a reputable and good place for an accountant to get his foot on the ladder – when his father died by drowning in the Slaney River. Corbett took some time off work to go home to his family and grieve, a process cruelly delayed by the week or so it took his father's body to surface. It is hard to estimate the impact of grief on a young person – the mark left by the untimely death of a parent – but we can safely assume that the young Pat Corbett was still raw with agony by the time he returned to work. Since Corbett has declined to speak about himself or Steorn for years, it is impossible to know precisely what he was thinking in those grief-stricken weeks and months, but he eventually decided to strike out on his own, slowly building up a clientele of farmers, builders and small businessmen.

Corbett is a deeply private person so his early career is difficult to track, particularly how he ended up making his money. In one way, it's not a mystery at all: his accumulation of wealth came at a time when Irish people were striking deals and making money and growing their portfolios in a way never before imaginable. Corbett was at the centre of that as an accountant, since each of his clients constituted a small point in a web of connections through which he could have legitimately met and struck up personal relationships with dozens, maybe hundreds, of people who could have cut him in on part of a deal for, say, advice on a particularly profitable tax structure, a heads-up on a property coming to market or consulting services on negotiating a deal.

Having built up such a network in parts of the country such as rural south Leinster and Munster – especially in Offaly, Kilkenny, Waterford and Tipperary – he was suddenly in touch with a large number of land owners, buyers and sellers: builders, developers, bankers, farmers, state agencies looking to buy fields to expand motorways – and it's likely that Corbett found himself at the centre of myriad deals. He was no longer merely signing off on annual accounts: he was now talking to people, helping to put them in contact with other clients, brokering and facilitating deals. In such an environment, it would be easy to identify deals of your own, to spot tracts of land that could be bought cheaply and sold for a profit.

In such deals, it was likely that Corbett's personality – his combination of professional competence allied to a charm and charisma that often came across as boyishly enthusiastic in its zeal and unguarded enthusiasm – could have engaged and ingratiated him with a great many people who were looking for a trusted advisor and financial counsellor.

Yet, surprisingly, no accurate record of his wealth can be gleaned from the usual records. He has a few companies to his name but not many properties, according to the Land Registry. He doesn't appear to be a massive shareholder in companies, private or public. What wealth he has he made quietly and kept privately, but it cannot be separated from the otherwise ebullient, effervescent and extravagant manner in which he spent it – on those rare occasions when he did.

One of those instances was Marcus Fearon. The two men had met through Tony Quinn, a purported faith healer to the stars.

Quinn, born in Dublin, is now a millionaire who has run positive-thinking and yoga seminars and has become famous for appearing at ringside during Steve Collins's world-title boxing match against Chris Eubank. Collins seemed to suggest he had been hypnotised by Quinn before the fight with Eubank, who would later acknowledge that the claim had unsettled him, in particular because he had once nearly killed a man in the ring. The idea that Collins would be insensible to pain made him worry that he would do permanent damage to him. (In the end, Collins won.)

As a well-known hypnotist and positive-thinking guru, Quinn is a harmless enough character, and his followers are free to spend their money as they choose. However, there's a darker side to the Tony Quinn business. For starters, he's been described as a cult leader, and many of his followers believe him to be the reincarnation of Jesus Christ. Quinn has never claimed this explicitly, but several former supporters have described a messianic zeal among his inner circle of followers.

There was more of Caesar than of Christ about Quinn, however. He displayed a terrific ability to convince people to part with their money in a variety of business ventures that turned him from an apprentice butcher into a millionaire mostly through the power of his personality.

It is probable that Pat Corbett and Marcus Fearon were unaware of any of this (Quinn guards his private life fiercely, and not everyone who attends his courses is part of his inner circle) when they met for the first time at one of Quinn's expensive business conferences in Monte Carlo in 1999. They were both fervent adherents of Quinn's brand of stubborn positive-mindedness and were wedded to the idea that wishing hard enough could overcome even the biggest deficits in talent or ability.

That was particularly apt for Fearon, whose life's dream was to be an international recording artist. Such a career usually takes time and hard work, building a following through small, poorly paid gigs before eventually hitting the big time. But Fearon was keen to shortcut that arduous process, which is where Corbett – and more particularly, his money – would be instrumental.

Marcus's father, a businessman who ran a builders' supply company in Dundalk, had stumped up some of the cash to help his son's band Why, made up of Marcus, his brother Philip and Fearon's first cousin Darren – as well an expensive-looking music video, set in a church and in which Marcus rapped over a gospel choir's backing vocals.

Fearon became a solo artist after Philip and Darren dropped out, the latter explaining, 'I realised it wasn't for me. I was basing it on money, success, fame … That's not what I want in life, so I stepped back and took a closer look at myself.'

Fearon would later describe the album as 'the largest demo ever produced in the history of music' and, in an interview shot at that time, outlined his 'one simple goal', which was to 'produce the biggest group the world has ever and will ever know. That's where our future lies; that's the aim, the goal, the dream we'll be chasing after.'

To achieve that goal, Fearon would need more than just his father's money, and that's where the meeting with Corbett at the Quinn seminar proved fateful. Corbett immediately took to the young man, describing him as 'an enigma. Every so often there is an enigma in the music industry, whether it's someone like Madonna or someone like the Beatles. Marcus is one of these gifted people.'

In preparation for his shot at fame, Fearon wanted to produce three albums virtually simultaneously: a hip hop–gospel album, a gospel album and a light classical album. Corbett provided the money for Fearon to get in shape with a diet that involved six weeks of eating nearly a stone of protein a day in ox hearts, porridge and beans to build ripped abdominal muscles to grace an album cover. He sent Fearon to the Bahamas for six months to imbibe the Quinn philosophy and get his head in the right place for success, and then he began to set Fearon up with meeting after meeting in London, Los Angeles, Italy and Dublin to deliver on Fearon's plan. He also hired a personal secretary.

A film production company working on a documentary about Fearon followed him on a number of his meetings, and these provide an often unflattering portrait of the gulf between his belief in his abilities and his actual talent. In one meeting with the London Symphony Orchestra's director of planning, Sue Mallet, Fearon showed a tin ear in relation to the subtle advice he was being given.

Fearon described his plans to record and rerecord all his songs, telling Mallet that

> the way I work is I'm not necessarily trying to work within a budget. I use the best elements I need, and then I look at budget, if you follow me. If my sound is going to sound better with a full orchestra, then I use the full or-chestra, and then I address the budget. I don't want to address the budget and say, 'Okay, well, I can only have this amount of players because of my budget.' So, it's a little bit differently how I work, because, to me, I can't sac-rifice the sound for anything.

Mallet, seeming crestfallen, observed that Fearon must have some wealthy backers, which Fearon confidently confirmed.

'Right, you'll need them,' Mallet replied.

However, in a black cab outside after the meeting, Fearon was positively giddy. 'I just know that went perfect. I can pick up on those things,' he said of his meeting with Mallet. 'I would go so far as to say I'll even get a phone call from her saying the music's great.'

He met producers, agents for producers and studios all over the world. He even spent money on travel to Stockholm to meet the famed pop producer Max Martin. But this ended in failure when it turned out that Fearon hadn't set up a meeting in advance, meaning a lot of money had been wasted on flights.

On their trip to Los Angeles, Fearon and Corbett met Dionne Perrineau, a stylist for the likes of Will Smith and Michael Jackson. Perrineau archly observed – after Fearon explained that he needed two looks (one for his hip hop–gospel album and another for his light classical album, or a look that would comfortably straddle them) – that 'star quality is for someone who is mediocre at what they do, but something in them draws people to them'.

Fearon was not listening, however, leading Corbett to chide him for his headstrong approach and point out that Perrineau was an expert and ought to be listened to.

When Fearon's personal secretary asked if he would be willing to give way to Perrineau's expertise, the supremely confident Fearon replied, 'I'd say let's leave that till it comes,' leaving the evidently amazed Perrineau to once again observe that 'star quality is something that, if you don't have a lot of talent, you have to have'.

The matter of whether Fearon could sing was answered definitively on that trip to Las Vegas when he had a $645 vocal-training session with Seth Riggs, a famed voice coach. With the two men seated at a piano, Riggs ran Fearon through a series of drills, but the exercise served only to highlight his limitations as a singer. Throughout, Riggs maintained a concerted mask of neutrality while Corbett smiled on beatifically, apparently pleased at what he was hearing.

At the end of the Las Vegas trip, Corbett seemed pleased at having met several serious movers in the industry. 'I can now get a total feel for what I'm investing in and where he wants to go with this.'

Fearon's conclusion at the end of the trip was that he had to go home to 'develop [himself] as an artist' and work on his music, fix the elements that were broken and develop those that were right. Most important, though, was to 'write incredible hits … You can polish up anything … [but] the songs have to be right; the songs have to sell.'

By February 2001, Fearon and Corbett had rented a luxurious apartment in well-heeled Ballsbridge, Dublin, with views onto the sea and a space for writing and installing a IR£130,000 recording studio. It was a huge sum – the apartment cost more than IR£3,400 in rent – but Corbett made it clear that money was no object when it came to helping Fearon realise his dreams.

In the documentary about Fearon, Corbett explained how Fearon convinced him to loosen the purse strings.

Marcus said to me, 'Pat, I've found this perfect apartment. It's exactly where I want to work', and I said, 'Great, where is it?' He said, 'It's in Ballsbridge.' Okay, I said, right, and my mind immediately goes – there's a logical accountant! – £3,400 a month, and it's perfect? [But Marcus said,] 'You have to see the rooms, and they're fabulous, and there's three bedrooms, and it's this and it's that.' I says, 'Right, okay.' And, I suppose, the guy wanted to do this, and who am I to question?

Of course, being the man holding the purse strings, Corbett could easily have said no several times, but it is clear that he never did.

One thing Marcus never says is no … So, if Marcus says, 'I want to do this,' I've never said, 'No, you can't do that.' That doesn't exist between us.

Budgets really go out the window with all of this. … When we set out to look at this, we were of the opinion that something of this nature would probably take a quarter of a million to put together. That figure has long since been passed. … I suppose the project to date … is somewhere in the order of £850,000.

Nearly a million pounds had therefore been spent on a man whose ambition was to become a recording artist, even though the best sometimes don't make money for years. For Corbett, it was an exceedingly long shot, any financial return likely to be years off – or non-existent. The Celtic Tiger hadn't even properly kicked in, and Corbett was already showing an appetite for risk that would've shocked property speculators in even the most cock-eyed investment.

Worse still, Corbett had virtually no protection should Fearon flop and the money evaporate. Corbett had no contract, no loan agreement, no lien over Fearon's assets as a kind of insurance policy. He had no guarantees whatsoever.

And yet it didn't seem to bother Corbett. Smiling into the camera, he said, 'Am I an accountant that doesn't worry about money? Yes, I am. I don't worry about money.' He seemed to have supreme confidence not only in Fearon's ability to make it, but in the strength of their connection, which seemed at times to verge on the spiritual. 'It's not even a gentleman's agreement,' Corbett said at the time. 'It's just two human beings that meet on a particular level and just agree that this is something that must get done.'

For Fearon, too, there was a sense that this investment was more than a financial outlay designed to generate a return: there was something deeper that bound the two men.

> I met this guy [Corbett] six months ago, literally. He undertook the whole thing then and invested a lot of money into it since – a lot of money. And we never signed a piece of paper. We operate on the basis of trust and belief …
> If we operate that way, I'll make a lot more money, and he'll make a lot more money, and we'll both be very successful because of that.

Clearly, much of that spiritual connection was based on their subscription to Tony Quinn's quasi-cult, something Fearon alluded to when he described his own mental process.

> If I buy an apartment like this and a car like the car I'm getting, and living this lifestyle and staying in places like the Beverly Hills Hotel, I'm conditioning the mind into thinking that it's not really, in that I haven't anything concrete there to say this is my success as such. I believe, by doing all this, the mind will fool itself into thinking it's successful so will very naturally and very effortlessly and very easily become successful just from that alone.

Fearon had believed that the Ballsbridge flat and the songs he would write there would make or break him as an artist – 'I've no excuse not to come up with any of the goods now' – but apparently his neighbours in Ballsbridge didn't agree with the noise coming from the flat, so Fearon moved back to his native Dundalk – a move that appeared to concern Corbett deeply.

> When Marcus mentioned to me he was going to move back to Dundalk …
> I said, 'Are you sure?' because … I always found, when Marcus came back from Dundalk, his state of mind wasn't as good as it could've been. … I can't maybe explain that, but Marcus, for want of a better word – a genius is never accepted in his own hometown.

Nevertheless, Fearon managed to write some material, and by July 2001 he was ready to record in Windmill Lane Recording Studios in Dublin, where the likes of U2 and Sinéad O'Connor have recorded million-selling albums. As well as hiring the studio, they hired conductor John Finucane and musician Gloria Mulhall to help Fearon with the technical elements of conducting and recording an expensive orchestra, but the album was not a success and sold virtually no copies.

Eventually, Fearon and Corbett – having now sunk so much money into the project – decided to roll the dice on one final gambit: Fearon would audition for the television programme *Popstars*, in which aspiring amateur singers compete before such music industry legends as Louis Walsh (manager of Boyzone and Westlife), Linda Martin (a Eurovision winner) and the producer Bill Hughes.

The problem was that Fearon had never sung on stage before, and while his confidence was as high as ever – he told the camera crew before his audition that he had 'never done anything like this before, and I thought I'd be nervous, but I feel amazing' – most of his music to that point had been based on rap rather than on singing.

Still, he acknowledged that there was a chance that his inexperience might prove to be an obstacle, particularly to his state of mind.

> I don't get stage fright or anything like that when I get up there. I just hope they let me rap, because that's what I do, and I'm very confident if I rap. So, I'm keeping my fingers crossed that they don't stop me after a line and say I'm supposed to sing.

They didn't. And although he threw in a token few bars of a self-composed rap in a sleeveless vest in front of the judges, when it came to singing a song – Ronan Keating's 'When You Say Nothing at All' – it was hopelessly out of tune and husky. Fearon even managed to fluff the lyrics, forcing him to wing it and make up his own words after he had barely sung a full line.

The judges' conclusion was damning, Hughes quietly noting to Martin and Walsh that 'with the best will in the world, even though yer man did the rap, he can't sing. He hasn't got a note in his head.'

Money had by now become a major issue, Fearon himself acknowledging that 'it doesn't look good, as in I've got loans of huge amounts of money to do what I've done'. It's not clear whether this was an admission that he had borrowed from Corbett in a formal credit arrangement or whether it was just an informal recognition that he had burned through a huge pile of someone else's money. Either way, it was beginning to dawn on Fearon that superstar riches were not guaranteed. 'It's looking as if – and I'm looking at this outside of myself – it's looking as if that money might be a total loss.'

Corbett, however, was still relatively hopeful.

> I still have huge amounts of faith in Marcus. There has been a lot of dark days; there's no sense in saying there hasn't. It has taken longer [than I thought]. I would have felt that the results would've come maybe a year ago.

Corbett was keen to express his gratitude for having been brought on the journey, though.

> In a lot of ways, I was brought to places that I never was before, and I prob-ably just went with it. And all of a sudden, it got to a stage that I was just so deep into it I said, like, 'What do I do? Do I get out or do I keep on digging?' So, I kept on digging … My belief in him will just come through, and that's ultimately what's going to win through at the end of this day.

It would prove not to be the case, however. Soon after, Fearon emigrated to Thailand. He is no longer working in the music industry.

––––––––––––

The story of Marcus Fearon is not merely illustrative of Pat Corbett's willingness to throw good money after bad – even in the pursuit of a good cause. It was one of the routes through which Corbett got in touch with Steorn. Corbett was attempting to hawk Fearon's CD to as many industry people as possible and was working his way through his contacts book to get as much advice and help as possible. Corbett had contacted Shaun McCarthy before in relation to a possible technology investment that he wanted Steorn to run the rule over. Although that investment came to nothing, when Corbett wanted to find someone to evaluate Fearon's CD, he asked McCarthy for advice. During their discussion, the matter of Steorn's odd discovery came up, and McCarthy mentioned that he had been attempting to raise funds for it through the formal venture capital channels. That's when Corbett came up with the idea of raising the money himself.

Shaun McCarthy: Pat Corbett

Pat was an absolutely fantastic fucking guy. You'd really have to meet him and spend time with Pat to realise the power of the guy's personality. It's just phenomenal. He's an incredible person.

He was also a very private person, and I think a lot of that was because we were generating a lot of media attention. … He'd been involved in the Marcus Fearon documentary, and that was a complete shafting of Pat that he didn't deserve. We had some guys in filming us for some fucking thing, and the cameraman had been the main cameraman for the [Fearon] doc, and I had to step in. What they did … was a complete shafting and mischaracterisation of Pat and the reason he probably won't speak to the media again.

Like anyone, we had disagreements on belief systems, but ultimately, Pat is a force of nature. If he had been born in the States, I have no doubt he'd be a multi-millionaire by now.

Far be it from me to judge. I mean, I think Tony Quinn's a fucking cult leader; the fucker can sue me all he wants. I despise Tony Quinn, everything he does and has done. But if someone wants to believe in Jesus Christ or Mohammed, fair play to them. I don't care. That was never an issue between me and Pat – we used to take the piss out of each other all the time about that. There was no fractious relationship between me and Pat.

Except at the end.

7. THE INVESTORS

S haun McCarthy was right about one thing: everyone was a millionaire – or at least wanted to act as if they were. Just as Steorn was beginning its fundraising drive in 2005, Eddie Hobbs was beginning to gain what passes for fame in Ireland as a personal finance guru. Hobbs had started his career in the pensions firm Zurich Life and had spent more than a decade there before quitting in 1991 to set up his own financial advisory firm, TIPS, with Tony Taylor.

Taylor, it turns out, was a fraudster: he would later be charged and plead guilty to five counts of fraud, forgery and destruction of documents, having fled the country after Hobbs's decision to lodge a complaint about him to the regulator in relation to Taylor's handling of client funds.

Hobbs came out with his reputation intact – he was described by a High Court judge as having shown 'efficiency and determination' and praised for 'not standing idly' – and from there began to build a public profile as a people's champion, tackling the insurance industry, the government and the investment-funds industry over its use of the tax code. He acted pro bono as a spokesperson for the Consumers' Association of Ireland through the late 1990s and was eventually rewarded with a number of television programmes on RTÉ in which he gave advice to cash-strapped consumers or editorialise against hidden costs and unfair practices.

By the 2000s, though, the mood had changed, and Hobbs had clearly noticed the shift. People were suddenly less interested in saving a penny than in spending a pound – or more. By 2006 he had turned his attention to a now infamous state-backed savings scheme called the Special Savings Incentive Account. The SSIA was the brainchild of Charlie McCreevy, a former Minister for Finance, who was notorious for his cavalier approach to drawing up annual budgets for the government, often refusing to tell even the Taoiseach what he was planning.

In principle, the SSIA wasn't a bad idea: Ireland was so wealthy that inflation threatened to accelerate to feverish levels. The special savings account encouraged people to save the money rather than spend it; if they took that prudent course, they'd be rewarded with a euro for every four they saved.

In 2006, households therefore found themselves sitting on an impending bonanza of cash, and newspapers, radio stations and TV programmes generated tens of thousands of words and broadcast minutes with speculation and advice on what the first tranche of SSIA payouts would be like – and, more to the point, on how people should spend them. For RTÉ, when it wanted advice from a trusted voice – and a proven ratings-winner – there was only one man: Eddie Hobbs.

In 2006, he hosted the programme *30 Things to Do with Your SSIA*, its theme, tone and production values reflecting the mood of the time. The opening credits showed Hobbs sprinting down an alley in homage to the intro to the film *Trainspotting*, implicitly offering himself up as the guru of the ordinary investor while channelling a film about the dangers of addiction and the risks of heedless consumption of your narcotic of choice. The famous opening lines of *Trainspotting*, recited over Iggy Pop's 'Lust for Life', had become:

> Choose right: choose a saving account, choose a new motor, choose a bloody big television, choose plastic surgery, new teeth, a new partner, a holiday home in the Baltic; choose an education plan, a pension plan; choose shares, commodities, gold and rubies; choose a hot tub, an attic conversion, the holiday of a lifetime; choose anything, but let it slip through your fingers or pissing it against the wall and having nothing to show for it after five years of saving; choose something worthwhile; but, for God's sake, choose right.

Now, there were plenty of sensible suggestions in the programme. Hobbs warned that foreign property investments could be the 'graveyard' for a lot of SSIA money; but such was the orgy of consumption that he could float a three-hour programme on a hefty dose of highly unserious suggestions (such as getting elected, getting divorced or getting a sex change so that women could get paid the same as men) and only slightly less unserious ones (such as buying fine wine because, even if it didn't appreciate in value, you could still drink it).

However, one of these ideas today sticks out like a sore thumb: to buy an Irish investment property. It's best to let Hobbs himself explain it in the language of the programme:

> Eddie, you're nuts, you've lost it. Surely today is the worst time to invest in Irish residential property. Now, the idiot's guide to invest in property is that the first rule to investing in property – and there are three rules – is location, location, location.
>
> But the second rule is cash, cash, and cash, because if you run out of cash, you're in very serious trouble.
>
> So, the third rule … is about gearing: using the least of your own cash and the most of the bank's that you can.

The principle behind gearing was simple, Hobbs explained. If you have €1 million and buy a property, and a year later it's revalued at €1.1 million, you've made a profit of 10 per cent. But what if, instead of spending the whole million, you put in only €100,000 and borrow €900,000 from the bank? When that house is revalued at €1.1 million, you've made a profit of 100 per cent, less the cost of borrowing. And what if you've used the other €900,000 to buy nine other properties?

In the audience, and around the country, a population who had learned to flick to the property section of a newspaper before the front page was now watching the euro symbols tick up inexorably, with only a few auld interest repayments needed to keep the whole endeavour ticking over.

It didn't matter that Hobbs made other, more sensible recommendations, such as investing in property companies, and he also warned against the temptation to become a full-time landlord. None of that mattered in that heady climate of rampant property price acceleration and paper millionaires. Nor did it matter that Hobbs painted gearing in the most dramatic terms possible: 'Gearing, of course, is like rocket fuel. It propels you up in a rising market, but can bring you crashing down in flames in a falling market.'

The idea of taking a million euro, splitting it 10 ways to buy 10 properties and then using someone else's money to make up the difference – safe in the knowledge that the ever-upwards revaluation would take care of the risk – well, that was just too intoxicating for Ireland to resist.

Shaun McCarthy: €20 Million

So, we were doing the whole thing that every tech company does. We decided that this is a lovely idea, so let's get a bit of money. Except in this case it was quite a large amount: around €20 million, we figured.

Pat [Corbett] got in touch through a friend of Fraudhalt's CEO, Phelim O'Doherty. Pat had got himself stuck on this music thing [with Marcus Fearon], and he knew I had a couple of buddies in the music industry, so he asked me if I would pass on Marcus's CD to them.

Pat dropped in the CD and I gave it to my buddy Dan. Now, Dan's a very nice man and he keeps his views to himself if they're negative, and Dan said very little about the CD. So, I said to Pat, 'I don't think there's anything here. The production values are blah blah blah.' Pat asked if there was anyone I could think of to help Marcus through the shark-infested waters of the music world, and I didn't know anyone else.

The conversation went from there. Pat asked me what I was doing, and I started spoofing, telling him where we [Steorn] were, and I said we were raising money. He said, 'Ah, let me have a go.'

I went, 'Yeah, this is a lot of money, Pat. We're looking for €20 million.' And Pat's a very confident guy, so he wasn't put off by that. From our point of view, we said, 'Sure, why not give it a go,' and it went on from there. He just kept delivering, and at that point we'd met with Mike Moriarty, who was working on the corporate finance side, and he said, 'Mate, if this guy can deliver like this, then why are we talking?'

Eventually, myself and Pat fell out, and that happens – nothing against Pat – but in hindsight that was probably the biggest mistake we made. That wasn't Pat's fault, but we had decided to raise money from people who probably didn't understand the risk. We did try to say, 'Look, this is the 100/1 bet at Leopardstown Races,' but all they could see was us controlling the battery world, which was of course our business plan, but it was a long shot.

But anyway, we'd started this process on a coincidental meeting, and it just worked, at least in terms of raising money.

It's a decade and a half ago, but you can see how easy it was from the company filings. The first thing he [Corbett] did was set up some meetings where he'd set up the presentation, and we'd go in and do a pitch: we've discovered this effect, we have validation from a couple of postgrads, and we've had several engineers look at it and confirm the [anomalous energy] effect, so this is not made up. It's not a case of 'Just believe Mike [Daly] and Shaun'.

Within a day of the first meeting, we had a quarter of a million. Not joking: it was a quarter of a million the next day.

So, the question then became: what do we do with all of this? We had become more attuned to the project now after working with Mike Moriarty, and we had identified the ambition, which was to patent it and license it to mobile consumer-electronics companies, and we felt that the fundamental Steorn/Orbo concepts were well put together at this stage.

We were in the office, building stuff and testing stuff and putting together terabytes of test data, but the message was – and it was the same message we've pushed ever since – to get further validation, further validation and further validation. Because ultimately, if we can get this validated, we will not need to do any heavy lifting; we'll just license it to someone who has the actual capability to put this out in the real world.

There were questions, of course, but to be honest, I can't remember what they were. We had four or five slides at the end of the presentation saying here are the risks: that we're just fucking wrong or that we can't raise the money, and the first money coming in is basically screwed and all the usual risks of an early-stage start-up.

A little of that came back to the fact that we were kind of embarrassed – being highly educated and trained engineers – at how this would appear to anyone. I still am embarrassed. When it comes down to it, I know it works, and a lot of other people know it works, but it's still slightly embarrassing to be claiming you've got an over-unity device – a machine that puts out more energy than it takes in.

But it was the height of the Celtic Tiger, and we were getting calls asking if we would do a presentation here and a presentation there – in Wexford and Waterford and all over the countryside – and the money just flooded in. There's no other way to say it. It was absolutely an eye-opener for me about the amount of money that was residing in Ireland at the time.

A lot of people said to me, 'You went around and defrauded a bunch of farmers,' and I argue that on two counts. Firstly, yes, there were a lot of farmers, but Pat's contacts were primarily in the countryside, so that's who we ended up presenting to, and that's who ended up investing. There was no 'We better avoid those smart Dublin people because they'll see through our scam' kind of carry-on or anything.

Secondly, I would maybe have been of the lazy, Dublin 4 view that farmers are stupid or gullible; but these were some of the smartest, most intelligent people I'd come across. They were canny as fuck.

You have to understand that not everyone invested for the same reasons. Apparently, everyone in Ireland except me was a millionaire at the time, so – and this is the bizarre thing – the mood among some of the bigger investors – the people who'd written cheques for more than a million – was that, meh, this was just one of my investments that I discuss over cognac and cigars at the end of the evening, because it's such a small part of my portfolio.

But to a lot of people who were investing, they were doing so not as a financial investment – or not *just* as a financial investment, because obviously everyone wants a return – but because they were very much into the impact that it could make on the world if we got Orbo into the market.

I know that sounds clichéd and maybe a bit naive, but, sincerely, there was a huge number of people who wanted to use us to win for Ireland and because, if we pulled off what we hoped to pull off, it could be a big win for the world.

I understand that people will be sceptical about that, but I still get calls from them today saying, 'You need to pull this off, Shaun. Fuck the money: you still need to pull this off.'

––––––––––––

There wasn't a huge market for bull semen in the 1990s in Ireland. But the market was about to get bigger, and the Cork farmer James Murphy and the Tipperary veterinarian Folke Rohrssen knew that if they got in early, they could build a comfortable business. In 1997, with a friend, Billy Irwin, they founded Eurogene AI, a company working on artificial insemination in cows, and it soon took off. Before long, they hired another man, Robert Seale, a former farmer who had retired early with a small nest egg. All four men would put money into Steorn.

James Murphy grew up in rural Cork in a family of five on an 80-acre dairy farm. Like the rest of his family, he has a restless mind, always turning to new things, burrowing deep into something, however complex or technical. It is, to his mind, a family weakness that when they 'get something between our teeth, we're very focused and very intense'. His parents were both orphans, and Murphy has described them as not knowing much about raising children, though it's clear that he doesn't mean this as a criticism: it's more an indication of the unburdened approach they took to child-rearing.

Murphy grew up in awe of his father, whom he has described as perhaps 'not a natural farmer' – by which he means successful, of course, but not necessarily a man who loved farming with the intensity that some other farmers possess. The family was, in Murphy's telling, slightly out of kilter with the culture of the time. They didn't spend much time in the pub and they weren't much into sport. Since there were few other pastimes in Ireland in the mid-1960s, they relied on each other and on books for their entertainment.

Murphy likes to tell a story to illustrate his father's intelligence, and it revolves around an American academic who met James's brother Gerard, also an academic, in Dublin. The American had written a lot about James Joyce, and, in the course of the conversation, Gerard told him that his father was reading *Finnegans Wake* for the third time and laughing his way through. It's something of a cliché in Ireland, a means of displaying your wit and erudition, to say that not only did you finish *Ulysses* and *Finnegans Wake* – both notoriously difficult books – but that you also got the jokes. Murphy the elder went one further: not only did he get the jokes, but he recognised the echoes of the east Cork vernacular that peppered the text, since Joyce's father had grown up in Fermoy. The American was immediately intrigued. Could he, he asked Gerard, come to Cork to visit and go through the book so that the elder Murphy could point out the subtle references that had passed under the noses of even the most astute Irish Joycean students? So, the American arrived, notebook in hand, and had the text read to him, the visitor scratching down references all the while. His father, James Murphy recalls, enjoyed it 'down to the ground'.

James Murphy had applied some of that intensive inquiry to farming when he took over the family farm, in particular applying it to breeding more productive strains of cow. Along with being a man of science, Murphy readily acknowledges that he's given to some of the more superstitious influences of rural Ireland. If you ask him, he'll tend to disclose it in an offhand way, slightly sheepishly, as if he were confessing to a fondness for cheap airport romance novels.

As Murphy tells it, he was drawn to Steorn almost unwittingly, with the universe – or whatever energies that determine fate and destiny – laying a trail of messages and clues for him that he would recognise only when Steorn was finally laid before him. Murphy says that his mother also had that strange power of heightened intuition, though he knows that being intuitive can often lead to being intuitively wrong. Even so, he believes that there are people who can intuit feeling before the event, and it allows him to sometimes suspend his disbelief.

In any case, in the years before the arrival onto the scene of Steorn, Murphy's youngest son, John, had been born with a heart defect. Murphy recalls the paediatrician telling him there was no hope for John. Murphy had a strange inkling that his son's defect had been in some way caused by the nuclear disaster at Chernobyl in 1986 – he had been reading for years about the number of birth defects on the rise in western Europe that some people attributed to the fallout carried on the wind from Ukraine. As a dairy farmer, Murphy knew the stories of millions of gallons of milk being dumped in the aftermath of the disaster.

He had spent many an eerie day in his fields after the news broke, watching the skies and wondering if they were filled with cancer-causing radiation, and it reminded him of his childhood during the Cold War, when he was terrified to look at the drawer containing the iodine pills the government had circulated in case of atomic warfare. To him, these dangerous forms of energy generation became mixed up with his farm and his son's illness.

Then there was the local dowser – a water diviner, that is – in Fermoy. She was a woman born in a man's body, who lived in a house so ramshackle that 'it was fascinating in its awfulness', he recalls. The dowser lived among cats and dogs, usually in pitch darkness. When Murphy visited the house, he came across a mystical book that had a lengthy passage on electrical energy that had happened to fall open on that page – a memory that stuck with him because of his fears about Chernobyl.

Thankfully, despite Murphy's worries, his son John's heart was healed, though he would require occasional check-ups in Dublin. On the last of those, Murphy took a spin home through Offaly to the home of his friend Kevin Flanagan, who was also a dairy farmer and who had a fine herd of Rotbunt cows, a German breed known for its red hide and a high protein content in its milk, making it more valuable. On that trip, Murphy was feeling relieved and unburdened: his son was healthy, his business was thriving, the fear and anxiety of Chernobyl seemed a lifetime ago and all was well in the world. As Murphy walked out the door to head home, Flanagan made what seemed an offhand remark. 'James, you and I will do business ourselves one day.'

Years later, when Flanagan approached him about Steorn, the words came flooding back to Murphy, and suddenly the breadcrumbs – the fears over Chernobyl, the hospital check-ups, the cows on the trip to Flanagan's, the water diviner and the book improbably open on a page about mystical energy – all seemed to come together in a flash.

Yet he remained reluctant to believe. He knew that what was being proposed would break the first law of thermodynamics, and that, to him, was impossible. But Flanagan kept nagging him, urging him to come to a meeting in his house about Steorn, at least to hear him out. So, he went.

Robert Seale is the kind of man who gets described as a decent auld skin. A broad-shouldered man who tends to stoop when he walks, a physical manifestation of his self-effacing character, he is a man of morality and integrity, honesty and transparency. He doesn't aim to take what's not his or promise what he can't deliver. Wanting only what he's owed in this world, he will also give more than that if he can. You might pass a hundred people like Seale in any given day and never notice them because they neither court attention nor seek validation: they're happy with their lot and take the vagaries of life in their stride.

Seale grew up on a farm in Laois. He was an intelligent boy, attending the elite Mountjoy boarding school in Dublin. He performed well in science, often topping the class in his exams.

When he was 11, his father died and his mother had to take over the running of the farm. Then, in 1963, aged 15, he had to leave school to return home to help her, never getting a chance to sit the Intermediate Certificate exam.

This left him with a nagging sense that he had missed out in life; but, being a quiet sort, he knuckled under and managed the farm, eventually taking it over. He had a good deal of success as a farmer but didn't find the work fulfilling; it was demanding, certainly, and required competence in a range of skills, and it was often a physically gruelling job. While he could manage all of that, he just never felt cut out for farming.

He got married young and raised a family, but his children did not seem to have a passion for farming. Moreover, the improvement in the economy meant that they had other professions open to them, and they began to drift away from the farm and into their own lives.

By then, Seale was beginning to realise that he was getting sick of farming. In 1999, on the spur of the moment – as he would later describe it – he was made an offer of £1.1 million on the farm and he took it. In later years, he would wonder if he had done the right thing; perhaps waiting a few years would have netted him even more, or perhaps not selling would have insulated him from the financial difficulties of the next 20 years. In any case, he took the money and went, like so many people in the late 1990s and early 2000s, to invest it.

At that time, the biggest and smartest investment – according to those who knew, and those who claimed they knew – was property, so Seale went out immediately to buy land in Ireland, houses in Britain and apartments in Spain. Unwisely, as he would later acknowledge, he overstretched, borrowing to buy properties so as to build up a portfolio.

He also retained some of the land from his farm and got planning permission for seven houses, building one for himself and his wife. This wasn't just any house: it was a Celtic Tiger house – more than 4,000 square feet on 10 acres, with ponds and landscaping and all the rest. It was valued then at €1.5 million – more than he had sold his farm for a few years before. He sold the sites for the remaining houses to a developer, who gave him €500,000 for the sites, on top of which Seale got a generous tax break.

Seale now felt that he was finally in control of his destiny, finally forging his own path in life. The sums that were rolling past his eyes every month seemed to validate the decision to sell the farm and take a different course. To keep himself occupied, he went to work as a salesman for Billy Irwin, Folke Rohrssen and James Murphy at their company, Eurogene AI.

———————

Folke Rohrssen had grown up in Stuttgart in the 1970s, later moving to Hanover to study veterinary medicine and work as a researcher before he came to Ireland to work as a vet.

Ireland in the 1980s struck him as a grey place in the direst of dire recessions, with shabby, unpainted houses and a surprising – to him – amount of influence from the Catholic Church. Nor was it the kind of place that loved animals, as he might have imagined. He had worked initially for a vet in Fermoy, Cork, being paid tuppence, before going out and setting up his own practice in 1992. It was a risky leap for a young vet, and there wasn't the kind of income stream that vets today can expect. Big animals were certainly taken to the vet if they needed treatment – after all, they were expensive investments – but small animals, like cats and dogs, were not so well looked after, simply because people didn't have the money to spend on the treatments such animals need, and for the first few years Rohrssen relied heavily on his farmer clients to keep his new practice going.

During the 1990s, though, the economy began to pick up. Suddenly, people who might have taken a dog or cat in to be euthanised were getting them treated, even if that meant expensive titanium plates in legs, overnight stays or expensive medication. Rohrssen soon had to hire another vet to help with the volume of work.

However, in 1998, Rohrssen was kicked by a horse on a farm and lay in a coma for three months. When he recovered, he decided that a single business in which he was the principal was too risky. He opted to expand the business. He'd had an idea of artificial insemination for cows, and he and James Murphy and another local farmer, Billy Irwin, decided to set up a company they called Eurogene AI. In 1998, they each put €50,000 into Eurogene, and before long the company was the biggest supplier of dairy semen in the country. The risk had paid off, and now Rohrssen had another leg to his business. So, when Murphy came to him with news of Steorn, he was more inclined to consider it; after all, the country was beginning to boom, he had two successful businesses and he was only going to invest what he could afford to lose.

A meeting on Kevin Flanagan's farm, arranged by Flanagan through his accountant, Pat Corbett, attended by Shaun McCarthy and Mike Daly and heard by several members of the Flanagan family as well as by James Murphy, Folke Rohrssen and Robert Seale, is, as far as anyone can tell, the first of the big meetings of the new investors in Steorn. These were the post-2004 investors, as they would come to think of themselves, distinguishing themselves from the company's founders and the likes of Tom Byrne and his Davy colleagues who had invested in the belief that Steorn was a consultancy firm rather than a world-changing research outfit.

McCarthy and Daly drove down to the meeting in McCarthy's old Renault and gave the presentation in the front room of Flanagan's house. Before the meeting, each prospective shareholder was given a copy of the company's slick and glossy 'confidential information memorandum'. As professionally produced as the most blue-chip of stock market-listed companies, it projected an aura of competence with its muted, neutral palette that avoided a tone of gauche money-grubbing. It wasn't hard to see why investors could be so easily sold on the idea.

Throughout, the document emphasised just how much risk was inherent in an investment in Steorn and how much third-party advice an investor ought to seek. Repeatedly, it 'strongly advised [investors] to consult an authorised independent financial advisor who specialises in making investments of this kind prior to making any investment decisions'. An investment in Steorn, it read, was a highly speculative investment and an investment should be made only by those with the necessary expertise to fully evaluate the investment. In addition to the usual risks associated with an investment in a business with an unproven revenue stream, the following principal risk factors should be considered …

It then listed the usual risks associated with a company that hadn't yet developed a product, market or single identifiable stream of revenue.

Yet so much of that could easily read as boilerplate to those new to investment – as something no more serious than the sped-up warnings at the end of a radio insurance ad. Inside, the memorandum made a giddily compelling case for investment in Steorn. The company had been founded by a 'team with significant international experience in successfully building global technology-centred businesses'; it had 'developed a proof of concept unit in 2003/2004'; it had 'already filed five patent applications in respect of its technology and has agreed terms for the commercial engineering and manufacture of certain power products with a European specialist engineering company'; it had 'entered into discussions with potential customers, global brand owners in mobile communications, computing and entertainment'; and 'an Irish university has validated the core technology'.

The memorandum also claimed that the 'technical director [of a] leading electronics blue-chip' had told the Steorn team that the 'most attractive option would be for [Steorn's] technology to replace the battery', though the memorandum did not name the director or the company. Even so, the document made some juicy suggestions about the business connections Steorn was making and about the potential deals it was on the verge of striking. Steorn had already 'introduced its technology to two dominant brand owners / key component manufacturers in the mobile computing and mobile phone markets'. At those meetings – which it could not say more about because of non-disclosure agreements – Steorn had 'presented to the aforementioned brand owners and agreed a process for these potential customers to test the technology over the course of the first quarter of 2006'. The plan was to conclude a 'co-development agreement with these parties for the design, manufacture and licensed integration of Steorn's technology into their products for commercial release in 2007'.

If all that sounded implausible, the shareholder register was not. Together with McCarthy and Daly, there was Francis Hackett, managing partner of O'Donnell Sweeney Eversheds, one of the biggest law firms in the country, sitting on 9.9 per cent; Tom Byrne had 6.7 per cent; Shaun Menzies of the internet firm Zartis had 4 per cent; and Barry Nangle, another senior Davy executive, had 2.3 per cent. Bank of Ireland was also listed, representing a Business Expansion Scheme from which Steorn had got investment.

Meanwhile, the management team was stacked with heavy hitters. Roger Hatfield, the chief financial officer, was described in the memorandum as having '25 years of experience in corporate financial management including flotations, acquisitions, and raising capital for technology companies in the UK, Ireland and the US'. Hatfield, it read, was the 'financial director that took Alphamerica public' and was 'also a senior manager with Accenture'.

Michael Moriarty, heading up corporate finance and strategy, had 'worked in corporate finance for 17 years, most recently as Director of Dawnay Day Corporate Finance Ltd, where he worked on mergers and acquisitions and capital raising. Prior to joining Dawnay Day, he was investment director with the Carroll Group.'

On top of that, there was an apparent abundance of scientific figures. Richard Walshe, the marketing manager, had been involved with the Irish technology firm Microsol; Ciaran Mythen, the senior technical specialist, had an undergraduate degree in experimental physics from Trinity College, Dublin; had worked for Oxford Instruments; and had held the position of scientific officer and scientific consultant at Daresbury Laboratory (the national synchrotron radiation facility in England) as well as at Aarhus University in Denmark.

If the prospective investors didn't know much about physics – and, in truth, few did – they took confidence from the calibre of people who had joined the company. This fitted neatly into the Celtic Tiger model in a country in which investments were made on a nod and a wink and got benediction from those who pitched them rather than on what was being pitched.

Certainly, Steorn noted that its technology was controversial – a point McCarthy and Daly had made repeatedly and prominently in their shareholder meetings – and yet a prospective investor could be forgiven for having a thin grasp of the intricacies of the laws of thermodynamics but a clear understanding of the plain meaning of these lines: Steorn was on the verge of some very lucrative deals indeed. After all, the invention of the mobile phone had turned battery power into an acute problem.

Perhaps, given such urgency, the market could finally turn out a revolutionary solution. As the confidential memorandum set out, Steorn's

> technology allows for the production of electrical power without the need for external force or power input. The operation of power at point of use is similar to currently available power generation technology except that it allows for the generator to self-rotate, thus producing an output for no more than the natural properties of its components; this effect mirrors the requirements for a device to exhibit the properties of over-unity.

Using such language, Steorn's proposal didn't sound so controversial; in fact, it was 'similar to currently available power generation technology' but for a single difference: it allowed for the generator to self-rotate.

But that's where even the sober document began to look a little feverish. For starters, it acknowledged that, yes, this was indeed over-unity – one of the most controversial concepts in physics and a mirage that had for centuries driven countless amateur inventors to distraction. But in the pages of a legally airtight, fiscally prudent investment prospectus, one buttressed by promises of deals virtually already signed, it didn't sound as controversial as the physicists believed. It described the 'use of a multi-pole magnet array' that 'consists of a rotor that has a magnet array affixed in a defined arrangement and is attracted to the actuator'. This 'unique configuration' allows for the system to 'increase the energy gain by manipulation of the array while the energy required (loss) for operation is constant'. In short, the magnets moved the wheel more than the volume of the power input, thus producing a spinning wheel that could be harvested for yet more energy. But then it made a truly whopping claim.

Steorn's patent pending, over-unity technology can be installed within most energy operated devices/machines, is more efficient and cost effective than battery and fuel cell technologies and makes existing energy-storage and distribution systems largely redundant.

In fact, the reader was told, by 2010 the technology would be developed for mobile phones, computers and gaming; beyond 2010 it would be developed for auxiliary power units for RVs, lorries and forklifts through compact portable units of between 100 watts and 3 kilowatts; then it would be developed for back-up power units of between 500 watts and 50 kilowatts for critical communications infrastructure and railways, then buses, military vehicles and the holy grail of cars.

The company's sales would explode. Its modest profit of €69,000 in 2002 – when, it should be noted, Steorn was still a consulting firm – and losses of €12,000 in 2003 and €896,000 in 2004 would turn into profits of €19.8 million in 2007, €134.6 million in 2008, €590.2 million in 2009 and €808.7 million in 2010. Thereafter, profits would presumably surge into the billions.

To do so, it needed €20 million, which would 'provide sufficient funding to commercialise the technology, launch a strong marketing campaign, attract the appropriate senior executives, and underpin Steorn's negotiations with the major brand owners'. The goal was an IPO in year four, at which time the profitable company would be spitting out dividends to its shareholders.

———————

Robert Seale would later reflect on just what had motivated him to invest that night. Was it greed? Partly, perhaps, since Pat Corbett had presented a compelling picture of the profits to be made if the Steorn technology ever came to fruition. And even though those figures were based on no kind of reality, they were intoxicating to hear.

For Seale, though, there was something more to it. As McCarthy would later realise, it was a feeling shared by Murphy, the Flanagans and dozens of other investors who pumped money into Steorn in those early days. It was the feeling that, if it worked, it would be a world-changing technology of incalculable benefit to humanity. The term 'climate change' had yet to gain popular currency, but everyone in that room knew that pollution, the melting polar caps and the damage caused by fossil fuels were existential issues. If that could be solved there and then in that room in Offaly by their investing in an Irish company – an *Irish* company! – wouldn't it make all the risk worth it?

It may now seem gullible, even a little foolish, but most of those investors had already seen changes wrought that they couldn't have predicted, or even imagined, a mere decade before. Take the telephone, a piece of late-Victorian technology virtually unchanged for more than a century. Then, in little under a decade, it was made mobile and then converted from a telephone in your pocket into a tiny computer more powerful than the one that had landed people on the moon.

The laws of physics were, they knew, inviolable, untouched by centuries of people promising precisely this; but maybe, just maybe, this time it really could happen.

McCarthy and Daly gave a fairly unadorned presentation, merely outlining the anomaly as they understood it, and running through the potential applications and the technical aspects of working it out. But Corbett was – as Seale saw it – a kind of evangelist, using his considerable charisma to tap into that cultural excitement and conjure the possibilities inherent in Steorn.

If it seems reckless now, don't forget that most of them had the money. It was sitting there in the bank, waiting to be used. Plenty of it had already gone on safer investments in property – which was only going up – and in bank shares and bonds, the prudent stuff, the boring stuff. With so much money squirrelled away in the investments that would take care of their futures, what would be so bad about a little flutter on something that, if it could be pulled off, would make the heart race a little faster?

James Murphy, like the others in the room that night, was impressed with McCarthy's unprepossessing way and unpretentious airs. As well as noting McCarthy's earthy and compelling manner, Murphy recognised that he had a strong track record in business and consultancy.

But for most of the meeting – while everyone else was listening to Daly and McCarthy give their spiel – Murphy was having something close to an out-of-body experience. Five minutes into the meeting, he had been overcome, as he would later recall, by a strange feeling that took him out of himself, so that he was looking at the meeting as if from the outside. He is reluctant to talk about it now, but as McCarthy was speaking, Murphy – whether inside his own head or outside of it – was being told that McCarthy was right. As Murphy recalls it, it was a vision that told him that Steorn would be a long, tough road, but that McCarthy was right.

Murphy was, at that moment, attempting to struggle against it, to avoid giving into what he feared might have been a delusion, and he knew that delusions were a tricky matter: the world is filled with holy zealots and Murphy didn't particularly want to be one of those people, having a farm to run and a family to raise. Yet he knew enough quantum physics to know that time is merely a dimension, not a linear progression, and that maybe some of that old, pre-industrial intuition and spirituality might have been tapping into something unrecognised and misunderstood.

The Steorn presentation went on for two to three hours, by which point Murphy had regained some sense of self-possession. Afterwards, over a Chinese takeaway, they all talked about the investment. Murphy, in spite of himself, was intrigued. He reckoned it was a 10 billion to 1 chance, but he nonetheless made an investment in the company.

He wasn't the only one. In fact, everyone who attended that night wrote cheques for tens of thousands of euro on the strength of Daly's and McCarthy's presentation.

Neither Robert Seale nor Folke Rohrssen had out-of-body experiences, but they invested regardless. Within the first year, Seale would put in more than €120,000 at around €1,642 per share.

Rohrssen, who viewed an investment in an efficient battery as a good fit with other investments he had made in renewable energy, such as solar panels and wind turbines, put in €30,000.

By the time McCarthy and Daly got back to Dublin, Steorn was sitting on a quarter of a million euro. Pat Corbett wasn't prepared to stop there: he had a target of €20 million to chase.

In this, Corbett was helped by James Murphy, who had become just as zealous as McCarthy and Daly, particularly after a consultation with his brother Gerard, who confirmed the veracity of Steorn's claims of world-changing perpetual motion to James's satisfaction. As he recalls it, he 'selectively chose people to invest who would have a value system', by which he meant people who understood not just the financial value of the company, but the moral, economic and environmental benefit too. He wanted highly moral people, people with a sense of egalitarianism; above all, he wanted ordinary people who could get a share in this company that would not only secure their finances, but also save the world. He would later come to regret getting so many other people involved in Steorn.

The news of Steorn soon began to spread beyond the original group that had gathered in Kevin Flanagan's farm, and Pat Corbett arranged meetings up and down the country so that Mike Daly and Shaun McCarthy could do their presentation and so that Corbett could wow them with the investment returns they could expect.

Tom Byrne attended a few of those meetings in the early years as he watched the money flow in and the company change direction. He travelled to some of the country hotels, and one in particular, in Port Laoise, struck him because of the number of four-by-fours sitting outside – almost like a meeting of the Irish Farmers' Association.

Byrne was mystified by the amount of interest from what he supposed to be unsophisticated investors. He had, after all, advised another friend not to invest in Steorn, and he took it on himself only because he knew that he, by virtue of his financial wherewithal and investment experience, could absorb a level of risk that most other investors could not.

At one of the Steorn investment meetings, he struck up a conversation with the mother of a family in attendance. He asked her how much she had put in. A quarter of a million each, she replied. In total, a million euro. He was left wondering how this family had come up with a surplus million euro.

The net soon spread wider.

––––––––––––

In 2005, Edward Sheehan and his wife, Evelyn, were standing in the front room of their Georgian house in north Cork, from which they have sweeping views of the valley of the Blackwater, which runs along the border between Cork and Waterford. On a sunny day, with the Sheehans' house perched halfway up a hill overlooking the valley and a patchwork quilt of farms, the area is quietly beautiful. The house hadn't been designed to take in the view – after all, you can't eat the scenery – but by the beginning of the Celtic Tiger, the Sheehans had realised that their kitchen window was too small to capture the panorama.

Edward Sheehan is as sharp as they come. He grew up in the house and had attended school a short walk through the fields away. He had held onto some of the land while training as an accountant, working briefly in a local co-op before setting up his own practice and taking on a couple of local farmers as clients. He was also a canny businessman, having invested wisely in a chain of newsagents and a small but healthy portfolio of stocks and bonds and a smattering of property for rental income.

Sheehan is a man given to weighing carefully the value of money and to balancing the outgoings so that they never overwhelm the incomings. So, for him, the house surely seemed more than adequate.

However, Evelyn eventually convinced him it wasn't. He took a trip into town to his local bank, which catered to farmers and those working in the agricultural sector. He went directly to his friend in the bank, a man who had once introduced him to a senior bank colleague known as 'the million-dollar man' – an official who could give a loan up to a million euro without having to refer it to head office. This was a novelty that, in rural Cork, made this official something of a celebrity, at least among those businessmen and women inclined to go to him with a loan application.

'Joe, would you givvus a quarter of a million?' Sheehan asked his bank manager pal.

'I will. What kind of security have you got?'

'I've an apartment in Cork that's paid for.'

'Yeah, that'd be fine. You're looking for 250. I'll get someone to value that at 290 for you, and I'll give you the 250. You could pay interest on it for a while, and then you can pay the capital.'

That was fine for Sheehan, who took the money and did the necessary renovations, inviting the Blackwater Valley, in all its sunlit glory, into his front room. Moreover, he was left with a lump sum of roughly €100,000. Rather than take the money and wipe a chunk of the debt off at a stroke, he invested it. He put €70,000 into shares in Bank of Ireland, the biggest and safest bank in the country; he put another chunk into CRH, a concrete and gravel company that was one of the biggest blue-chips in the country – one so big it didn't even deign to list on the Irish Stock Exchange; and he put €30,000 into a property-investment vehicle, Belfry, that was being promoted by AIB, the second-biggest bank in the country.

So far, so safe. He had limited his exposure to risk by keeping his money with two banks, one directly and another through an indirect property fund; he had avoided putting any more of his money directly into property, instead allowing a bank to manage it for him as part of a collective investment; and he had stuck money into the shares of one of the most successful Irish companies in history. No investment manager would have regarded the investments as anything other than prudent and sensible.

The remainder, however, was burning a hole in Sheehan's pocket, and that's when he ran into James Murphy. Or, more accurately, his partner in his accountancy firm, Tony Glavin, ran into James Murphy, the local farmer and bull-semen salesman who had convinced several of his friends to meet with Shaun McCarthy and Mike Daly from Steorn.

Glavin and Sheehan's son Conor attended a meeting in Port Laoise and came away impressed. It was certainly a bold claim, they told Sheehan, but the two Steorn boys seemed honest and genuine. With so much of their money already wisely and carefully invested, surely they were allowed a little roll of the dice at the casino? After all, wasn't that what good portfolio management was about: balancing the low-yielding, safe investments with higher-risk, but potentially higher-yielding, punts?

So, that's precisely what they did. Edward and Evelyn Sheehan bought about €30,000 in shares, a friend put in €20,000 and Conor put in some money as well, as did Glavin. Soon after, Evelyn took €20,000 out of a life insurance bond and topped their investment up.

It wasn't hard to see why they did so: though the prospectus was a sober document peppered with appropriate warnings about the risk associated with the product, the potential for gain was enormous.

Edward Sheehan wasn't all that bothered about the substance of the Steorn claim. He had no training in physics, and the idea that it was controversial and that it up-ended the laws of thermodynamics didn't seem that relevant in the context of a small, risky investment at the riskier end of a safe portfolio. In any case, technology had developed rapidly in his own lifetime, so the idea of a more efficient battery seemed risky but achievable.

Meanwhile, Pat Corbett was telling shareholders that the first round of dividends could be €8,000 a share. Given the shares the Sheehans had bought, their dividends alone could be worth €360,000 a year, and that's before any talk of an investment return based on the sale of the company.

Sheehan joked that he could give up his job with the Law Society and live off the fat dividends; although, with his accountant's head on, he knew that this was an overestimation – even by Celtic Tiger standards – since even the biggest corporate measured its dividends in cents, not dollars, and certainly not thousands of dollars.

Alan Wallace has lived all his life on the family farm just outside Tullamore, Offaly, where the Wallaces have cultivated grain and bulbs since 1939.

The Wallace farm sits on a little ridge of land on the outskirts of Tullamore, on the road to the smaller town of Clara. Even after the rapacious years of the Celtic Tiger, the town has never quite managed to reach the farm – Beech Hill – giving it a removed feel, both from the town and from the construction.

While Steorn was stumbling on the discovery that would come to define it, Wallace was watching the changes take place – most vividly at the annual National Ploughing Championships, where the ploughing is a kind of novelty event behind which the real business of trading and striking deals is done and where, in the early 2000s, tents selling foreign property had begun to emerge.

Wallace had seen precious little land around Tullamore being sold. All of a sudden, though, farmers who in previous generations had been highly reluctant to sell land – for emotional reasons and because it was more lucrative to work the land than sell it – found themselves sitting on windfalls, or prospective windfalls, and a whole industry emerged to provide them with options either to save or to spend it.

One thing was certain: farmers were not putting it back into their farms and expanding their herds; they were buying houses and flats, and not just in Ireland but all over the world.

Nor was it just farmers. The property mania had spread to ordinary salaried workers, who had also begun to benefit from the loosening of bank lending and the increase in property investment. Wallace had been horrified by the reckless way in which Irish people were spending their hard-earned money, using money from land speculation to fund ever riskier land speculation, seasoned with liberal quantities of bank debt.

All this made Wallace deeply uneasy. For one investment seminar in Jury's Hotel in Dublin, rooms were set up for different regions of Europe. To buy a house by a pool in Spain, you went to the Spanish room; to buy a city apartment in Budapest, you went to the Budapest room.

On one such visit, Wallace had walked into the Spanish room to find it deathly quiet, people having concluded that the real value was now in Eastern Europe. He struck up a conversation in the Budapest room with one couple from Wexford. The man had his chequebook out and was putting a deposit on three apartments. Wallace asked him if he had been to see the apartments.

No, he replied, he wouldn't have time.

Had he spoken to his accountant?

To this question, Wallace got a slightly baffled look.

Why was he buying them, then?

'My neighbour bought two apartments in Berlin, and I want to go one better,' he told Wallace.

———————

Alan Wallace had known Pat Corbett for years, right back to Corbett's father's death. Wallace has an old-fashioned loyalty, and Beech Hill farm was one of Corbett's first clients when he started his own practice. But after Corbett retired from accountancy, they didn't meet again until an accidental encounter on a Dublin street one day in 2006.

They idled a while before Wallace asked Corbett what he was up to, and Corbett suggested they sit for lunch. Over lunch, Corbett told Wallace that the job he was doing was secretive and that Wallace would need to sign a non-disclosure agreement even to hear about it.

'What's a non-disclosure agreement?' Alan asked.

'It means once you sign that document, I can tell you about it; but if you talk about it, you can lose your house.' But, Corbett added, it was good; there was money in it.

So, Wallace signed the document – Corbett just happened to have one with him – and was told all about Steorn and its technology and about the meeting on the Flanagans' farm. Wallace was also told that the company had already raised a couple of million in the two years since the meeting.

It was the middle of the boom, and the Wallaces, like the rest of the country, were doing well. They had resisted the urge to sell their land and had resisted multiple offers on all but one of their fields.

Everything about Wallace, from the house on the hill outside the town to his diction and syntax, is slightly old-fashioned. His interpretation of the surge of wealth during the Celtic Tiger years is rooted in the middle of the twentieth century, and he was slow to leap on whatever fad had seized the country.

Yet the story Corbett was telling him seemed to be a godsend. It prompted Wallace to recall his childhood, when his grandfather ran the old vacuum-tube radio off a tractor battery. The battery would run for a week, at which point his father would take the second battery, which had been attached to the tractor outside, and hook it to the radio, using the tractor to recharge the first.

Just like Robert Seale, Wallace felt that the money was only part of the motivation. This was about being part of something that had a chance to save the world – a world-changing device, and Irish to boot. For Wallace, the chance that the beneficiaries would be ordinary Irish families rather than obscenely wealthy financial institutions was simply irresistible.

He offered to buy 100 shares at €1,642 a share. Six months later, he bought another 100.

Shaun McCarthy: When to Stop Fundraising

At some stage, we'd gotten to €16 or €17 million, and we said, 'This is too easy. Let's stop.' And only when we ran into trouble did we go out again. And again. Relative to our experience hustling money from customers and tech start-ups, this had been just simple. We'd managed it in two years, maybe three.

We could've kept going during the Celtic Tiger, and I'm sure we would've raised €40 million. But we did make a purposeful stop. We said we're going to go public with this thing; what we don't want – and this goes back to this tingle in the back of your spine going, 'You know how this looks' – we don't want any of the publicity that we're doing this only as an exercise to raise money.

Another reason was that we were going public, and the obvious criticism would have been that you're telling one of the greatest snake-oil stories in history, and you're making money on the side, so we purposely shut it down before that arose.

It was a lot of money to come in all at once, so we were sitting down with Pat [Corbett] and Roger [Hatfield], our accountant, and Mike Moriarty – who we'd gotten to jump ship from Dawnay Day and join us full time. We had a little office in Fumbally Court [in Dublin], and then we moved to East Wall and started hiring people. We had raised it to spend it, and we were spending it.

We had to go to [the legal firm] O'Donnell Sweeney because Francis Hackett was a lawyer there. We were ending up potentially, after the first quarter of a million, having multiple investors, so they put in this trust structure where, say, if someone looks for James Murphy on the Steorn share register, they'd think he'd invested €6 million, but he hadn't: he was just holding it in trust for others.

That sounds a bit Ponzi-ish, but it wasn't like that. It was done with full corporate finance advice and with the lawyers. We were very by the book. We raised the money from an unusual clientele or audience; but in terms of the documentation and legalities, it was led by people who had done this well for most of their working lives. And I was really just wheeled along to these things to do my spoof about the technology.

So, we had three full-time people who did all of the paperwork. There was money we turned down as well. We weren't taking just any money: we had full know-your-customer, anti-money-laundering and all kinds of management of the share register. There was a lot of money we didn't take, and I would imagine they wouldn't have passed AML [anti-money-laundering] processes. There might have been a fierce bang of diesel off it.

It was Ireland at the time; there were a lot of people running cash business – I'm sure they still are. It's not a world I have any great exposure to, but if you couldn't stump up all the documentation that we needed, that was it.

We also had meetings, annual meetings, and a lot more often than that. Because of the whole idea that everyone in Ireland is less than six degrees of separation from everyone else, we ended up with a situation where, for the last seven or eight million, we didn't even attend the meetings ourselves.

Then we hired Pat outright to manage not just the fundraising but the communication, and we would do meetings around the country, and we ended up doing them as often as required. So, we didn't have AGMs; it was significantly more frequent than that. But this wasn't pitching: it was 'What are we doing? Where are we going?' and so on. I guess you'd call them update meetings, and we did that right through to the bitter end.

Pat and Mike were the perfect combination, really. Pat is the best salesman on a one-to-one level that I've ever met. It's one of the most remarkable things. Meanwhile, Mike [Moriarty] was so corporate and formal and box-ticky that the combination of the two was everything you need in terms of brake and accelerator. This is what these guys did.

It wasn't Pat going off on his lonesome and selling snake oil: it was always that there was a balance between our need to raise money and also our making sure, in raising money, that we didn't fuck it up for the exit in the end. Because whenever we're looking to license or sell or IPO or whatever the exit turned out to be, everything had to be holier than thou.

8. A JURY OF YOUR PEERS

Shaun McCarthy: What Now?

The first part of that process of developing Orbo was to secure what we had developed, so we had started a long and expensive patent process because your patents are like your land deeds: they're the proof you own the thing. So, we had a guy, full time, responsible for managing the patents, and there's a whole world of pain in there.

Meanwhile, we had Mike Moriarty hire a couple of people, and they were looking at entry points into the market and who you'd license it to. So, if you licensed it to Apple, we'd all go home in our own helicopters; but when you dig into the detail, that's not actually where you enter the market. So, we had people doing deep dives into market structure to find out who makes Apple's batteries.

And I was primarily responsible for moving the technology forward and making it more and more compelling in a test environment. Our fundamental business objective was simple: how do we demonstrate in a way that's convincing enough to license this, or at least to start a process of licensing this. So, we were going around trying to get validation from anyone who was prepared to test this thing.

We needed to find people who we could spend some time testing with and who were prepared to document their tests and potentially allow us to use their test results. It would be slow progress, nudging it forward an inch at a time.

We approached everyone who would listen. Because we were engineers, our instinct was to approach other engineers. I honestly couldn't tell you how many engineers came in and tested. So, we were getting engineering validation, but a lot of it wasn't usable because even the engineers who were validating were saying, 'I'll write you a report, but you're not sticking that in the public domain, fuckface, because this is my career.'

We were also trying to get academics and physics professors, and we approached all the universities in the UK and Ireland. We got one university who was prepared to do some provisional testing, but all the other ones said no. We were developing a portfolio of what some people would consider lower-level validation (but I don't consider it that) of people who were just below PhD level, and we were trying to leverage that to get to ever more illustrious views.

Maurice Linnane is a filmmaker who has made music videos for the likes of U2, the Rolling Stones, Neil Young and Garth Brooks, and he was one of those things that Steorn, now that it had raised the money, decided to spend it on.

In 2005, Linnane was hired by Steorn to make a documentary about the company. Steorn was an odd commission for him, but he was intrigued by the prospect of a documentary that would follow Steorn's journey from discovering a freak reading on an oscilloscope to creating a source of free energy that would change the world.

Linnane had briefly studied science in university and knew enough to know that over-unity was part of a package of fringe science – to put it generously – along with cold fusion and perpetual motion. He had done some research to remind himself of those murky areas of magnetism in which people claimed discoveries that never quite panned out. But for Linnane, whether it's for a rock band looking for a dramatic and attention-grabbing video or an accountancy firm looking for a crisp and professional advertisement, his job is to help the subject realise their vision, not to judge their activities. Steorn was therefore just another commission. Or so he thought.

Linnane sat down to discuss the project and set the budget with Shaun McCarthy and Richard Walshe, Steorn's public relations manager, and immediately took to them both. McCarthy struck him as the kind of person who could be full of thigh-slapping, hilarious bonhomie one moment and of slightly uncomfortable menace the next, which made him a fascinating character for a filmmaker. Linnane would later reflect that he had never met anyone better able to convince a roomful of people of something that, on the face of it, was absurd, even if they had entered that room with rigid scepticism.

He sat down with McCarthy and listened to his description of MOAB – 'the mother of all bumps' – the spike in the monitor when the particular arrangement of magnets showed an acceleration at a moment when, according to conventional science, it should have been decelerating. He watched McCarthy tell him this in his trademark style – full of charm and disarming unpretentiousness – and realised then that McCarthy truly believed in Steorn. The science, and the fact that they were thumbing their noses at one of the foundation stones of physics, seemed not to bother McCarthy. They didn't know anything about scientific theory; it hardly seemed relevant when they had found this weird thing and had shown, McCarthy said, that it was repeatable.

'The rest,' McCarthy told Linnane, 'is just engineering – and we're engineers.'

Having made that pitch, McCarthy explained to Linnane what he wanted: a documentary-maker to follow Steorn on what they were convinced would be a short journey from discovery to fame. They would sign a deal with Linnane according to which the filmmaker would have full editorial control. Steorn asked only to have access to the documentary in the fullness of time so as to support themselves and use it as publicity.

It was – a year or two before Steorn went public – further evidence of their unshakeable confidence in what they had discovered and of its never being intended as a scam. Only the most foolish bank robbers record their crime. Steorn, however, wanted the world to see this; the video was for posterity. The idea that the film would record an abject failure never seemed to cross their minds; nor did they worry that they might want to place a provision in the contract to exert control over or ownership of the tapes. Since their plan could only succeed, why would they need to protect themselves?

Linnane's immediate sense of Steorn was that there was an air of excitement and possibility around the place, as if everyone believed that they were on the cutting edge of technology and that the property bubbles that had destroyed everywhere else in the world would not destroy Ireland.

He shot his first few hours of video in 2005, when Steorn was still working on the mechanical version of Orbo, which the Steorn team said was powered purely by the interaction of magnets. In effect, it was a big wheel the size of a manhole cover. The plan was to put the wheel into a flight case, put the flight case into a car and drive to the Cavendish Laboratory at the University of Cambridge, with a stop along the way at Isaac Newton's house so that McCarthy could do a piece to camera.

It was bold, even a little brazen, and, not surprisingly, when they got to the Cavendish Laboratory the staff members wouldn't even entertain the idea of testing the system, which later led Linnane to believe that it was McCarthy's intention all along to show how unwilling conventional physics was to deal with these upstart engineers before Steorn's discovery was eventually shown to be valid, with Linnane tagging along as the dispassionate, independent observer.

Linnane wrote a budget for the film project, based on the assumption that it would take mere months to execute. But things didn't quite go according to plan.

———————

While Shaun McCarthy was getting creative, Pat Corbett was still out raising millions of euro. The increased volume of financial filings with the Companies Registration Office was beginning to catch the attention of some of Dublin's more attentive business journalists – after all, raising several million euro in Dublin was still worth noting, even if growing volumes of private-company fundraising had almost become de rigueur.

In May 2006, Gavin Daly of the *Sunday Times* reported that Steorn had so far raised €3 million and was three years into a four-year development plan focused on 'revolutionising the consumer electronics market with technology to extend the lifespans of batteries in mobile phones and other gadgets'. While that was undoubtedly part of its aim, it was clearly a sign that McCarthy and his colleagues were intent, for now, on staying below the radar. Indeed, it's clear from Daly's article that McCarthy was attempting to spin a mundane version of the Steorn story. 'Striving to extend mobile battery lifespan' wasn't untrue, but it also wasn't the full story.

Nor was McCarthy being wholly candid about Steorn's fundraising goals or the figure of €20 million that had already been flung about. When asked by Daly, he said that €2.5 million of the existing fundraising had come from 'high net worth individuals' within the previous 18 months, which meant that Steorn was 'not under pressure to deliver a financial return in the short term'.

As to the substance of the technology, McCarthy described the products as being based on the same principle as kinetic-energy generators in watches, and he said the products would be ready by the summer of 2007. Again, this was a low-key description of what they believed they had.

'We are totally on plan in terms of development,' McCarthy told Daly. He then mentioned the 'voracious' market for battery technology. 'We have done it at the right pace, and are very confident in our technology.' Steorn would have low revenues for the foreseeable future and would continue to lose money, he said; but these losses would be according to a plan that would deliver in the future.

Daly didn't ask about Steorn's real goals because at that point in the company's development, there was no reason to believe that it was anything other than a standard technology start-up. Nor was it odd to raise money through private investors, since there were suddenly many private investors who had the wherewithal to invest. The sum of €20 million was not eye-watering, nor was it to be raised suspiciously quickly – or so it seemed from the outside looking in.

———————

Meanwhile, Steorn was working with McCarthy's former college, Dublin Institute of Technology, to sponsor a young entrepreneurs' competition that had a top prize of €5,000 and a prize pool of €11,000.

The goal of the competition was for students to devise the most commercially viable idea that would 'encourage and support a rigorous business planning approach to entrepreneurial activities'. In the public relations material for the competition, Steorn was described as 'a leading Intellectual Property (IP) research and development organisation' based in the Bolton Trust's Docklands Innovation Park in East Wall Road and as working closely with the DIT.

To external observers, Steorn was a respectable, viable, up-and-coming tech start-up with the funds to build out its commercial plan and with both connections and ambitions. In the background, though, the company was running up against some closed doors.

Shaun McCarthy: Getting Creative

By the end of 2006, we started the next phase of our little internal plan, which was this: okay, we've identified the people in the industry; let's go out and talk to them.

We had identified the guys who developed the power-management chips, the guys who developed the controller chips. If you wanted to license the technology to a company that had the biggest market share and the most production capability, you're not licensing it to some battery factory; you're not licensing it to the Nokias or the Samsungs. No, you're going to license it to the guys who, in turn, license it to the guys who develop the chips that control the batteries. They're the guys who decide whose power technology goes to the batteries you use in your phones and other devices. They are the US multinational chip manufacturers like Texas Instruments and Intel.

To get into meetings with them, we sent them the validation. There was enough meat in the validation we had got at that point for them to say, 'Well, maybe these fuckers ain't crazy!' We had done enough to get the meetings, and we felt we had enough to convince these guys to test it themselves. That's all we wanted, and that was the nub of our plan.

But when we got there they said, 'No, we want to see the top guys in the world say this is worth investigating.' That was very much a watershed moment. So, it was the meeting with the biggest manufacturer that reset our plan. Basically, we needed high-grade academic validation to move forward.

That was when everything kicked off into trying to go back to the universities and getting people who had already turned us down once. I don't want to sound slightly sour, but the most expert people on the planet who do magnetics and physics had already said, 'We're not even talking to you fuckers.' I already knew the door was closed, and it wasn't just [Prof. Michael] Coey: it was anyone in a position of authority and power in academic institutions. You're not even going to get a hearing. It was a fair request from the companies, I suppose, but our experience with it was 'shutters down'.

That's when we said we had to come up with a different way. We were sitting there, going, 'Plan A is out the window' – Plan A being academic validation, license the product, then buy a small house off Grafton Street. Everything was going in that direction, but, ultimately, if the guy or girl or company who's going to license it says, 'Well, yeah, that's what you think you need, but this is what *we* need,' you have to go back and rethink.

We had multiple options, as far as we saw it. One was to approach the second- or third-tier players in the market and try the same story. The view was that we'd end up in the same place and, commercially, down the road, it would be dangerous.

Just to give you the thinking behind that: it was never our plan, if Plan A had worked, to have an exclusive licence. Everyone would've had to get it for free. That was pure self-protection, because if we'd got the biggest chip guy in the world to license this, and they went exclusive, all that would do is force the guys who don't have access to it to develop a competitive solution because it's so compelling. So, if we went to a second-tier guy, they'd know we'd been rebuffed, and we'd get locked into an exclusive contract. Eventually, one of the big guys would come along and develop their own version.

The second option was to develop a product of our own, and €20 million wasn't even going to fucking touch it.

The third option was to try the one we ended up going for – to say, 'Okay, there's got to be some fucking way we can get these guys to look at this.' And that's where we ended up sticking our heads above the parapet. We had to get creative.

Meanwhile, Steorn was still fundraising and tapping some of the existing investors for more money. In August 2006, for example, the Steorn investor Alan Wallace got an email from Pat Corbett.

> A meeting is being held in the Days Hotel, Main Street, Tullamore, Co Offaly. [It] represents a major milestone in the company's development. The purpose of the meeting is to provide you, as an investor, with details of this exciting event. I realise the meeting is being held at short notice, but I believe once you have heard our plans you will appreciate the reasoning behind our strategy.

At that meeting, Wallace was showered with an array of figures that promised eye-watering returns if he invested. For his investment, he could stand to earn millions back.

The key, as it was outlined to Wallace, was the likely value of Steorn when the product was finally developed and ready to come to market. Every share was being sold that night for €1,470 – lower by €172 than the original price of €1,642. With 135,000 shares in issue (though, of course, only a fraction of them were sold at that point), this valued the company at a hair under €200 million, at least on paper.

Everyone knew that €1,470 a share was pricey – even the most blue-chip listed corporation, with guaranteed dividends and a strong probability of retaining or increasing its value, would reach a share price of only a couple of hundred euro – but that's where the real Steorn hard sell came in.

If the company was sold, Wallace was told, those shares would multiply in value to potentially fortune-making levels. He was told of one company that had sold in early 2004 for €8 billion, each share valued at €59,000 or so. That meant that someone with a mere five shares got €285,000 into their hands; someone with 10 shares got more than €570,000. Anyone who bought 20 shares was now a millionaire, with €1.1 million. And someone with 150 shares got €8.7 million.

Steorn's shares, though pricey, could rocket in value. That share Wallace bought for €1,470 might be a big outlay now, but the potential for returns was immense. Steorn didn't leave it to Wallace's imagination: he was told that if the company sold for €1 billion, every share would be worth €7,142. Buy 10 shares, and that's a cool €70,000, minus the original cost of the shares, resulting in a net gain of more than €53,000 – a fivefold increase on the original investment. If the company sold for €3 billion, the shares would be worth €21,428. If it sold for €5 billion, every share would be worth more than €35,000.

It is a sign of the sheer conviction of Pat Corbett, and his ability to sell a dream, that Wallace's handwritten notes from the night of that meeting show that they had calculated every permutation between €1 billion and €20 billion – at which point the shares were worth €842,857, and presumably the euro symbols were spinning like a fruit machine for anyone considering an investment.

———————

However, not every investor was convinced. For one, Edward Sheehan was beginning to have doubts. On one occasion while on business in Dublin, he had dropped in to the Steorn office to visit the team. He was given a coffee and a tour of the premises. He asked to meet Shaun McCarthy but was told that he was checking the size of the mobile phone market – an idea that struck Sheehan as odd, since it was either far too early to be checking that market (since there was no product to sell) or far too late (since they had apparently raised millions without having checked the size of the market until now). He was also wholly underwhelmed by the lab, seeing only rows of offices rather than the high-tech research and development facility he'd been expecting.

Sheehan came away with a nagging sense of doubt, but as he drove away, he tried to suppress it. They must know what they're doing, he told himself; they were engineers and consultants to some of the biggest companies in the country. And James Murphy, a polymath who could talk at length about the Steorn discovery and its application, regarded McCarthy as a genius – beyond a genius, in fact. So, Sheehan told himself to bear with them, to listen when they told him that everything was okay, and to believe.

Sheehan wasn't alone, however. Folke Rohrssen had also begun to have doubts. When Corbett, McCarthy and Mike Daly attended meetings afterwards seeking more funding, Rohrssen began to develop a firm scepticism that his money would ever come back. He declined to invest any more, believing that his original €30,000 was gone. He wasn't willing to throw good money after bad.

Rohrssen was also disappointed with the amount of information coming from investor meetings; they were less updates on the company than sales pitches for additional investment. Rohrssen and James Murphy remained friends, but the two tacitly agreed not to talk about it. Rohrssen had concluded that Steorn wasn't a scam – McCarthy and Daly truly believed they had discovered a world-changing energy system, he reckoned – but he felt they had overestimated their abilities and forgotten the practical applications.

Rohrssen was also growing concerned about some of the signs he was seeing in the economy. Like Alan Wallace, he had watched the National Ploughing Championships become a platform for people to sell properties off the plans in Spain and Eastern Europe, with people throwing down deposits of €100,000 without having seen the properties they were being sold. He was horrified by the idea. He had taken on the Steorn investment as a punt – 9.5 on the risk scale, with a great chance that the money could be lost – but the property speculators he was watching seemed to believe that things could only go one way: up. He wondered just how many of those investors had bailed in to Steorn believing it was a sure-fire bet. What was to happen next wouldn't improve his outlook.

9. PICKING A FIGHT

Shaun McCarthy: The *Economist*

Where did the idea [of placing an ad in the *Economist*] come from? I have to claim credit for that one. I wish I could blame this on some other fucker, but I just said, 'Screw this, man.'

The one thing science doesn't like is being embarrassed by a bunch of engineers. That much is clear. Also, I had developed a certain attitude towards some of the meetings I'd had.

There is one example I can give you: I went to Enterprise Ireland, and we were looking for the usual free money. You show them what you've raised and they give matching funds. So, they sent a scientist in and he sat me down and said, 'I believe you, but there's no way I'm putting that in a report.' That is 100 per cent true.

To be honest, I wasn't that interested in the quarter of a million from Enterprise Ireland; it's more grief than it's worth. If I want a quarter of a million, I can go and make a presentation somewhere down the country, and I can get a quarter of a million. That was the mood at the time; but seriously, I came away thinking, *Screw you!*

So, I developed this attitude through experience that this wasn't going to be easy, graceful or anything like that. That's where I said maybe what we need to do is slap these fuckers in the face. I think that's an exact quote from the time.

It's fair to say my back was up. I've been described as a contrarian – the one thing I won't argue with is that I like to argue. But there was absolutely zero agreement within the company about this approach. We're talking about bringing a world of pain on everyone in the company, everybody's family members, and potentially shareholders (although less so).

Most people are really media shy, and they certainly don't want to be going down to their local corner shop to be told, 'Hey! You work for those idiots, don't you?' But my job wasn't to make everyone feel fucking great; we were trying to achieve something.

So, there was highly reluctant acceptance that we had to do it; but once we decided to do it, that was it: everyone was saying, 'Okay, we're doing it, so it's all hands to the pumps.'

We were all standing on the edge of the cliff, and it just took someone to push – and I did the pushing.

———————

By 2006, Steorn was still – as far as anyone outside the company and its shareholder base was concerned – the consultancy firm one occasionally read about in the *Sunday Business Post* or the business pages of the *Sunday Times*. If it rang any bells, it was because it had a slightly odd name, because it was raising money (but not a huge amount, given the climate) and because it seemed to have had a connection to anti-fraud software. But in truth, few people would have paid much attention to it.

That would all change, and change utterly, on 19 August 2006, when copies of the *Economist* started to land on the newsstands and in letterboxes all over Ireland. Sitting on page 5, in vivid green, was an advertisement with a swirling dark-green circle, over which was laid, in white print, a famous line from a play by George Bernard Shaw: 'All great truths begin as blasphemies.' The ad was Steorn's coming out to the world.

> Imagine a world with an infinite supply of pure energy. Never having to charge your phone. Never having to fuel your car. Welcome to our world. At Steorn we have developed a technology that produces free, clean and constant energy. Our technology has been independently validated by engineers and scientists – always behind closed doors, always off the record, always proven to work.

It was part declaration, part challenge: a declaration that Steorn had developed an over-unity device and defied the laws of physics; and a challenge to scientists that they should come forward and prove Steorn wrong.

It was bold and provocative – and fiendishly clever. Instead of apologetically stating that they were right – like so many over-unity claimants in past decades – they confidently told the world they were right until proved wrong. Even the tone of their invitation to a scientific jury was designed to wrong-foot the academic critics who had blithely refused to even discuss the possibility that Steorn was right.

The challenge: We are therefore issuing a challenge to the scientific community: Test our technology and report your findings to the world. We're
seeking a jury of twelve – the most qualified and the most cynical.

The media circus immediately descended on them, and one of the first
journalists to visit Steorn's office was Steve Boggan of the *Guardian*. He
visited the office in Dublin in August 2006, describing Shaun McCarthy
and Steorn's public relations manager, Richard Walshe, as 'dynamic
and personable businessmen' who insist that 'they have found a way of
producing free, clean and limitless energy out of thin air'.

The *Guardian* article refers to McCarthy, Walshe 'and the other
28 shareholders of Steorn', but it glides past the ownership issue, only briefly
stating that, in the three years since the discovery, Steorn had spent roughly
€4 million. Boggan, however, was there to delve into the claim made in the
Economist ad, and he focused on the scene before him in Dublin.

> There is a test rig with wheels and cogs and four magnets meticulously
> aligned so as to create the maximum tension between their fields and one
> other magnet fixed to a point opposite. A motor rotates the wheel bearing
> the magnets and a computer takes 28,000 measurements a second. The mag-
> nets, naturally, act upon one another. And when it is all over, the computer
> tells us that almost three times the amount of energy has come out of the
> system as went in. In fact, this piece of equipment is 285% efficient.

A good chunk of the *Guardian* article is the well-rehearsed Steorn
story: the background of the company, their shock at their discovery, their
disbelief and the eventual conclusion that they were on to something. But
all this is most notable for being the first time that Steorn and McCarthy
had told the story publicly.

Boggan quickly injects a note of scepticism, though, referring to
the doubts about the power source and the anonymity of the supposed
independent verification by 'electrical engineers and academics' with
'multiple PhDs' from 'world-class universities'. None of those people,
Boggan notes, 'will talk to me, even off the record'.

Boggan was promised a diagram of how the system worked, but it never materialised because Steorn's lawyers 'are concerned about intellectual property rights'. Nor will Steorn's European partner talk, Boggan notes, a tad perplexed.

'It's the Pons-Fleischmann factor,' McCarthy tells Boggan, referring to the scientists Stanley Pons and Martin Fleischmann, who claimed in 1989 to have discovered cold-fusion reactions – that is, the splitting of atoms without the enormous release of 'hot' energy. They were pilloried for the claim by the scientific establishment because it wasn't believed that a nuclear reaction could take place at room temperature. 'No one in the scientific community wants to become embroiled in the kind of controversy that Pons and Fleischmann faced,' McCarthy continued.

McCarthy went on to describe the 'stick' he had got, including 'abusive emails and telephone calls – people telling us to watch our backs, that sort of thing. Someone even published my home address on a website.'

If McCarthy was expecting solidarity from either Pons or Fleischmann, it didn't come. Boggan contacted Fleischmann to ask his opinion on the Steorn claim. Although Fleischmann wished the Steorn team luck, his response disputed their claims.

> I am actually a conventional scientist ... but I do accept that the existing [quantum electro-dynamic] paradigm is not adequate. If what these men are saying turns out to be true, that would be proof that the paradigm was inadequate and we would have to come up with some new theory.
>
> But I don't think their claims are credible. No, I cannot see how the position of magnetic fields allows one to create energy.

———————

Steve Boggan's interview with Shaun McCarthy caused a stir, as did the surge of media coverage of Steorn, not all of which was flattering. Challenging a scientific law in such a brash way – and in so prominent a publication as the *Economist* – virtually demanded a response in kind, and Steorn certainly got it.

McCarthy was forced to address some of these responses in a question-and-answer press release on the Steorn website. In one example, a reporter who had visited the Dublin office described 'a door behind which the [Steorn] device was situated' and had said he was not allowed through. The reporter went on to say that an 'agitated Frenchman went through the door while he was there'.

But this reporter had misinterpreted the significance of the door, McCarthy argued in the Q&A.

> Our office has different security zones. The 'agitated' Frenchman was coming from an area where our engineering group work (no external parties are allowed in this area) – he was agitated because I was using a test system to show the reporter something – he was in the middle of a test and was upset [that] he would have to restart it. Note that we have a visitor test lab, this is where the interview was conducted.

The Q&A also provided other interesting facts about Steorn that were news to anyone who took an immediate interest in the company. There was a question about whether Steorn had devices operational in France or any other European country (this question was apparently based on the inference that the French engineer was evidence of formal transnational links).

There was nothing of the sort, McCarthy answered; but there was technology in development in another European country. Although it wasn't revealed in the Q&A, that country was the Netherlands and the company was Kinetron, a kinetic watchmaker founded by Thieu Knapen in 1984 to harvest the energy of movement to power watches. A few years later, in conjunction with the Swiss watch company Jean d'Eve, Kinetron developed the world's first automatic quartz watch, the Samara. Kinetron had form in developing innovative and intricate ways of generating and storing energy, so it made sense for Steorn to send the device to Knapen in Tilburg for testing.

As Knapen was testing it, Steorn also sent Maurice Linnane over to interview him for the Steorn documentary. Knapen was enthusiastic about the machine he had been sent. In a slick video that showed Knapen in his lab, working on a small, intricate machine with a tiny pair of pliers, he set out his credentials briefly – he had been working with magnets for 25 years – and said that the machine he had been measuring surprised him.

'I saw things I didn't believe. It was my first trigger to say, hey, maybe we forgot something in the past, and Steorn have found the trick to do it,' Knapen told Linnane. Producing energy from nothing was impossible, he conceded, but Steorn

> came with a special idea to bring in magnets in a certain way, and it was very new for me as well. The principle is you have two magnets – a very small one and a big one – and you bring in the small magnet into the area of the big magnets, and you do it in such a way that you gain more energy than you put in. And even from the data we had and the measurements we did, we see that we gain energy.

Now, Knapen continued, the idea was to develop this into a working model.

> Even with all the mechanical losses in it, at this moment it should be not possible that we reach this moment yet. So, it's already a miracle in its way now. It can be two times, three times better than this. It's just the beginning. I'm sure of it.

All this went down a treat with Steorn's investors. Though they may never have heard of Knapen or his company, he appeared to have all the right credentials: an inventor himself, he was non-Irish so was unburdened by the begrudgery that the investors were sure was motivating the rejection of Steorn, and he was evidently a serious mechanical engineer. It seemed a perfect dose of public validation.

However, since McCarthy's visits to those major chip manufacturers, he knew that Knapen's praise wouldn't be enough. During those visits, Steorn had been asked just how many scientists had verified their anomaly, as well as how many had completed the testing and then didn't verify it. To this, Steorn answered – without, in fact, answering it at all – that 'we stopped the testing once it became clear that the tests would produce no publicly usable validation – this defeated the purpose of the tests.'

This addressed a problem at the core of the Steorn story – and at the heart of McCarthy's insecurities: so far, they had not a single piece of credible testimony that the Steorn device actually worked. So, if they couldn't go to the universities, the *Economist* ad was an attempt to bring the universities to them.

Shaun McCarthy: The Jury

We had gone around the brand-name universities from day one with this bloody thing, and the whole game was always reputable validation, and that was reinforced when we went out to some of the big companies, who said, 'We're not going to test this thing, but if you're right – right being defined by reputable validation – then of course we'll license the thing. We'd be stupid not to.'

We had a bunch of semi-academic and a lot of engineering validation. We did the tours of Cambridge, Queen's [University, Belfast], Trinity [College, Dublin], UCD and anyone who'd talk to us, basically. We just didn't get anywhere. Mostly what they said was, 'We're not even interested in testing it.'

The jury process was a direct result of that. We were not going anywhere without enough PhDs and reputable scientists saying, 'Fuck it, the lads have something here.' We weren't getting anywhere in any acceptable time frame doing it quietly-quietly. So, bang! We thought: let's create a mess; let's create a fuss.

Initially, it was pure marketing and spoofology. We'd pick a jury of 12, originally. We ended up with 22, and we had a real long process about how we scored and how we qualified them, because if it had gone the way we thought it should've gone, we'd be hand-picking the jury – and that wouldn't look right. So, we ended up with 22 because we couldn't bring it down to 12 without getting subjective in the process.

There was a variety of people. The ones I remember, obviously, were the chairman, Ian MacDonald, as well as some CERN [European Organization for Nuclear Research] guys and some NASA guys. They were from all over Europe and the US, probably 50–50 Europe–US, while some were from commercial research, and some were professors emeritus.

We tried to play it straight, but it became obvious very quickly that it was going to go nowhere.

Ian MacDonald was sitting on the beach in Bonaire, an island claimed by the Netherlands in the southern Caribbean, just off the coast of Venezuela, when that issue of the *Economist* dropped into his letterbox.

Life had been good to MacDonald. He'd been an academic in the University of Alberta for a while, he'd worked for the US government and he had spent the seven years before his retirement working in private industry. His field was photonics, which is the science of light and how it is manipulated.

The company MacDonald been working for before he retired was JDS Uniphase, a half-Canadian, half-American conglomerate that worked on a range of commercial applications of photonics. Its share price exploded throughout the late 1990s as most countries and companies built out trillions of miles of fibre-optic cables during the great internet capital infrastructure boom. The company's share price at one point reached $153 per share, making millionaires of any staff members who had stock options – including MacDonald. The company was huge in a way that's hard to recall now because we have forgotten a time when the internet wasn't a ubiquitous part of our lives. On paper, at least, JDS Uniphase was worth more than the Royal Bank of Canada or the Ford Motor Company, and it once had all the excitement that Facebook, say, carries today.

But it wasn't to last. In 2001 there was a collapse in the company's share price – not unrelated to the tech-bubble crash that had wobbled Steorn so badly – and its shares fell to as low as $2. By then, though, MacDonald had cashed in his shares and gone into retirement.

So, when he picked up the *Economist* on that morning in 2006, he was that perfect combination: solvent, free of encumbrance and curious as hell. Moreover, his wife was Irish, and a visit to Dublin would give them a chance to see her family home on Ailesbury Road in Dublin. In spite of the likely backlash from his friends in the scientific community – some of whom would turn out to be critical of him for being so open-minded about an obviously unscientific project – MacDonald applied, along with hundreds of others, to be on the Steorn jury.

He tried to convince himself that maybe, just maybe, someone had achieved the impossible – after all, wouldn't that make life interesting? But his logical mind refused to allow him to consider a discovery that would overturn laws that had been the basis of his career.

To his surprise, MacDonald was among the final panel of 22 selected to go to Dublin. Steorn announced the formation of the jury in December 2006 with typical braggadocio, explaining in a press release that it had finally signed contracts with the independent jury, which it described as 'the latest milestone in Steorn's efforts to get validation for its technology, which began when the company issued a challenge to the world's scientists'. The technology, Steorn said, 'can be applied to virtually all devices requiring energy, from cellular phones to cars'.

The jury process had been oversubscribed several times,

> with hundreds of qualified scientists applying to be part of the jury, [who have all] agreed to see the testing process through to its completion and have their names and findings disclosed once the testing is complete. Steorn has agreed not to identify members of the jury until the results are made public, to protect their privacy and avoid unnecessary interruptions to their work.

It included scientists from all over the world with expertise in cold fusion, electrical engineering, magnets, lasers, particle physics and in the case of the self-penned biography of one researcher for NASA named Creon Levit, 'heretical (that is not a typo) physics'. The jury also featured academics and commercial scientists. The ground rules of the jury's task were simple. To prove its claim, Steorn would have to hit certain targets – which it called 'gates' – the first of which was a working demonstration that its claims were true; it would then would give the jury a description of a machine – an Orbo – that bore out its claims.

The second gate was that the jury – having been convinced by a display of a working prototype – could go away and build their own versions of the machine to test and examine the principle behind it.

It was a reasonable process, most thought. If the jury saw a working Orbo, they could at least take away the instructions and figure out what was happening and, crucially, discover whether Steorn had made an elementary mistake that was creating the anomalous finding.

Although Steorn was keeping its cards close to its chest – even the names of the jury members, who were bound by non-disclosure agreements, were kept private for a number of years after the demonstration – it did define its claim in one of the documents related to the jury agreement.

> The angular velocity of a loaded rotating element of a device, constructed solely of permanent magnets and mechanical elements, can be sustained without input power under laboratory conditions.

In short, it was an over-unity device. The company further claimed that

> the device can produce more energy than is contained in its magnets; the production of energy by the device is not accompanied by a significant change in the magnetization of the permanent magnets nor by a change in the overall mass of the device under test.

If the first phase – or gate – established that there was indeed something to examine, the jury would proceed to the second, formulating a plan to define the steps required to satisfactorily conclude the process. That meant building and testing it themselves – a process that could be facilitated by a number of labs to which the jury members had access. They were not short of facilities. Michael McKubre was a New Zealander who had studied cold fusion and had been injured in an explosion in a lab in 1992 when a cold-fusion cell exploded, killing one of the researchers. He was director of the Energy Research Center at SRI International in California and offered up the SRI lab. Meanwhile, Dr Emil Prodanov of DIT's School of Mathematical Sciences offered up a lab in DIT.

In June 2007, the jury members were put up in Jurys Hotel in Ballsbridge, Dublin, ahead of their first meeting. McCarthy recalls that one member invited him out for a pint and offered him money. McCarthy immediately recognised it as a ham-fisted sting operation and thought, 'He thinks we're committing a fraud here.'

The sting didn't work – McCarthy had enough money to run the company for several more years – but things didn't get any better from there. At the jury's first meeting in June in in the Steorn offices, McCarthy first explained what he could about the Orbo technology and told the jury it operated on the principle of magnetic viscosity, which refers to the time dependence of magnetisation in a constant magnetic field and temperature and is related to McCarthy's claim of having developed a 'time machine' of sorts. It was a loose discussion of the concept rather than a detailed explanation, though, which would prove to be typical of the jury process.

As they talked, a small group of Steorn employees in an anteroom was working on the simple demonstration model. The idea was that someone with an airgun would blow the wheel, setting it moving, and that the arrangement of the magnets would spin in such a way that the magnets would maintain and increase the wheel's momentum, allowing it to spin by itself long after the force from the airgun had dissipated.

However, the demonstration wasn't working, and MacDonald sat in the main boardroom with the jury listening to the airgun being repeatedly triggered. Eventually, McCarthy entered the boardroom and apologised, telling them that the demonstration wasn't going to work.

The jury was then told that a better version of the first magnet motor would be flown in from Kinetron in the Netherlands. In the meantime, the jury found themselves at a loose end, with nothing to study and nothing substantial to discuss. So, they did what any tourist to Celtic Tiger Dublin would have done: they went on an expensive holiday. MacDonald and his wife took an impromptu historical tour of the country, visiting Newgrange before heading north to Belfast, all the while eating and drinking quite comfortably – at least partly on Steorn's dime.

MacDonald was struck by the wealth in Dublin, with cranes dotting the skyline and providing a canopy over expensive restaurants, skyrocketing property values and streets full of new cars; but he developed a bad cold – he had been travelling by bus, which, even in the middle of summer, was a great deal less balmy than the beaches of the Caribbean – so he returned to Dublin to see if the Kinetron model had arrived.

When the jury returned to Steorn's office, they were told that the courier from Kinetron's offices had missed the flight to Dublin, so the device wouldn't be available until Friday. Then, on Friday, they discovered that the airline had no flight that day.

Meanwhile, it had become clear that McCarthy's plan for the jury wasn't to have a panel of scientists observe a model he had built, but simply to provide them with an instruction manual to build one of their own, which few jury members considered a task worth their time. It was a leap past gate one to gate two, and it would prove to be a sticking point between Steorn and the jury.

Eventually, the time came for MacDonald and the jury members to leave after a singularly unproductive trip. Not only had they not seen a working demonstration model, but they had left without having had much in the way of technical conversation with McCarthy. He'd talked a lot, of course, and they had been taken out for a hugely expensive dinner in a very loud pub, during which he had laid on the full promotional spiel; but, not having been given any details, MacDonald left Ireland as unedified as he had arrived.

If Shaun McCarthy was the stereotype of an Irishman to Ian MacDonald – brash, confident, talkative and fond of the drink – MacDonald seemed equally stereotypical of Canada: quietly confident but soft spoken, mild mannered and not given to sweeping statements or characterisations. If MacDonald had left Dublin frustrated, he didn't express that frustration openly. Another jury member, David Powell, a lecturer in aeronautics and astronautics at Stanford University, was similarly relaxed about a trip that had turned out to be a dud. He had been alerted to Steorn's ad in the *Economist* by a friend in Italy who thought he might consider it a lark. Powell had done a lot of work on mechanical engineering and had designed outboard motors before his graduate degree, and he clearly wasn't closed-minded. He believed that the manner in which the laws of nature had been changed in the past showed that they could well be changed as further evidence came to light. But his scepticism surged when it became clear that Steorn couldn't even demonstrate the effect with its own model in its own office. After deliberations, Powell and MacDonald and their fellow jury members concluded that the first condition had to be met: an experiment that would remove all doubt.

Powell left Dublin believing that Steorn sincerely thought they had something – which explained why they were willing to spend so much money to bring experts to Dublin – but he found it odd that they couldn't then produce a working model. Like the other jury members, he was expecting an experiment at the very least. Instead, he got apologies and explanations and presentations on what would have happened had the model been working.

Powell didn't conclude that the entire thing was garbage or a hoax, and he peppered Steorn with questions about the apparatus; but without a demonstration, he had to fall back on the laws of physics – which had obeyed all known observations for the past 700 years on the principle that energy cannot be created from nothing – and exercise his scepticism.

Shaun McCarthy, Powell concluded, didn't have a heavy scientific background, but, oddly, he seemed to view this as a strength rather than as a weakness – a sign of what a can-do, practical character he was. He wasn't lying, Powell concluded, merely self-deceiving.

Not everyone was so generous about their time being wasted. Davor Pavuna was one of Croatia's most eminent physicists. He worked at the Institute of Physics, in École Polytechnique Fédérale de Lausanne, focusing on physics, chemistry and a highly specialised field of science called micro-opto-electronics. Pavuna came away feeling the whole thing was a bluff. Like MacDonald and Powell, he had sent his application on a whim and enjoyed the luxurious hotels and, of course, the creamy Guinness. But the jury had seen nothing technical they could validate. Pavuna left unable to understand how Steorn had raised the money, given how little they had to show for it.

Pavuna had seen plenty of scams that had pulled off a level of technical sophistication that might have fooled many – even those with scientific backgrounds – but Steorn hadn't even presented a demonstration. It felt to him almost like a joke. Perhaps a mistake had been made and they'd been invited too early. It was clear to him that, at that moment, you could easily lay your hands on money in Dublin, and he joked with jury members that they should pull a similar scam and grab a quick €10 million.

In the end, the jury left without having reached a conclusion.

10. PUTTING ON A SHOW

On the other side of the jury table, Shaun McCarthy had, predictably, once again begun to lose patience. In fact, the jury hadn't even got a chance to start their work before he began losing faith in the process. The failure to produce a working demonstration – and the jury's refusal to proceed with testing until they had seen something, *anything* working – signalled to him that this would be a long-drawn-out process. What he had wanted was a quick hit of validation, but that was proving to be more and more elusive. Steorn had gone to universities and had either been scorned or given validation that they couldn't use with anyone else, because it had been given anonymously. They had gone to engineers who could provide only qualified assessment of their anomaly, and they had gone to the major industry players, who were demanding a much higher threshold of validation than Steorn, with its small office and meagre resources, could provide.

Now, a few months into 2007, McCarthy's latest idea was getting bogged down in debate after debate over pure, theoretical science rather than progressing to practical engineering discussions. He was beginning to see that the jury process would go nowhere.

He would later conclude that the problem wasn't that Steorn could present nothing to the jury, but that after three years of its own rigorous testing of the anomaly, Steorn couldn't agree on a common test language with jury members.

It frustrated him, and in his frustration he decided on a parallel approach. He would later conclude that this would be yet another impulsive – and bad – decision, but he was convinced that they needed something to run alongside the jury process – something that wouldn't impede the jury but that might make its process and deliberations less relevant. He had convinced himself that the result of this new idea wouldn't affect the jury process, which he thought had very swiftly got lost in the kind of hard, quantitative analysis that had bedevilled Steorn in the previous three years. He began to pin his hopes on yet another high-profile and attention-grabbing idea: a public demonstration.

_____

In fact, had anyone been looking closely, the idea of a demonstration had been signalled well before the jury idea.

The Kinetica Museum of kinetic art in London, which had opened in October 2006, had given the game away with a pamphlet issued late that year that advertised its schedule for January 2007, showing that Steorn had been considering a public demonstration long before the jury process failed to produce the immediate validation it had wanted. The pamphlet described a demonstration by Steorn that sounded more like an art exhibition than a scientific display.

> The History of Kinetic Energy and Beyond: Man's harnessing of kinetic energy, from the dreams of Leonardo to the future. [Shaun] McCarthy, CEO of revolutionary Irish technology company Steorn will be presenting their new technology to the UK, for the first time, at Kinetica. Steorn has developed a technology that produces free, clean, and constant energy. This provides a significant range of benefits from the convenience of never having to refuel your car or recharge your mobile phone to a genuine solution to the need for 'Principle of the Conservation of Energy', considered by many to be the most fundamental principle in our current understanding of the universe.

Anyone with any knowledge of physics would surely have bridled at the suggestion that the conservation of energy principle was merely 'considered by many' to be the fundamental principle in current understanding.

So, why London, and why Kinetica? For McCarthy, if it were to be done, it couldn't take place in Steorn's office in Dublin or in Kinetron's office in Tilburg. A demonstration in its own office would look rigged; one in Kinetron's – to whom Steorn was paying thousands of euro – would be interpreted as a scam. No, it would have to be neutral territory: somewhere open to the public, open to scrutiny and immune to cynical questioning.

So, the Kinetica Museum – which aims 'to encourage and promote collaboration and cross-over between artists, scientists, technologists, engineers and academics' – was an apt place to show off Steorn's machine.

Then there was the question of when. McCarthy knew it was cheeky to choose 4 July, turning American Independence Day into world energy independence day, but it was yet another example of how McCarthy simply couldn't refuse a vivid, attention-seeking hook. He had a genius for marketing, provided he was offering himself up as the lightning rod for the attention, just as Ryanair boss Michael O'Leary uses gauche, uncouth comments and stunts, regardless of the mockery he might suffer, to draw attention. The difference was that O'Leary seemed to suffer no ill effects from his buffoonish behaviour. By contrast, McCarthy seemed to be burning huge amounts of his reputation with every eye-catching statement and presentation. However, in the run-up, all that was apparent was McCarthy's overweening confidence that this, finally, would convince everyone of Steorn's validity.

This sense is evident in an interview posted on the company's website in early 2007 in which McCarthy, asked about Steorn's progress with continuous-motion testing, answered, 'We have made huge progress on this – I would say 80 to 90 per cent of the way.'

When he was asked about the reason for the public display after such a lengthy period of secrecy – which he attributed to the 'risk of giving counterfeiters and competitors a heads-up' – he said that the decision about the July demonstration in London 'was a risk/reward decision for us – we feel that the public exposure will be worth taking some of the risks … And it's also about the time that we need to engage with the mainstream media again.'

It was bullish and typical of McCarthy, but even he knew it was a gamble. He had convinced himself that the odds were in his favour, but the closer the demonstration got, the longer the odds got – and he knew it.

Steorn was dealing with highly sensitive equipment hand-made by Kinetron's team of watchmakers. That equipment would have to be tested, taken apart, brought to Dublin, reassembled, tested again, broken down again and brought to London to be reassembled for the demonstration.

Any one of those stages could introduce an error or an accident that would derail the effort. The pressure was mounting.

Once again, McCarthy had invited enormous public scrutiny. As he put it in conversation, they were 'putting their balls on the line'.

———————

Dr Mike Rosing was a lecturer at the University of Wisconsin and a scientific polymath. He had studied nuclear engineering and engineering physics in the 1970s and early '80s at the University of Wisconsin and, later, at the University of Boulder, Colorado. He wrote software for a time, designed diagnostics and measured neutral particle beams for Ronald Reagan's Strategic Defense Initiative (the so-called Star Wars programme). By the late 1990s, he had got involved in psychology and neurophysiology, supervising a group of researchers at the University of Wisconsin's psychology department who were designing a robot to imitate a baby monkey for controlled stress in adult tamarin monkeys.

Rosing followed that by working with Wicab, Inc., developing prototypes for medical devices that would help the blind. Like many, Rosing had seen the ad in the *Economist* and was perplexed by it. He found the Steorn website and dug in, intrigued by the claim and perhaps intoxicated by its audacity. By his own admission, he got hooked. How could a company be so bold with these public claims and spend so much money on a proposition that clearly could not work?

When Steorn created an online forum, Rosing was one of the first to sign up. He noticed that there were three classes of people on it: those who believed everything Steorn told them and didn't understand the science; those who understood physics and were trying to debunk the claims of over-unity in a disrespectful way; and those, like Rosing, who tried their best to engage Steorn on philosophical and physics grounds, giving examples, showing evidence and trying to reason with the more fervent supporters.

But after six months Rosing realised that he was wasting his time. No amount of explanation would convince the zealots that the science couldn't support Steorn's argument. (Presumably, no amount of setting a good example could convince the disrespectful doubters to take a more mannerly approach.)

A few months after giving up on the whole thing, Rosing got an email from Steorn asking him to be an observer at the public demonstration on behalf of the forum. So – with the promise of a paid trip to London to reward his patient and respectful debating – he agreed to travel to the Kinetica Museum.

Because of the secrecy surrounding the demonstration, Rosing hadn't been able to tell anyone about the arrangements, and he was doubtful in the days after the invitation that it would take place.

He was then sent technical papers with which to brief himself. The first, he would say soon after the demonstration, 'did not explain any detail, but the second was a full technical report. [McCarthy] had mentioned magnetic viscosity as the key to the effect he was seeing.' This caught Rosing's attention, and he wanted to combine whatever it was that Steorn was demonstrating with a fundamental physics test.

So, Rosing came up with a pendulum test, which would look at the physics underpinning the company's claims 'without giving away any technological secrets'. McCarthy agreed, and a plan was put in place to test the system by rigging it up to Rosing's pendulum. If the pendulum swung by harnessing the energy that was produced by Steorn's demo model, this would surely be evidence of its validity.

Rosing, a belt-and-braces kind of guy, built a second data-collection device using magnetic field probes to ensure that if the pendulum didn't work, he could collect data some other way.

He had also brought with him an array of tools and electronics. He hadn't planned much sightseeing, so, on the flight to London, he boned up on Emmy Noether's theorem on time invariance.

———————————

Maurice Linnane, the filmmaker commissioned by Steorn, was on a family holiday when McCarthy contacted him about the London demonstration.

Linnane had begun to realise that no matter how confident and forceful McCarthy could be – and how convincing he was in person – Steorn was never going to produce this world-changing technology. What struck him most forcefully were the contradictions in McCarthy's character. For a man of such conviction and confidence, and of such obvious intelligence and leadership abilities, it was his salesmanship alone that left a lasting impression on Linnane.

It was also clear that McCarthy could find himself struggling with some of the most basic logistical elements of life. On their past trip to Cambridge to test the Steorn device at the Cavendish Laboratory, for example, they had travelled from Dublin to the ferry port in Liverpool, having needlessly spent money on cabins on the ferry despite the brevity of the journey. Their informal convoy from Liverpool to Cambridge took twice as long as necessary because they made many impromptu stops and got lost several times. At one point Linnane's mother phoned him to tell him she had fallen and broken her hip, but he couldn't tell her where he was, so hopelessly lost were they.

So, when McCarthy phoned Linnane on his holiday to tell him about the London demonstration, part of him was aghast. Was he to quit the holiday and leave his wife and children behind so that he could film what would in all likelihood be a flop? Moreover, the short notice meant he hadn't informed his regular team, so he'd have to ring around for a back-up team.

Nevertheless, he decided to go. He arrived in Steorn's office in East Wall Road in Dublin the day before McCarthy was due to travel to London and he spoke to one of the Steorn employees there, asking him how serious this plan was.

'I don't know,' he answered. 'He's convinced us all again, but I think it's all mad.'

Linnane watched some of the engineers that night and got the impression that some of them felt uncomfortable as they worked on the Perspex wheel within another Perspex wheel, which had precision holes into which small magnets had been fitted. The engineers whizzed the wheel around with a large air compressor, all the while measuring it for bumps in energy output.

McCarthy was giving his usual spiel. 'Forget the science bit and the rest of it is just engineering, and we're engineers.' Late in the evening, he announced that he and the team were off to the pub.

Linnane couldn't believe it. 'I'm going to have to risk divorce to come back to London and meet up with you fuckers?' he recalls asking McCarthy, incredulously. 'And just let me get this straight: you don't have a unit yet that has revolved on its own without the big air compressor?'

'No, no.'

'Shaun, you have tonight to manage it, but you're going to the pub. At some point tonight you'll have to break it down and bring it to London, where you'll have to rebuild it, where you'll have to put it in a unit that's going to have cameras and live streams pointed at it – and it still doesn't work!'

'But it will work,' McCarthy insisted.

'But it doesn't work yet, and you're going to try to do it in a bit of a weekend?'

'It's just engineering.'

Linnane left the office and rang the Steorn employee who had expressed doubts earlier. 'It's not going to work,' Linnane told him.

The reply: 'All we can do is try.'

———————————

The Steorn online forum had been watching Dr Mike Rosing's progress closely, ravenous for details on the company and the public demonstration. On Sunday, 1 July, the morning after he arrived in London, Rosing was sent a pay-as-you-go phone by one of the forum members; another member wrote on the forum that he had sent his wife from Wales to Euston Station to give Rosing 'a very expensive laptop and a brand new, never used before cell phone' so that he could keep in touch with forum members. The plan for the laptop had been to use it to take the data from the demonstration and crunch and analyse it; it ended up being more useful for posting to the forum about events as they unfolded.

Meanwhile, the Steorn investor Alan Wallace had – at short notice – travelled to London for the launch. Part of him wanted to be there to support the team so that he could 'enjoy the prospect of good financial things to come in three to four years' and part of him wanted 'to be in some small way a part of history', as he wrote in a letter to McCarthy a few days after his arrival. When he stepped out of Liverpool Street Station, he struck up a conversation with a newspaper vendor. He explained he was there for Steorn's demonstration and the vendor wished him luck, which bolstered Wallace's hopes.

Indeed, there was plenty of hope in evidence as the week began. The demonstration was to begin on Wednesday 4 July at 11 p.m. on an internet stream; the museum would open the next morning to the public. Steorn and McCarthy, they believed, had done everything to ensure success. The machine was simple: a free-standing device you pushed with a finger. This would start the rotation, which would be accelerated by the magnets. It was then to continue by itself, producing more energy than had been put in and more energy than was lost by air friction and friction at the bearings. Hypothetically, that is.

As McCarthy explained before the demo, what they were showing was

a very simplified version of the technology. It's virtually all clear plastic and magnets, so we are demonstrating … that there is no battery hidden … What the system will be doing is … lifting a weight, demonstrating work being done for free.

It all sounded simple and confident and achievable – after all, they'd been preparing for this day for months. But behind the scenes, things were chaotic.

Linnane arrived one evening early that week to find that McCarthy and his two main engineers had been up all night arguing about the machine and its readiness. Meanwhile, Linnane's documentary crew buzzed around and shot footage of what was to be the historic moment.

The pressure was understandable. Steorn had organised a party and promised a trick, but they were rapidly finding that it was easier to gather a crowd than to impress one. The focus of the world was now on Steorn – scrutiny from some of the most prominent physicists and from enormous technology media publications such as *Wired*. Steorn was no longer sitting in blissful obscurity in a drab industrial campus on the East Wall Road; in a couple of hours, it had to have this thing working and be ready to turn on the webcam.

Except the Steorn device wasn't working. Linnane had come to Kinetica Museum the night before only to find that in their lab upstairs, the Steorn team had re-created the model, to a point. Except that the beautiful clear Perspex case was now covered in clumsy, gluey fingerprints and the crew was looking frazzled.

McCarthy was continuing to tell everyone that it was going to be all right: everything was going to work. But with each passing hour, his assurances rang hollower. Under such circumstances, they weren't behaving like rational people, McCarthy would later concede. They threw everyone out and worked through the night.

To escape the madness, Linnane took his crew off for dinner in a bar near Tower Bridge, where they discussed, in some disbelief, the chaos they had just witnessed.

The next morning, over breakfast, McCarthy asked Linnane where he had gone. 'You should've stayed,' he told Linnane. 'We had the thing going. We had it going for about 40 minutes before we stopped it.'

He asked two engineers for confirmation, but they were non-committal. It was then that Linnane realised, finally, that he was documenting something entirely different from the original commission. This wasn't a scientific documentary: it was a psychological one. He knew he could no longer charge McCarthy money for this. The Steorn story – at least the Steorn story McCarthy believed in – was over. An entirely different story was taking over.

On the night of 4 July 2007, with the world watching online, viewers, instead of seeing an Orbo machine pulling a weight on a pulley – thus changing the world forever – were given the news that a test unit

> was built yesterday in Kinetica, in the temporary lab we have set up. Once we had signed off on the final magnetic configurations we went to transfer this magnetic config to the display unit & casing on the exhibition floor.
>
> Here [the engineers] ran into some technical issues, firstly a problem with the bearings, which was fixed once identified. The next issue appears to be an environmental issue. We think possibly the temperature from the lighting system in the immediate area, but this has to be further assessed in the morning.
>
> The current plan of action is to have a technical meeting in the morning and we will update you … [We] are planning to turn on the web streaming by lunch time so we can give you an ongoing update on progress (and you can see some stressed Engineers working in real time, if it is not fixed by then!). The demo will go ahead as soon as we fix the small outstanding issues. Please accept our apologies on this …

The message gave a clear impression of having been written hastily, even in panic. It was the first indication – at least publicly – that something was profoundly wrong.

The Steorn team tried again the next morning for the public's visit to the museum, which had been set up in typical Steorn style, with posters plastered on the Kinetica Museum's windows bearing inspirational – and pointed – quotations from Claude Bernard ('True science teaches us to DOUBT and in ignorance, refrain'), Orville Wright ('Isn't it astonishing that all these secrets have been preserved for so many years just so we could discover them!'), Frank Herbert ('The beginning of knowledge is the discovery of something we do not understand') and Oscar Wilde ('I can believe anything, provided that it is quite incredible'), among other quotations such as 'People who say it cannot be done should not interrupt those who are doing it'.

Inside the museum, though, all was not going to plan. Early in the day, a notice from Steorn went up in the window.

We are experiencing some technical difficulties with the demo unit in London. Our initial assessment indicates that this is probably due to the intense heat coming from the camera lighting. We have commenced a technical assessment and will provide an update later today. As a consequence, Kinetica will not be open to the public today (5th July). We apologise for this delay and appreciate your patience.

Dr Rosing was outside Kinetica, reading the notice and talking to several people who had arrived for the demonstration. One of those was Richard Walshe, Steorn's marketing manager, who had gone outside to tell Rosing that there were still plenty of problems.

Rosing could see this for himself just by looking in the window at the team. Even the live stream wasn't working quite right: though it was officially running, the cameras were working only sporadically.

Photographs from the day show just how chaotic it was. In the upstairs lab, a table was strewn with the detritus of the demonstration's construction phase – this scene serving as Steorn's own exhibition of panic. A Perspex disc, a drill, a hammer and a hacksaw sat on a workbench alongside an open packet of Blu Tack.

During the day, one blogger at Kinetica pulled Pat Corbett to one side. Corbett, dressed in a big red windcheater, was on the receiving end of a serious dressing down over the sheer incompetence of the demonstration. He conceded that there had been no load-bearing Orbo device in the Kinetica Museum, as promised. The device they had was not, in short, going to display its effect by lifting a weight. The load-bearing device was in Dublin and, according to Corbett, the device that wasn't working was a spinning device of some sort. They'd changed tack at the last minute and brought an entirely different machine, he said. Whether or not this account of this conversation is accurate – and Corbett no longer talks about Steorn – it conveys some sense of the disorder of the day.

At around 7 o'clock that night in Alan Wallace's hotel room in London, he, McCarthy, Corbett and a handful of others convened for a post mortem. It was a sombre affair and Wallace jotted down notes as they talked. These notes show that they still hadn't got a handle on what had happened. Though the notice posted in the museum window had blamed the failure on intense heat from the camera lighting, they discussed the possibility that a bearing had been removed and replaced improperly. They wondered whether the machines had been tested long enough before they were brought to London. They had been run for only two days. They asked what had to be done to get it right and wondered whether it could be done in two hours, as they had been told earlier. (It couldn't, they concluded.)

They would try again tomorrow, they decided.

On Friday morning of that week, Dr Rosing returned to Kinetica, the prospect of failure seeming greater than when he had arrived. There he met Hal Puthoff, an American engineer and parapsychologist mildly controversial for his belief in psychic ability (he once claimed to have demonstrated that Uri Geller had psychic powers). Puthoff was there out of personal interest. His employee Michael McKubre was working in parallel on the Steorn jury.

By noon, the public demonstration had been cancelled. It was announced that McCarthy would give a media presentation at 3 p.m.

So, a few hours later, McCarthy, dressed in an ill-fitting black T-shirt with a Steorn logo on the front and *CREW* written on the back, got up in front of a roomful of journalists and interested interrogators, a camera whirring behind him, and issued the *mea culpa* that would ultimately define Steorn. Winding up for what would be a lengthy process of making himself the scapegoat for the debacle, he began his presentation.

> We screwed up. I should say specifically I screwed up ... We arrived here on Sunday. We brought three systems with us ... We got one operating on Tuesday night. On Wednesday evening, we installed it into the display cases ... and the system ceased to function. So ... we spent quite a few hours trying to analyse what the problem was.
>
> We stripped down the system, and what we found is [that] the friction in the system had gone to hell. So, we stripped it down to core components, which

was either alignment – it's a very simple system – alignment of the shaft or the bearings. And the bearings are bust; why they're bust we don't know. We swapped out the bearings live – we probably shouldn't have done that – and we bust the other bearings. These are small watchmaker bearings. We have additional bearings, not here. One of our engineers is with our supplier at the moment with the additional bearings.

However, we made the decision that until we have it operating, that we wouldn't try to put any more pressure on the engineers working on it, and so we're deferring it.

We don't know when we're going to defer it until. I want to make that absolutely clear. I want to equally say that's a technical explanation. Whether people believe it or don't believe it, I can do nothing about that. It's just a statement of the truth.

But, he implied, there was a greater truth, and a greater problem: human error. The error had happened

because I had put a three-day timeline to get this up and running. It was against the advice of everyone else in the company ... against our engineers' advice, so I have to take this on the chin.

One journalist then pointedly asked how long they had had it running for the night before, to which McCarthy answered, 'Four hours on Tuesday night.'

Another journalist asked him why no video of that night's successful running existed. McCarthy, not pausing even for a second, launched into yet another justification for the failure by reference to his own failings.

I need to say something. Obviously, this has failed; this event has failed. It is a deferral. We will be back, but equally, I have to recognise we have lost what little confidence that people would have done.

So, as a company, we're going to have to do some other things in addition to redoing this demonstration when we're ready to do it. Some of that may involve videos and so on. So, whether they're believed or not believed is a different thing.

But, his questioner responded, something to disbelieve would be better than what they currently had: nothing.

Whether this journalist knew it or not, he had hit on a *leitmotif* of the Steorn story: if extraordinary claims need extraordinary evidence, so far Steorn hadn't produced anything, not even a working demonstration to prove its claim. It had failed even to pose the question, let alone provide the answer.

In that moment, however, McCarthy was mired in self-flagellation and self-recrimination – another *leitmotif* of the Steorn story.

> Again, I'm not here in the situation I want to be. I've put the company in this situation and I have to take that on the chin. The only defence that I can make – and it's poor comfort to everybody – is that if I were here to rig a demo [fake a demonstration], we'd be here watching a wheel spin.
>
> It's the nature of who I am: when there's good news, I'm happy to take the kudos; and when there's bad news, I'm quite happy to take it on the chin.

———————

In a later press release about the failed demonstration, Steorn would conclude that 'due to certain difficulties with some of the materials selected for the display device, we were unable to get the system to function within the Perspex case'. The different expansion rates of the polycarbonate and brass components within the display device put stress on the bearings and triggered a failure, they said. Though they had tried to replace the bearings, they had been working under pressure and had damaged the replacements.

They 'had to make the decision to postpone the event', as Steorn would phrase it in later letters to their shareholders, but they knew it wasn't merely a postponing. The event was dead in the water and the company's reputation wasn't far behind.

Steorn tried gamely to pass it off as a simple mechanical error caused by anxious repairmen, assuring shareholders that

> it should be noted that the display device was fully operational on Tuesday evening and the failure discussed above happened only due to the extreme

heat in the display case. While some negative media is to be expected, we want to personally assure that Steorn is not only operating from a strong financial base but continues to have the support of the jury members, staff and advisors [and] leading scientists and our shareholders.

This excuse was met with worldwide derision. Even the most supportive people had questions that McCarthy and the rest of the team simply couldn't answer. How could a world-changing technology be so sensitive that a few lights could upset it? How had they, the world-changing engineers, not accounted for this possibility? Why in the world had they come to demonstrate a product that wasn't ready? Were there no test runs?

For those who weren't supportive – and they were undeniably in the majority – it was proof that Steorn was either a scam or, far more likely, fundamentally ignorant of the nuances of what they were claiming. This ignorance made the demonstration, well intentioned as it may have been, a prominent and highly embarrassing exercise in burning piles of other people's money.

For all his confidence that he could soon produce a live demo, McCarthy knew how that would look. Steorn had taken the gamble in the fervent hope that the pay-off from a successful display would more than compensate for the years of ridicule from the media. Success would make the brand stronger. But the converse was equally true: failure deepened suspicion of a con – and of McCarthy being the conman.

It was a shot in the gut for him, and he knew he needed to get out straight away and talk to the shareholders and bloggers, buy them a few beers and explain his story to them.

He was now also privately expressing doubt that he could proceed. In a taxi journey from Spitalfields in London afterwards, McCarthy sat with Maurice Linnane and his crew and with Richard Walshe and Pat Corbett. On that journey, McCarthy lamented that this seemed to be it; it was his moment to fall on his sword. Corbett tried to convince him not to.

The next day, McCarthy continued to make the rounds, explaining what had gone wrong and appealing to the base not to lose faith. Not surprisingly, a good number of meetings were held in pubs and as McCarthy spoke, people drank. One of those people was Dr Rosing, who later wrote in a blog posting that watching McCarthy

and listening to him talk (and boy can he talk!), I am convinced he has seen everything he describes. Unfortunately, the rest of us cannot. I am certain Steorn really believed I would see something that resembled their claim. They spent a lot of money setting up this demo and some £2,000 sending me over and putting me up. There are much cheaper ways to pull a con.

If it was a hoax, the whole upstairs [of Kinetica Museum] would not exist, nor would [McCarthy] have taken the time to go through all the details of how he thinks it all works.

My conclusion after going through all this is that Steorn is neither hoax nor scam. It is delusion. The reason it seems surreal is because it *is* surreal – we are the real part of someone else's imagination.

Shaun McCarthy: Aftermath

We – and by 'we' I mean 'I' – rushed the decision to do this [public demonstration] in London. It was for the right reasons, but at the time we had enough money that I could have said, 'Let's do this in three years.' We needed to get to a point where I could stick it in my briefcase, fly to Moscow, fly back again and the fucking thing's still working.

We didn't do that. We did it because the pressure that a professional jury process was creating on us – which was nothing to do with the jury; I have nothing bad to say about the jury and, bizarrely enough, I'm actually still friends with a lot of the guys on the jury – but we had backed ourselves into a corner of validation. We'd gone public, and we were sitting there two years later having nothing demonstratable for the jury, nothing demonstratable for a public point of view, and we decided we needed to do something. We had shareholders and they want to see progress, rightly ... but we didn't know how stacked the odds were against us because of our own actions.

There is some video of me getting interviewed – I don't know where the fuck it's from – which would put it into context. And I've no problem saying this now, because I've said it on camera: it was the first time in my life where I felt like rigging the demo. I could have. I could have done something where it looked like it worked. I wouldn't say it was a fleeting minute [in which I thought about this] – it was 15 minutes where I was standing outside the museum having a smoke at 3 o'clock in the morning, going, 'This is not going to be good.' Then immediately ruled it out. Didn't even discuss it with anybody.

We just completely miscalculated how high the risks were in trying to do this. … It was a kick in the balls; there was just no other way to view it. And it's not one of these kicks of the balls where you can go, 'Fucking referee!' It was 100 per cent on me.

It's one thing doing all the publicity, saying, 'We've got this.' But when push came to shove, we couldn't show it and we'd built it up, so we got everything we deserved in the media because of that.

We had a bunch of shareholders who travelled to London to see this. The day we pulled it, I spent most of my time hopping from one hotel room to the next, just wondering who was going to be the first person to punch me. I mean that sincerely. But I've always found the great advantage of being followed around by camera people is that people generally don't punch you on camera.

Look, no one was happy. Everyone was going, 'How the fuck did this happen?' I had one of the believers saying, 'I can blow up the building and we'll use that as an excuse.' I'm not fucking joking; I *think* he was.

I had had a ridiculously stressful career up to starting this whole Steorn thing, and this was on a par with some of the most stressful moments I've had in my life. And it's not just me – I'm a big boy – but walking into the company the day I got back was like walking into a morgue. It was horrible. The whole place was punch-drunk.

It was them and everyone associated, and even to this day they have to deal with it. I recently met a guy who used to work for us, and we were having a yap, and he was saying his friends and family still say, 'C'mon, what's the real story?'

When all the suffering and mental anguish is over, you sit around a table, and we're stuck with the same fundamental problem: how do we ever get any validation? Because there was only ever one plan, and that plan was to license it. We'd clearly been told, with no equivocation, that no one was going to test it; they wanted credible people to say it works before they licensed it. The jury was never going to go anywhere in a credible time frame.

So, all those plans were all of a sudden over. We had to say, 'What are the options here?' We went through a process of getting more and more engineers in to validate this. That was more to do with the shareholders, because they're sitting at a distance, saying, 'You lying fucks. You have our money.' So, we got more engineers, friends of friends – anyone to come in and say, 'You test us; tell us what's going on.' That dealt with confidence in terms of shareholders, confidence in terms of us; but it didn't move anything forward.

There were two responses after that. First, we needed to engineer this in a different way that's not so sensitive. So, let's look at this technologically, and we see that we've engaged a watchmaking company, and everything they're going to do is going to be finicky watchmaking stuff – and we're not in that league.

So, let's look at this electromechanically, and we started a project in-house to do it electromechanically. What that means is that a pure mechanical approach is like building a perfect clock: it's all 100 per cent mechanical intricacy and complexity. But electromechanical uses small bursts of electricity that cause things to happen, and then you recharge. That's a much easier engineering challenge, and it's something we took complete control over in what I call Generation Two.

Second, we asked: is there anything we can build? I don't care if it's just an executive toy that sits on someone's desk; there's got to be another way to validate this, and surely if it's in someone's hands and working, that's a good compromise.

We started to re-engineer version two so we could turn it into something someone could stick on their desks – even if it's just a curiosity. And if it's still moving in six months, they've got to say, 'Hang on. This is worth a look at.'

Then we sort of fell off the radar.

The company went quiet for a few months after the demonstration. For some reason, the President of Ireland, Mary McAleese, was photographed at the Steorn office, having accidentally arrived there on a tour of the East Wall business campus. But that was about the height of it. Steorn was by now a footnote rather than the story.

Steorn had fallen off the public's radar, maybe, but the shareholders were still shell-shocked in the aftermath of the failed London demonstration. While McCarthy continued to work behind the scenes, he was suddenly putting up with grumbling that he'd never had to deal with before.

In December 2007 the company wrote to its shareholders to tell them – perhaps for the first time – what had happened in the months since the Kinetica demonstration.

Following several months of extensive testing of the Kinetica devices and consultation with our engineering partners, it was agreed that the Kinetica physical implementation of our Orbo technology had some fundamental mechanical flaws. Specifically, these flaws affect the robustness and reliability of the operation of the system.

Several 'quick' fix mechanical solutions to these flaws have been tested and implemented [but] these fixes in themselves tended to reduce the mechanical reliability rather than ... increase it.

During this process we have of course continued to develop and research our core technology (time variance of magnetic transactions). In recent months we have identified the key drivers to these time variant transactions (the substantial slowing down of magnetic fields). This discovery, which is in reality a discovery within the existing discovery, has a substantial impact on our ever deepening understanding of the physics behind the technology and more importantly it opens up new possibilities for rapid and robust physical implementation.

Physical prototyping of these new methods of implementation will start early in the new year and we anticipate a shareholders demonstration in the not too distant future.

———————————

For small Irish investors, the Steorn event in London was a new and unpleasant experience. Alan Wallace – a gentle soul far more comfortable being in the business of growing and selling daffodils than being in a high-profile situation and receiving a high volume of abuse from both mainstream newspapers and a growing number of online commentators – sat down in April 2008 to write a letter to Pat Corbett to express his unhappiness with how the entire thing had panned out.

I am very sorry to have to write this letter to you, but I feel I have to for the following reasons.

We (the shareholders) always knew that it would take time to get Steorn's energy breakthrough accepted and passed by the scientists. We have accepted that to do this Steorn have to make working motors to enable the scientists to sign off.

We have been told by you (to the best of your knowledge) that it would be October or November 07 period for the failure in London to be rectified. We were told then in November 07 that it probably would not be in December 07 and to look forward to mid–end January 08. This enabled [my wife] Barbara and I to go to Australia last December happy.

Jan 08 went into Feb 08 and then we were aiming at March 08; and then end of March 08 and then mid-April; to the latest – the end of April 08.

I would like to stress that I and other shareholders understand that you can only tell us what you have been told.

The talk of the shareholders coming to Dublin to see a machine working has come to nothing and once again we are all in the dumps.

I feel I and another shareholder have annoyed you enough. I/We know it's your job to keep us happy, but at the end April 08 it is not fair for us (and you) to be still in a vacuum.

At this stage I am calling on Steorn at the TOP level to meet at least SOME shareholders – maybe those that showed the most interest and went to London etc or whatever to tell us how near we are – or, if it is a failure and is all over.

If it is all over and a failure, there will be no recrimination from me to you or anyone in Steorn, but only a closure on this most exciting adventure I have ever been on, and move on.

If, on the other hand, it is going to be the success and earth changing as hoped, I call on [Shaun McCarthy] to take a little time as a friend to take us out of our vacuum/misery etc.

Wallace values loyalty and positivity above all other traits, and this letter, he feared, might be seen as too critical and harsh. So, having written it, he decided not to send it.

Nonetheless, he was frustrated with the lack of communication and, two months later, wrote to Corbett – after a meeting with McCarthy in June – asking when there would be an annual general meeting for shareholders (pointing out that 'all it takes is one disgruntled shareholder to contact the Office of the Director of Corporate Enforcement to make big trouble'); about the second- and third-generation Orbo machines, based on electromagnetism rather than simple permanent magnets; and, most importantly, asking about what needed to be done now.

The next communication the Steorn investors got from the company was in relation to what would become known as the Rice Report – prepared by a Waterford-based engineer called Sean Rice – which would become the touchstone for many investors who had been let down by the Kinetica demonstration and by the jury process. If anyone told investors that Steorn was a scam, even a failed experiment, they would point to the Rice Report, citing it as their validation.

Except that the report fell short of full validation. For one thing, it was not an independent scientific test, merely a 'report on specific tests carried out at Steorn Ltd'. As Rice sets out in the report's introduction, his role was to

> observe a series of tests which aim to support the above mentioned claim [that] kinetic energy can be gained when permanent magnets, producing a [magnetic field], are rotated in a closed loop … As part of its ongoing test work, the company invited the undersigned to formally observe specific tests which support the claim.

The tests did support the claim, according to Rice, since a rig with a ferrite magnet included showed a net energy gain compared with a rig with the ferrite magnet removed. This, Rice wrote, 'is the key outcome of the tests'.

This finding, if true, would prove that Steorn was producing more energy from its machine than the machine was taking in. Rice summed his findings up in a series of questions.

- Is the test equipment appropriate and suitable for purpose? YES
- Is the particular test rig, and its component parts, controls and IT systems utilised in a manner which delivers accurate, consistent and repeatable test results? YES

- Are the applied methods and procedures as observed during the tests objective and pertinent? YES
- Do the test results provide clear and explicit support of the claim? YES

The report was distributed to shareholders, though they were not told that the jury had also seen it and that in the words of its chairman, Ian MacDonald, it 'did not impress us much'. Along with the report, Steorn told shareholders that

> with respect to the development of Orbo, we have identified the technical reasons that made robust implementation problematic. The prime issue relates to the mechanical forces acting on the system due to the nature of magnetic interactions. These mechanical forces can cause substantial resonance and associated loss of system energy to friction.

There were, Steorn said, two steps to resolving this technical challenge. The first was 'physical prototyping' based around research they had already done on variations in the speed of magnetic fields, which had allowed them to 'design and implement magnetic interactions with a substantial reduction in the problematic forces'. The second, still in progress, was 'system design that is less prone to problems caused by the remaining mechanical forces'.

If that sounded simple – as an explanation, it boils down to a promise to build better machines with fewer flaws – the investors had to acknowledge that

> the engineering solutions that are necessary to deal with these forces are unique, and have not previously been addressed by any other industry. As a result we cannot simply contract in engineering resources that could help in designing solutions to the issue; it remains an engineering challenge we must resolve internally. We are confident we have the necessary engineering skills in-house.

Steorn also made it clear that it couldn't make promises about when anything would be ready, given that 'the nature of the development of such a new technology has not allowed us to schedule the completion of robust prototypes with a degree of certainty'. Steorn also explained that it would be restructuring the company to 'create a clear market and commercial focus; i.e. to move from a development-led organisation to a market-focused one.'

———————

In July 2008, the jury came on their second visit. Although there had been plenty of correspondence, little of it was constructive in relation to helping the company get the validation it needed. Worse, a few of the jurors had by then fallen by the wayside. David Powell of Stanford University, for example, had decided that he couldn't countenance leaving the university during exam time. His refusal to visit was an indictment of Steorn. When he had to choose between the chance to see at first hand a technology that could change the world (as Steorn saw it) and tending to the business of supervising exams, he was not about to leave students high and dry when he knew Steorn was going nowhere.

The remaining jurors were still arguing over the first point of agreement that had to be reached before the jury could proceed. Step one, or gate one as Steorn called it, stated that a team selected by the jury would visit Steorn and verify that the claim made in the *Economist* ad was true. But the jury hadn't even got that far. Steorn still wanted the jury to build the machines themselves, but the jury insisted that they wouldn't progress beyond gate one until Steorn showed them a working model the company had itself built. Not unreasonably, several members of the jury – including Ian MacDonald – concluded that the company still had, in fact, nothing to show.

Powell, by that stage, had begun to believe that McCarthy was acting dishonestly – not maliciously, mind you – having found himself in too deep to admit that there was nothing to show and in too deep to withdraw. In fairness to McCarthy, if he was pretending to be convinced of the merits of Orbo, he was doing an Oscar-winning job and would show unparalleled stamina for it, going on to keep it up for a decade. But Powell's view was informed in large part by the odd decision by Steorn to try to silence the jury.

All jury members had signed a non-disclosure agreement, and part of that agreement was that Steorn would get some say over the wording of the jury's final statement. When it became clear that the jury's statement would be devastating, Steorn made sure to exercise that power and try to stall the statement.

For Powell, it couldn't have come at a worse time. The jury was already split – not between believers and non-believers, but between those who wanted to eviscerate Steorn and those who wanted to give the Steorn team a bit more time before eviscerating them.

On that second trip, MacDonald and the half-dozen jury members who joined him took a long walk on the beach at Sandymount to discuss what they ought to do next. Half of them were ready to write the Steorn project off and make a robust statement. More of the jurors then resigned, some evidently feeling that there was no merit in the process, while others were frustrated at the decision not to send a negative verdict earlier in 2008, after the company had failed to produce a working prototype.

'A declining number thought we shouldn't shut them down, to let them have a chance to at least display something before coming to a conclusion and the rest of the jury's deliberations were basically around that matter,' Ian MacDonald later explained. A full year would pass before they came to a conclusion on it.

———————

In September 2008, Ian MacDonald wrote to Shaun McCarthy to nudge Steorn along in providing the jury with the material it needed to come to a decision – or, as the case was, even to define the question. At least early on, there was no unanimity on the jury, as MacDonald would later say of the process. It was not necessarily that anyone believed in the technology, but some jurors were prepared to assume that there might have been something elusive there and wanted to give the company more time to make its pitch. At least one juror had done some considerable analysis on the matter. Others, however, had reached the end of their patience. So MacDonald decided to outline the position to McCarthy:

As you know the jury contract specifies that Steorn pass Gate 1 by 19 August [the previous month] this year, the date having been amended from 1 August by mutual agreement of the parties to accommodate the availability of the jury investigation team. In view of your statement at that meeting indicating Steorn was not in a position to make the required demonstration, the jury must declare that gate 1 has not been met within the required time frame, and the jury test procedure specified in the contract therefore lapses. In this situation the contract specifies that the jury will determine how to proceed. The members of the examination team were generally impressed by the improvements in Steorn's ability to characterise and measure the magnetic interactions in question. However, further improvements must be made and further information obtained before an assessment can be made whether there is promise that the requirements outlined in Gate 1 might ultimately be met.

MacDonald then listed technical conditions that needed to be met, such as the manner in which Steorn was to set up the mechanical test system and other issues related to measurement.

The jury has therefore determined that it will defer for a short period its decision whether to proceed so that Steorn can address the issues noted above and also provide data from the testing which has been claimed already to have shown evidence of energy imbalances.

Steorn had, MacDonald wrote, until 15 December 2008 to meet those conditions.

Throughout late 2008 and early 2009, meanwhile, Steorn and Shaun McCarthy had been focused on developing better test systems in parallel with giving talks and presentations wherever they could get an invitation. Every time the company popped up in the news – buried in the business pages or played for jokes in the main section – it would prompt the same question: what are those guys still doing? How have they managed to keep going, and how have they failed to produce a single product?

It was on the minds of their shareholders too, but Steorn was still stuck on square one in the game. To develop the technology, it had to spend more and more time, money and effort delving deeper into the process of developing tests for electromagnetic systems, jigging and rejigging the magnets, refining and redefining the parameters of the hypothesis and spewing out terabytes of test data.

It stood to reason. The Steorn team was never going to build a battery on the kind of mass scale that was required; the business model was still about licensing it; to license it they needed to prove it; and to prove it they needed to test it. What nobody seemed to notice in all this was that spending millions on developing test systems amounted to one enormous bill that showed, like a neon sign above the office, one incontrovertible fact: they hadn't proved it yet.

They had already done presentations to universities and institutes of technology in Ireland, talking to engineers all around the country with their usual rough-edged panache, shoehorning quotes from Isambard Kingdom Brunel – the great British engineer – and facing down the bad publicity and reputational damage with insouciance. But it was harder to open doors now and fewer people were inclined to regard this as a fun diversion, not just because of the failures of the past years, but because people's personal finances were being squeezed, increasing their anxiety.

Once again, Steorn was trying to shortcut the process. They figured that the jury wasn't going to work as a way to shortcut academic validation; the demonstration hadn't worked to shortcut the jury; but perhaps engineering validation would work to shortcut the science process and help Steorn lurch closer to being a business that could license what, they had to admit, was still only a seeming anomaly.

In January 2009, the jury finally told Steorn it had come to a unanimous decision: they would announce that the company had not proved its thesis.

Steorn objected to this, claiming that it had projects that would soon come to fruition. MacDonald and his fellow jurors gave Steorn until June 2009, at which time they would made a public announcement.

McCarthy was not pleased and the relationship between the company and the jury was beginning to sour. When it became clear that the jury had reached a conclusion, there was a series of what MacDonald would later describe as 'fairly public tussles', which led to McCarthy threatening to block them from speaking. According to MacDonald, the jurors received

> a threat to invoke the NDA [non-disclosure agreement] against us. It came by email from [McCarthy] himself, reporting that Steorn's lawyers had informed him that we were in breach. Since we had been quite careful to stick to the strict letter of the NDA, we disagreed, though it caused some concern for a while.

The relationship continued to deteriorate into the summer of 2009 as McCarthy and Mike Daly embarked on a trip to the Middle East – specifically, to any university in the United Arab Emirates and Oman, where McCarthy had worked for several years, that would have them. Their trip to Saudi Arabia gave rise to a rumour, entirely unfounded, that they had been tapping up rich, gullible sheikhs for investment. This was typical of the coverage Steorn was getting after Kinetica. Word soon spread on the internet that they had gone to raise money. McCarthy would later say of the coverage that people started to believe that 'we were going there to defraud the oil industry or raise billions of dollars'.

Even though the company was not trying to raise money, some of the jurors began to feel like their continued deliberation was being exploited by the company to do precisely that. As long as those deliberations continued, some jury members believed, Steorn could leverage some credibility by association. For his part, McCarthy felt like the misconception that they were raising money in the Middle East had hastened the jury's decision to issue a negative verdict.

However, the fact is plain: for most of 2009, the jury had been ready to render its decision.

On 23 June 2009, the jury finally issued its statement in a public posting on a specially set-up jury website. There was no report because they'd had no material to analyse and experiment on. Their statement consisted of two short paragraphs of relevance:

> In August 2006 the Irish company Steorn published an advertisement in the *Economist* announcing the development of 'a technology that produces free, clean and constant energy'. Qualified experts were sought to form a 'jury' to validate these claims.
>
> Twenty-two independent scientists and engineers were selected by Steorn to form this jury. It has for the past two years examined evidence presented by the company. The unanimous verdict of the Jury is that Steorn's attempts to demonstrate the claim have not shown the production of energy. The jury is therefore ceasing work.

It was signed off by Ian MacDonald.

Later that month, Shaun McCarthy wrote to the shareholders to address the release of the jury's statement. 'Due to the nature of the contract between the jury members and Steorn, we are not in a position to enter into the public debate on their findings at this time,' he said, noting that the company had issued a press release.

McCarthy then told the shareholders that the following was a confidential summary of the events leading to the jury's decision to release a statement, saying that in the summer of 2008

> representatives of the jury came to Steorn to witness tests demonstrating the key magnetic effect behind Orbo; these tests took place over a two-day

period. During this time one of the Jury members broke (accidentally) our key test system. Due to this we were unable to conclude the tests to the jury's or the company's satisfaction.

It was agreed with the jury on the last day of this meeting that there were two potential drivers for error on the test system (axial distortion and radial deflection). The company, in agreement with the jury, decided to place additional sensors on the system to demonstrate that these in fact did not cause significant test errors. Finally, a test plan was then developed in conjunction with the jury whereby we agreed how the error rate of the system would be determined and how actual tests would be concluded.

The above set-up involved some 3000 individual tests, the detailed data and net results of which were provided to the jury for consideration in December 2008. (I have also attached the summary report for your information.) The tests concluded that the net energy gain demonstrated was a multiple of over six times the maximum error rate of the test system.

On the 19th of January 2009, the jury reported back to Steorn stating that: 'We have not observed positive results from any experiments that could be directly indicative of energy production. Both the torque-integral and the wind-down experiments in which rotations in opposite sense are compared, are indirect. Interpretation, which is open to debate, is required to come to the conclusion Steorn claims.'

The key point in the above jury statement is that they were unwilling to interpret the data provided due to the potential for debate in future. It should also be noted that the tests witnessed by the jury are the same tests conducted by our engineering panel, who publicly supported our claims. While we will undoubtedly receive some flak in the media and on the internet, the jury decision in no way affects our plans for the commercial launch of Orbo.

It was an extraordinarily bullish letter, accusing the scientists of the jury of closed-mindedness rather than acknowledging that Steorn had failed to give them anything to wrap their minds around. The letter also contained astonishing claims of future profits that even McCarthy must have known were more ambitious than sensible.

By contrast, Ian MacDonald was generous in his comments about the jury process when asked about it some years later. Though concluding that the whole thing had been a bust, he described Steorn as having been 'remarkably co-operative', given that it had 'acceded readily enough to the criteria set by the jury'.

His comments were made on an online discussion board devoted to – or, more accurately, obsessed with – Steorn, and while MacDonald was magnanimous, he expressed a degree of befuddlement over one issue. Though the company had not been able to demonstrate anything of substance to the jury – beyond an unconvincing 'product for measuring magnetic interactions' – it had

> nevertheless attempted to show one [device] within months in London at the Kinetica Museum. There had been no mention made of any such plan to the jury. Given that the idea of the jury was to validate the device, this seemed very strange.
>
> I don't believe I ever thought that Steorn had a working perpetual motion machine. My interest was in what it was they did have that would generate enough interest to sponsor the level of activity they were showing, i.e. the advertisement in the *Economist*, the expense of assembling the jury, the cost of running a small company etc.
>
> I simply can't assess the motivation. My guess would be that some were deluded by others, but I have no way of knowing whom by who.

MacDonald concluded that although he would subsequently encounter

> other companies with claims that appear fantastic, some having quite a bit more investment than Steorn … I never have encountered anything as brash as Steorn's jury exercise.

But long before Ian MacDonald's remarks, Shaun McCarthy had got his retaliation in first, and his words seemed to convince the investors. When Alan Wallace came to visit the Steorn office in September 2009, he came away impressed, primarily by the measured approach everyone was taking. He wrote to McCarthy soon after his visit that it was nice to see Steorn staff members (including Mike Daly, Pat [Corbett] and yourself) not wildly excited over the imminent launch, but calmly confident about what is coming.

But there was a warning embedded in the letter, too, to maintain that prudence rather than get overexcited again.

I feel that Steorn need several demonstrations machines/models on display. These hopefully will be manufactured/made by some of the 300 people who have received free licences recently.

Various models doing different operations are needed to silence … what I call the chattering class, and to make it plain to ordinary people worldwide what Steorn has achieved and what will now happen.

[I] hope to live long enough to be able to purchase an Orbo-powered generator and to be able to ring the ESB and ask them to disconnect their supply to my house. I would also enjoy my son installing a large Orbo-driven generator into both of his industrial units and not to have to pay the ESB an exorbitant fee to provide power to his planned development of industrial units of which he has planning permission.

So to close, well done on all the progress over the last two years, and sock it to everyone … It will be a joy to watch.

11. THE CRASH

On 15 September 2008, the American investment bank Lehman Brothers filed for bankruptcy. The collapse of one bank doesn't usually trigger a global crisis, but the previous decade had seen a massive housing boom in the US and Lehman had grown fat on the exceedingly lucrative business of trading financial instruments that were derived – and in some instances derived and derived again – from aggregated pools of mortgage debt.

The interconnectedness of the dealings between banks in those pools, which were not traded in a straightforward fashion but were bet on and bet against and sliced and diced and resold, meant that pulling even a single bank like Lehman out of the system would destabilise the global financial network. Lehman didn't cause the crisis, but it fired the starting gun.

By the time Lehman fell, Ireland's economy had already begun to weaken. The country's vulnerability had been flagged years before, but people recoiled from it, as they often do from the truth, by branding it lies. Irish economists, including Morgan Kelly, who warned that the crash was coming were accused of being insufficiently patriotic, of not wearing the 'green jersey' – a garment fashioned from pure patriotism that makes the wearer immune to anything that would undermine Ireland's perceived economic strength.

The plain economic fact is that house prices simply cannot go up indefinitely: they must plateau or even fall. But much of the nation's wealth had been underpinned by pillars of debt based on overvalued property, and now those properties were worth less than the debt, making banks antsy. That the economy was too reliant on the output of the property sector all of a sudden became painfully apparent.

In 2007, tax revenues fell by 5 per cent from the projected level – around €2.3 billion of what was expected – a marked difference from the surpluses of previous budgets with which so many fiscal gifts could be given to voters.

Businesses began to struggle, jobs were lost and emigration began to rise. In the last year of the Celtic Tiger, many people who had feared that airing negative assessments would be tantamount to talking down the economy had begun to see that a plain vanilla recession was likely to be the least worst option. Pretty soon, the talk of soft landings had all but vanished and the green jerseys were shelved as it became apparent that the economy was tanking.

A month after Lehman Brothers filed for bankruptcy in 2008, Ireland declared itself to be in recession and the first of what would become known as austerity budgets was presented. These budgets levied a range of new taxes and cut spending to the bone. So bad was the situation that another budget had to be brought to the Dáil in April 2009 because, with unemployment exceeding 10 per cent and construction collapsing, the government feared that the shortfall in tax income might be close to €5 billion.

Irish banks were at the centre of that tanking economy, having borrowed billions by issuing bonds to foreign investment funds so that they could turn the money inwards, lending to house-builders to build more houses. It worked, at least in the beginning: annual house completions had soared from 19,000 in 1990 to 50,000 in 2000 to 93,000 in 2006. By the end of the Celtic Tiger, construction accounted for 13.3 per cent of all employment. So much of the economy was driven by house building that when prices began to fall, so did Ireland.

Although the banks were all suffering, the ticking time bomb was Anglo Irish Bank, which had grown large from straightforward property lending (unlike Lehman's more complex financial trickery), firing out hundreds of billions in loans to the new class of Irish builder: the property developer. Such loans were fine when property was selling for higher prices than the loan had cost to take out, but when the market collapsed, Anglo was left with very large debts that couldn't be repaid. To stay afloat, it attempted to pull off a bit of accounting sleight of hand that led to €7.2 billion being moved between Anglo and two other financial institutions – Irish Life and Permanent and Irish Life Assurance – to make the bank appear healthier than it was.

Anglo would end up costing Ireland around €34 billion – nearly €7,000 for every person living in the country – making it one of the most expensive single banks, relative to the economy, in the world. But Anglo wasn't the only bank that took public money; the entire bailout required nearly €65 billion.

With such a hole to plug in the nation's finances, the government was struggling to contain the crisis. The US ambassador, in diplomatic cables that would be leaked only years later, said that the Irish government had found it 'almost impossible' to come up with a rescue plan, that it was lurching from crisis to crisis and that it failed 'to be straight with the Irish public' about the difficulties that lay ahead.

By November 2010, it was inevitable that Ireland would need outside assistance, striking a funding deal with the EU and the IMF to send in the troika of the European Central Bank, the European Commission and the International Monetary Fund (IMF) to in effect run Ireland's fiscal affairs.

The financial crisis had hit Steorn shareholder Robert Seale hard. With so much of his property tied up in mortgage debt, the banks closed in on him to squeeze out whatever value they could to solve their own liquidity and balance-sheet problems. Having chucked the money at him, they now wanted to drag it back, whatever the consequences for him.

Seale's honesty served him poorly during these years. He could easily have jetted off, taken the few hundred thousand he had in cash and gone to live in one of his Spanish properties that was unencumbered by debt. It was a route taken by plenty of property developers and investment speculators before him, who were safe in the knowledge that the banks might well be too distracted by their struggles on the home front to pursue an absconded debtor.

But this idea didn't sit well with Seale, who struggles to tell a lie. Instead, he sold his Irish house – the grand Celtic Tiger ranch – for a reasonable sum of €650,000 and allowed the banks to seize and sell anything with a mortgage attached. He also sold the Spanish properties to pull cash together to settle the balance with the banks.

When he went into his bank branch to cut a deal with the manager, presuming his good-faith engagement would carry some weight, he was told bluntly – after a consultation with head office – that no such deal was on the table. It was a ruthless process, greatly at variance with the exuberance and free lending of the past few years.

Seale took the honest approach and attempted to deal with the banks on their terms, trusting them to show mercy. Instead, they left him with the only property he had left: a small apartment in Port Laoise, his old-age pension and his shares in Steorn.

Many of his fellow Steorn shareholders were starting to get agitated. Like Seale, the property crash had hit them particularly badly, and their shares in the banks – which they had been told were solid and safe – were now worthless.

In that environment, funds for Steorn would surely be hard to come by.

By contrast, after the crash, another Steorn shareholder, Edward Sheehan, suddenly became very busy. Several of his investments had crashed spectacularly, his Bank of Ireland shares had in effect been wiped out and his rental income from his various apartments around Cork and Dublin had plummeted. However, he was arguably busiest in his day job as an investigating accountant for the Law Society.

By late 2008, conveyancing – the legal work around acquiring and transferring property – had stopped in its tracks. Fee income for solicitors had fallen by half in such work. Sheehan went into legal practices to look over the books, finding many of them simply abandoned. Going through the books of some of those law firms was like being a financial archaeologist, piecing together the artefacts of a cataclysm. In one firm, he came across a three-page letter to a solicitor relating a nearly €350 million loan from Anglo Irish Bank, which had cost the taxpayer billions because of its reckless lending. The letter recorded an arrangement fee of €2 million on the first €40 million of new money drawn down – money that went straight to the bank's bottom line. This was evidence of just how much incentive banks then had to lend.

Meanwhile, lawyers who had been too exposed to the property sector had started to go out of business, some of them with serious questions to answer.

In the early days, Sheehan was closing a practice a month on behalf of the Law Society. On a single day he referred four lawyers to the disciplinary committee. On another occasion he had a queue of 15 people awaiting disciplinary hearings, and he wasn't the only accountant working on such cases.

What struck Sheehan most was that these weren't property speculators; these lawyers were supposed to be the professionals overseeing the transactions, making sure they were legal and airtight. Yet so exuberant had the market become that many were acting in a cavalier fashion.

Today, headlines from some of the more egregious cases are displayed on Sheehan's wall: a solicitor whose assets were frozen after a claim that he had used the cash to buy a boat; another had sat on nearly a quarter of a million in a client account. This is not to say that Sheehan himself was untouched. He had got caught up in AIB's series of Belfry property funds, which, between 2002 and 2006, had raised nearly €300 million from the bank's customers, to which the bank added nearly €1 billion in loans to buy commercial properties in Britain just as the property market was reaching its peak. Although the first fund returned a profit for its investors, investors in the following five were wiped out.

While Sheehan had put in only the surplus money from that home-improvement loan on his Blackwater Valley home, he still had to pay that loan off and work hard to keep his businesses and apartments above water. More to the point, he still had time to reflect on the money he'd spent unwisely during the Celtic Tiger years. The last thing he was still thinking about was Steorn.

———————

Robert Seale, however, still believed in Steorn. During those bad days, he approached Pat Corbett on the urging of his wife, Anne, to see if there was anything that could be done about realising some of the value in the Steorn shares. The Seales met Corbett in a hotel, where Corbett rolled out his now familiar reassurance spiel: Steorn would work out; it was just a matter of time and patience. Anne Seale replied that she had heard this story dozens of times, then burst into tears.

Corbett, impassive, simply sat there.

After a while, the Seales left, nothing having been resolved yet. On his way out, Robert noticed Corbett speaking on the phone, now returned to his usual smiling demeanour, as if their conversation had never taken place.

And yet, during that period, Robert Seale was one of those who stepped up to push even more money into Steorn when it returned with the begging bowl. Having sold off the house and largely settled his debts with the bank, he was left with a small sum of money. Of that, he directed nearly €80,000 into Steorn in one of its austerity-era fundraising rounds, bringing his investment in the company to more than €206,000.

Much later, around the spring of 2015, Seale would get some small return on his investment, selling his shares to another investor for around €55,000. He would be one of the few to make even a fraction of his money back. It was, needless to say, a cold comfort.

Shaun McCarthy: The Impact of the Crash

By 2009 we were balls-and-all into the soft landing, or whatever the 'experts' told would be happening by that stage.

A lot of these people – the shareholders – obviously had huge exposure to property and to bank shares. If you ignore Steorn for a minute – and a lot of people would've said that it was good money after bad – a lot of the commentary was that everything else is fucked and Steorn was still standing. A lot of the psychology of that – and it's not something we pushed, because we were on our knees in every way – was this view that your property portfolio is in NAMA or so underwater it's embarrassing; your bank shares have gone from 30 bucks to 30 cents or whatever the hell the numbers were; but at least we're still there and giving it a box.

That, in a bizarre way, helped us to raise the additional funds that kept the show on the road. We probably shouldn't have. We probably should've drawn a line under it and said we need to do this a different way, but that's neither here nor there, because we didn't.

There was this kind of relativity – relative to everything else that people had invested in, we were still going.

And it makes sense, in a perverse way. Obviously, it wasn't our narrative, going back out again to raise money; but when you're speaking to these people, and a lot of them had a huge exposure to property and bank shares, it's a horrible thing, but we were outperforming them because we hadn't gone to zero.

That's probably more a psychological reason as to why people followed their money; clearly, it proved not to be a rational reason, but it was certainly part of the mix that Steorn was still alive, if not kicking.

We'd raised €20 million or so, and during the Celtic Tiger we could've raised €50 million, easy. It was just a simple process: everyone was a millionaire or a billionaire. Not me, of course, but everyone else was. One guy described it to me as something to discuss over dinner, and he'd written a cheque for a million. That was, I suppose, more a commentary on the Celtic Tiger than on Steorn, if you see what I mean. Things were different after the crash.

Also, we weren't running away from anything. We didn't wash our hands of it. We were always prepared to go and meet them in sometimes quite hostile meetings – because I don't want to paint the picture that it was all lovey-dovey and that people were saying, 'Ah, sure, they're lovely lads. Let's write them a cheque for a million.' We got our kickings, but we also went out and fought our corner. That we were prepared to face up to the mistakes and to criticism was part of the psychology of it.

But there was almost a commentary that at least we were still going, where everything else wasn't. You can call that a Celtic Tiger hangover investment, and it probably was, in certain ways.

We were struggling to pay salaries, and that was the same for every company in the country; but it was a new experience for us. This was the period during which Pat Corbett really showed what an extraordinary fundraiser he is.

Pat was and is one of the most remarkable salespeople I've ever met. I'm not sure that even covers it. He was just one of the most remarkable *people* in terms of human interaction I've ever met. To an extent, he has the ability – and it's not some kind of bullshit ability – that when he believes in something and walks into a room and starts talking, everyone fucking believes him.

It's an unbelievable talent that we were fortunate to have access to. When you come down to it, Pat is an incredibly powerful person. He did an unbelievable job in keeping people informed and on board. We had people coming in and out; it was kind of open – not like floods of people, but if someone wanted to come in and see if we were still giving it a go, they could do that too.

Now, we were also long enough in the tooth to understand that there's an inherent danger in that. So, we had Mike Moriarty, who's the polar opposite of Pat. Mike is Mr Suit, Mr Venture Capital, Mr This Is What the Law Says, and if anyone had stepped close to that line, he would have broken their fingers.

Mike had found it slightly different to work with Pat, and under doctors' advice was told he needed to leave. Which meant that, towards the end, calling a spade a spade, Pat was 100 per cent free to use his God-given talents, which are amazing and frightening at the same time.

That's not me washing my hands of any of that: I don't get to do that. But in the end, of course, it was oversold, because we didn't do what we said we'd do. So, it was oversold, but not knowingly oversold. We all believed what we were saying, but what we were saying didn't turn out to happen.

We were the underdog, and everyone loves an underdog. Inherently, people wanted us to win – that's the funny thing. A lot of the scientists absolutely just laughed at us and wanted us to be discovered for the frauds they thought we were; but just about everyone else who was close to us and knew we weren't Bernie Madoff wanted us to win.

There were people who are fundamental believers in the technology and what it can do. For a proportion of people, like [the Steorn shareholder] James Murphy, it was far bigger than the money. Obviously, everyone wants to make money, but it was more about what the technology would mean if we get it out in the marketplace.

I'd be more than 50 per cent in that camp myself, but we weren't the majority. The majority wanted to make an absolute metric ton-load of money and, fair enough, that's what they invested for.

There had always been people who rightly expressed their frustration, even before 2007. Why were we going through scientists? Why were we doing this? … People always questioned us. By and large – even in the better times – it was well-behaved questioning, but they were also very pointed. This was people's money, and it mattered to them an awful lot more after 2010 than before.

The case we were making to them didn't change. We said, 'Look, we have these challenges; we have these issues.' But the fundamental thing is that everything we ever did had only one fucking purpose: a demonstrable fact that this technology did something anomalous, something unusual.

In hindsight, we should've pared back to the bone – which we didn't because we still had marketing people. We should've just cut it and then just four of us lock ourselves in a room, tell the media to go and take a flying shite and write what they want, and we would focus on the problem at hand. But we didn't.

12. ANOTHER DEMONSTRATION

Shaun McCarthy: Waterways

With Kinetica [the public demonstration in London in 2007] and then with the jury, we'd rolled the dice again and come up with nothing. The mission, or the fundamental thing that gave the company value – which was the question of whether this technology does something or doesn't – hadn't changed.

We'd tried to publicly demonstrate and fallen on our faces. We'd engaged twenty-two of the field's leading scientists, and they turned around and said there wasn't sufficient evidence to support it (that's an exact quote). So, we were back to square one again.

Probably it was difficult to see a path forward when your prime option has proved not to work out. The secondary option, which was really related to the public display, was always going to be tough.

See, we weren't stupid: we knew that even if it had worked in Kinetica, we'd still be seen as a fraud. There are people who have committed perpetual-motion demonstrations that are fraudulent.

We knew, going into it, how this looked … We knew every time we stuck our head above the parapet with what we're claiming that this is snake-oil salesman territory, absofuckinglutely every time. This area of perpetual motion is full of scams and frauds and so on; but just because the space is very scammy doesn't mean everything is a scam.

It wasn't going to prove anything other than that we weren't prepared to cheat … But a public demonstration was going to give us an opportunity to reach out further into the engineering community.

If you come back to the beating heart of this: how did we end up where we ended up? We went to the biggest tech company; they said they needed validation, so we attempted to do that – which, with the beauty of 20/20 hindsight, was a fucking mistake. We tried to prod and probe with demonstrations and lectures and all this carry-on, and that got us nowhere.

After all of that, we rolled up our sleeves and started to think maybe that the problem here was that the format of the technology was difficult to assess. So, we went off and developed an electromagnetic system [E-Orbo] instead of the pure magnetic system. We disengaged with Kinetron, we took the beating heart of the battery, and we went off and redeveloped it along the same principles in very different engineering constructions.

That's what we ended up demonstrating in Waterways [in Dublin] in 2009 – these electromagnetic systems, these things we'd gone off and redeveloped. We stopped all the work on the first version of Orbo – this is part of the problem here; the bloody thing is part of the problem. So, we started on version two – a version that's easier to work with, easier to test, easier to demonstrate.

The first version of Orbo was a bunch of permanent magnets like the shit you have on your fridge, with no wires attached, and normally when you measure the interaction between these magnets the amount of work done is the same. The energy released when they come together is the same as when they're pulled apart. The first version of Orbo found that, 'Look, in certain circumstances this is not true; we have this energy imbalance.'

The second version had these permanent magnets, but we added electrical generators and electrical activators, so it was a combination of the original Orbo and an electrical motor. It's got wires, power, storage devices, batteries and all this carry-on. It's a lot easier to build and an awful lot easier to demonstrate – but significantly less compelling because people were saying, 'Look, there's a fucking battery.'

In any case, we put them [the E-Orbos] on public demonstration. They were on Perspex glass cases, a bunch of them sitting spinning away with 24-hour webcam streaming.

––––––––––––

Phil Watson was an officer in the Naval Service with a degree in electronic engineering, who also lectured at his alma mater, Cork Institute of Technology. Like most who understand a smattering or more of physics and engineering, he had always been fascinated by – and sceptical of – the claims of those who said they'd built an over-unity machine.

By the time of the Waterways demonstration in 2009, Watson had been associated with Steorn for nearly five years. A colleague had approached him in 2004 during a conference organised by the Sustainable Energy Authority of Ireland and told him about Steorn. He was intrigued. The company was putting together a panel to test device equipment and Watson's friend had been asked to go but couldn't. Could Watson go in his place?

He had to think about it. He'd heard of the company and thought it was like crackpot scientists claiming to have turned lead into gold. It's one thing being intrigued by these companies and reading about them on the internet; it's quite another to visit one and risk guilt by association. He was dubious, being risk-averse, but he eventually decided to go along and see what they were claiming. However, he resolved, he wasn't about to invest money in this company, whatever its claims.

On his first visit to Steorn's office in 2004, he was one of several engineers who had been brought up to view the machine Steorn had built. As Watson recalled it, the engineers had built a test rig (a rig being an engineering machine for virtually any test version of a machine) and it was set up on the principle that the large circular disc with magnets embedded in it would rotate through a magnetic field based on the arrangement of magnets. That arrangement of the magnets' magnetic fields would ensure that once the wheel had been given an initial spin, the magnet arrangement would ensure enough attractive pull to draw the wheel forward at moments when it should have slowed; other magnets would give a propulsive kick at other points. All this would generate enough motion and momentum to keep the wheel spinning long after the energy from the initial push should have dissipated.

Steorn also had a testing device attached that would measure the torque, the force that can cause an object to rotate about an axis. For two days, Watson and the other engineers were to test and retest and run experiments of their own. The Steorn team would leave them to it.

Despite his initial scepticism, Watson was stumped. It did indeed seem that there was a marginal amount of energy coming from the Steorn machine more than was going in. It did, at least from his testing, appear to defy the laws of physics. The output was never going to power a town or a city – it was tiny – but it *was* happening, he thought. Watson, who was guarded, concluded that it needed more testing. After all, it was too early in the process to make grand claims about over-unity, but it was certainly enough to say that something unusual was happening.

Watson even explained his findings in a video shot by Steorn. In it, he said that the gain is so outside the measurement error that [I can] definitely stand over this one. The potential for the Orbo is phenomenal, but it needs development behind it; it needs someone to get it by the scruff of the neck and just develop it into a product.

He was joined in the video by another volunteer tester, Hugh Deasy, a physics graduate who lived in Germany and worked as a flight-dynamics test and validation officer for the European Space Operations Centre. Deasy had written several self-published books, some of which were science-related and some of which weren't. *Humpty-Dumpty Disaster: The Ghost or the Machine,* for example, was about 'some aspects of modern science that are not compatible with a simple materialist philosophy'. Another book, *Grannies and Time Machines,* is a book of adventure stories about 'an epic voyage on a medieval planet' that 'leads beyond the furthest horizon'. In one story, a 'heroic couple travels to a seer to save their world from a vengeful monster breaking out of an age-old prison'. In yet another, 'an Irish grandmother helps rescue a brave cat from a church steeple'. The book includes a 'mixture of stories, comic strips, political cartoons and skilful illustrations' along with 'a joke story, crammed with one-liners'.

Deasy was a true believer in over-unity devices and bragged in the video that in his experiments on Steorn-like devices he had built, he had registered energy gains of up to 320 per cent – meaning that he had got more than three times the energy output from the initial energy from pushing the wheel. In the video, Deasy, like Watson, talked about how his finding was comparable to Steorn's previous tests and about how his finding had 'pleased us' – though he never gave the details of the tests or said who the 'us' was.

A third engineer present in the video, the Englishman Craig Coates, claimed he had squeezed 307 per cent energy output from his experiment. He explained that he had tested the anomaly on his own system at home, adding that he knew the gain was there. 'I could smell the gain,' he said. But now, in Steorn's lab in Dublin, he was convinced of it.

Steorn message boards hummed with comment and activity for several years, even during the duller years after the crisis in the company. Perhaps that's not surprising: the claims gave people something to talk about that wasn't higher taxes, restricted public services or their own money troubles.

Meanwhile, Phil Watson speculated that the Steorn device was absorbing energy from the ether, from radiofrequency waves, from the fluorescent lights, from vibration in the ground or from something that was being harnessed and allowing the device to put out a marginal amount more than the input. Maybe, he would later reflect, he was overlooking something brutally obvious that a material scientist would have spotted. Nevertheless, blindly disregarding the need for further study, he believed, was simply unscientific. But after the Waterways demonstration, Watson would change his mind.

———————

In December 2009, Steorn launched a promotional video. It began with the traditional Steorn approach of running through the remarks of those who had slammed the company, such as Engadget's reference to 'magic fairy powered rotary and magnetic systems', the *Economist's* 'perpetual nonsense' quip and Dr Michio Kaku's blunt opinion that it was a 'fraud'. Two years ago, this approach to criticism seemed bold and confident; by 2009, after a failed demonstration and a damning jury verdict, and in the midst of the first year of a financial slump that would last more than a decade, the humour seemed forced and threadbare.

This new mood was only enhanced by the appearance of Shaun McCarthy, standing on a footbridge above the Grand Canal basin, the Waterways building visible behind him. Wearing a light-brown trench coat open at the chest and an unbuttoned shirt, despite the cold, he looked tired. His usually mischievous smile was nowhere in evidence and his eyes betrayed a new guardedness. McCarthy addressed the camera.

> Six years ago, our company, Steorn, discovered a magnetic anomaly. We did this during the course of developing another technology, and the anomaly is very simple: the anomaly is that we could gain energy from magnets with no apparent sources.

Six years on, what we're doing is we're launching that technology; we're launching it with public demonstrations.

He then invited people to visit the Waterways building for the demonstration or to watch it on Steorn's website.

He also offered an explanation of the device Steorn would be demonstrating and the video showed live shots and illustrations of how it was to work. A flat, square Perspex panel – thick, with bevelled corners – was shown lying horizontally. On top of that panel, at each corner, sat four flying-buttress pillars made of solid Perspex. Into the bodies of those buttresses was embedded two circular magnets each – both wound around by electrically conductive copper wire – so that, at each corner, two magnets were directly across the panel from two others. In the centre, around an axis, spun two thick Perspex wheels, each of which had four sets of twin magnets arranged at the north, south, east and west compass points – making for 16 magnets on the two wheels. From each buttress, and from the bottom of the column, ran electrical cables to a battery, which would store the energy. According to McCarthy,

> what you're seeing here is basically an Orbo-powered motor. You have an energy reservoir, which in this case is a battery. This is feeding electrical energy into coils around the system, and the system operates very much like a traditional electrical motor. What is unique about this versus any other electrical motor is [that] the amount of energy we're drawing from the reservoir is substantially less than the work done by the rotor.
>
> What we've added to the system now is a generator. It's a sequence of pick-up coils, [which] … take some of the kinetic energy of the rotor and convert it to electrical energy. This is fed back into the battery with a very simple current rectification circuit, and this recharges the battery.

The new, electromagnetic version of Orbo, the E-Orbo, was substantially different from the previous version. Whereas the predecessor relied solely on the interaction of asymmetric magnetic fields, the electronic version would use electromagnets – certain types of metal rendered magnetic by running an electric current through them – giving Steorn the ability to turn the magnetic fields on and off by a process of saturation.

Therefore, as the wheel swung around, the field that would ordinarily repel it was switched off. The magnet-bearing wheel would then simply glide by. As soon as it did, the electromagnet was switched back on, giving it a kick just at the right moment, accelerating its motion.

The idea, like all over-unity machines, was beguiling. Like kicking the wheel of a bicycle every time it passes your foot, the wheel would continue to spin. A generator attached to the wheel would draw all that foot energy off and store it as, say, a light on the bicycle. But the problem was – apart, of course, from the body of theoretical and practical research that insisted that such a thing was not possible – that the energy that goes into saturating the magnet and thus turning it off was, in practical terms, greater than the energy derived from the spinning rotor. None of which fazed McCarthy in that video, as he asserted:

> What we're offering is not just some new cool technology: it is a real opportunity for us as a species and us as a society to change everything.

Steorn would conduct a number of public demonstrations, showing lines on an oscilloscope that it said proved that the device was producing more power than it was taking in. However, the door to the public was opened at the Waterways building from 15 December 2009, just before the rush of Christmas shopping and late-night parties. Between the pain of austerity and the collapse of Steorn's remaining credibility, McCarthy wouldn't quite get the attention he had hoped for.

Shaun McCarthy: After Waterways

No one bothered to come and see them [the demonstrations]. It was open and accessible to the public six hours a day, and in addition to that we did a bunch of live-stream experiments to show each step of this.

They were physical devices working away for months and months. But there was no reaction. No one gave a shit.

We had never had a problem getting media attention before. We'd invested a lot in this, and it was very professionally done, and we had shit that actually worked. But the first public attention – and this could be sour grapes on our part – was that AP [Associated Press] or one of the wire services came along for the opening, and it was opening for investors, and the only article we saw said that we were pitching to investors, which was not true. They came back and they apologised.

The only thing of note was that Brendan O'Carroll dropped in – the guy from *Mrs Brown's Boys*. It was completely by accident; he didn't come in to see us. He said, 'That's fascinating,' and wandered off, clearly thinking, *They're fucking mad, those lads*.

———————

In fact, this account of a lack of public interest in the demonstration wasn't entirely true. Plenty of people did visit; they just didn't see exactly what McCarthy believed he was seeing.

Plamen Stamenov of the physics department at Trinity College, Dublin, had discussed the possibility of visiting the demonstration with Prof. Michael Coey. The latter had considered going but decided against it because he would be too recognisable. Stamenov, however, had never met McCarthy and knew he could slip in unannounced and unnoticed and have a look around to see what Steorn was demonstrating.

He did so just before Christmas. He was left waiting a long time in the visitors' centre before McCarthy and one of his engineers wheeled out a standard scientific workbench on top of which was the E-Orbo device within a Plexiglas box.

Stamenov could see immediately what was intended by the demonstration. The wheel would be spun by the electrical motor, which would interact with the magnets. The system would try to extract more power from the spinning magnets than it had put in through the motor. This would be shown on the oscilloscope screen by measuring the voltage and the current, which would produce a measurement of the energy output.

However, Stamenov could see an error in how the machine was being measured: the Hall probe, used to measure the current, was misbalanced.

It hadn't been zeroed properly. That was enough for him to conclude that the demonstration simply couldn't produce any worthwhile findings.

He wasn't the only one to come to this conclusion. Someone else who travelled to see the Waterways demonstration was Phil Watson. He was surprised that Steorn had moved to a new version of their system; that in place of a purely magnetic system – the one that had failed two years before at Kinetica in London – Steorn had moved on to an electromagnetic system, which would be easier for sceptics to criticise, given that it was harder to say whether it was purely a magnetic effect, since the battery built into the system could lead people to conclude that it was the battery doing all the work. For Watson, Steorn had gone off on a tangent.

The company had invited him to the Waterways building to conduct more tests. This was no surprise, as he had tested the purely magnetic version of the system and had found a 200 per cent gain. (Notably, he had found less than his fellow testers, Craig Coates and Hugh Deasy.) On testing the battery-assisted electromagnetic system, though, he found something entirely different.

Before delving into his finding, it's necessary to consider how electronics engineers measure the output of a system. It's complicated and mathematical, but it can be boiled down to a simple formula: voltage is multiplied by current to calculate the power output. The problem was that Steorn was doing the calculation wrong, measuring the power input one way and the power output another. To Watson, Steorn should have stuck to a consistent system of measurement. When he asked why it hadn't done so, he was told, 'It's easier to measure that way.'

The company gave Watson an E-Orbo system to take home to Cork. There, he threw out Steorn's measurement technique and used his own more sophisticated testing machinery. When he used Steorn's systems the result was a net gain, showing apparent over-unity, but when he used his own system, it showed a net loss.

He went back to Dublin and told McCarthy that Steorn's measurement was wrong: the E-Orbo was actually losing 10 per cent to heat.

McCarthy, in typical fashion, replied, 'Aw, bollocks.'

This was an awakening for Watson. He knew that his measurement of the permanent magnet was rigorous. Of course, other engineers and physicists had come to different conclusions, and Watson, an electrical engineer, knew that his understanding of purely mechanical systems was not infallible. He believed that the device still deserved further study. But this error in the most basic method of measuring electrical input and output had led him to the only possible conclusion: Steorn was wrong.

Watson produced a report on his findings, which contained a substantial data set of readings and figures and an explanation of the technical approach to gathering each set. He stated his findings bluntly.

> The [Steorn] measurement method … results in an inaccurate measurement of returned energy. The method used to produce the energy integral in Dataset 1 is not a valid method of ascertaining the recovered energy from the Orbo. As demonstrated by dataset 2, the Orbo releases energy in line with the first and second law of thermodynamics.

In another report on the same experiments, he made the same point:

> Unfortunately we were unable to replicate Over Unity (OU). Using Steorn's measurement technique we did get results that appeared to demonstrate OU. However, we cannot agree that their measurement technique is valid.

In short, Steorn had measured incorrectly; when measured accurately, the production of energy was lower than claimed and was exactly in line with the laws of physics.

Watson walked away with a clear conscience, never having invested money and thus never having lost money.

Also in Dublin for the Waterways demonstration was Guido Stockhausen, a former member of the jury that had concluded that Steorn had demonstrated nothing that could be tested or evaluated. Stockhausen had been scratching his head since the first jury meeting, not because he believed the claim could be valid, but because he was sincerely mystified as to how Steorn's engineers might have convinced themselves they had discovered something real.

After the first jury visit to Dublin, Stockhausen spent several months investigating the claim and the various pieces of evidence that Steorn had put forward. It was no easy task. He spent months investigating, growing convinced that there was an explanation for Steorn's experimental magnetic anomaly buried deep in a textbook somewhere.

First, he tried to figure out the way in which Steorn actually measured their energy gains. In a report he would later write on the matter he said:

> Their 'main' evidence was always based on a measurement of the torque on that rotor magnet which was moved by an external force (a powered step-per motor) around a closed loop. For that they created their sophisticated 'torque measurement system'. If you do this over one round you will always get an energy loss because there are loss processes even in this 'static' set-up. To account for these losses they applied a well-known procedure and moved the rotor magnet one way round – say clockwise – and then turn it the other way counter-clockwise around. Then they calculated the difference between both values and assumed that this procedure cancels the losses while giving a net energy result which would correspond to an energy gain in one direction and an energy loss in the other.

This apparent gain in energy, Steorn claimed, was evidence of their theory of magnetic viscosity – or, as McCarthy more colourfully described it, their time machine. As they explained it, these asymmetric magnetic fields would propagate at different times and that the energy lost or gained between the delays could be exploited as a form of energy.

Stockhausen simply knew this could not be true, so in order to properly evaluate it, he ran the experiments using Steorn's arrangements of asymmetric magnetic fields. As he put it himself later, 'I fully expected that my simulation would show a zero result and nearly fell off my chair when the screen showed a non-vanishing value for the torque integral over a closed path. This would indeed correspond to an energy gain or loss depending on the direction of the rotation.'

It seemed to bear out McCarthy's time machine explanation – that if you walk up a hill slowly and then run down it fast, you've somehow gained energy.

But Stockhausen knew there had to be a reason for this non-zero result, so he wrote a paper titled 'The Improbable Coincidence'. In that paper, he presented his non-zero findings, yet stated:

> To avoid any misunderstandings I want to point out that this definition nei-
> ther EXPLAINS the effect nor PROVES any violation of energy conservation!
> But the similarities/agreements/coincidences between experiment and sim-
> ulation … are so perplexing that I'm convinced that there exists a MISSING
> LINK between them and that this coincidence can't happen by any chance!

To his consternation, it began to circulate – more as a rumour than a piece of work anyone actually read – that a jury member had actually validated the finding.

Then, when the jury made its final public determination, Stockhausen was a tad crestfallen. He agreed wholeheartedly that Steorn had failed to present something for evaluation and had, by its own yardstick, failed to demonstrate over-unity, but he still hadn't found that missing connection that would explain how McCarthy had convinced himself so thoroughly of his 'discovery'. So Stockhausen decided to continue with his investigations. He knew Steorn was wrong; he just desperately wanted to know why.

That's when he stumbled across the concept of 'rotational magnetic hysteresis'. In technical terms, it describes an energy loss mechanism due to irreversible magnetic domain movement on a microscopic level. As he would later put it in an email to some of his fellow jury members, the kind of asymmetric magnetic field that Steorn was talking about could lose energy at different rates because of this magnetic hysteresis effect, depending on which direction the magnets were being rotated. This difference in energy losses, he said, was interpreted as an energy gain by Steorn.

It was an understandable measurement error because of Steorn's imperfect understanding of some of the deeper, more complex and layman-unfriendly reaches of magnetic theory.

By then, however, the jury had already made its decision to announce and for a time Stockhausen found himself holding the answer to a question no one was asking anymore. Then, in later 2009, McCarthy – ever forgiving – sent an email to the jury members asking them if they would like to be interviewed as part of Maurice Linnane's documentary. He also asked them to attend the Waterways demonstration, attaching data files that apparently supported the claims he made about the working prototype of the second-generation E-Orbo device.

No one but Stockhausen accepted, and even he wasn't particularly interested in seeing a working prototype, since he now knew how Steorn had made its error. As he put it in a later account of that time,

> I was warned [not] to accept the invitation because Steorn would spin any-thing critical I could tell them against me. [But] at this time I was confident that I would win any argument with Shaun and decided to accept this offer.

He visited the Waterways centre at Grand Canal Dock in January 2010 to observe the demonstration and to have that argument. It didn't matter that the system had changed from a permanent magnet arrangement to an electromagnet system – it operated on the same asymmetric magnetic field configuration. He felt confident that Steorn would still be interpreting the delay in the way the magnetic fields were created and collapsed as an energy loss or gain.

The morning Shaun picked him up from his hotel, he complained to Guido that 'he was really upset that only three jury members had downloaded [some] data files [in] which Steorn had invested a lot of time'. It was yet another example of just how sincerely McCarthy believed in the discovery, but Stockhausen told him – bluntly – that it didn't matter how many jury members had downloaded the data, since they all believed he was fundamentally wrong in his scientific approach. Stockhausen reminded McCarthy that in any case, the data Steorn had supplied was the wrong data: the jury had wanted what's known as wind-down data, meaning data derived from the slow winding-down of any over-unity device (which, of course, would be slower than a non-over-unity device because it was powered by an unseen source of energy, and thus wouldn't slow according to the accepted rules of physics).

McCarthy simply said, 'Ah, Guido – you know how difficult these wind-down tests are.'

Ignoring that, Stockhausen told McCarthy that he knew how to explain the magnetic anomaly and that no conclusive wind-down data could ever exist. According to Stockhausen, McCarthy changed the subject to E-Orbo and they drove on.

At the Waterways centre, Stockhausen sketched his equations on a whiteboard. These, he felt certain, would show McCarthy where his error lay; they had taken Stockhausen more than a year of hard study and calculations to formulate and he felt they identified the very heart of the flaw in Steorn's theory.

Instead, Stockhausen later recalled, McCarthy stared at the whiteboard bearing the equations and simply said, 'Ah, Guido – I'm not sure if the equations can describe this set-up.'

Stockhausen was beginning to get the picture. McCarthy was in too deep and was too skilled at, as Guido put it, 'fading out any inconvenient truths'.

Later in the day, filmmaker Maurice Linnane and his crew arrived. To his surprise, the Steorn team, including McCarthy, left the building. Linnane explained to Stockhausen that the movie was his project alone and that Steorn wasn't allowed to have access to the recorded material.

During his interview with Linnane, Stockhausen was asked about the jury process and then about what he truly thought about the 'discovery'.

> I took care that I emphasised the patience and goodwill of all jury members and that it was alone Steorn's fault for not showing any real evidence. Maurice knew some details of the static torque experiment, so I could explain to him my theory about the hysteresis effect. I [said] Sean still believed in his interpretation but if he would have been right and all physics as we know would be wrong then at least there would exist a wind-down experiment where the supposed effect of the interaction between the stator magnet and the rotating ferrite would increase the wind-down time as compared to a configuration without a stator magnet.

Finally, Linnane asked him, 'Do you think that they might have something with this E-Orbo configuration?'

He later recalled:

> I'm not sure why, but in this moment I recognised the bizarreness of [the] whole situation (our long jury process, a real film crew, this big fridge in front of me with all the cables coming in and out, my time and energy spent during the analysis, the Waterways location with all the big monitors displaying curves from all the temperature sensors) and broke out in laughter and said, 'No way!'

When he finally finished the interview, Stockhausen needed to rush to get his flight home. Before they left, McCarthy copied a huge volume of Steorn's test data onto a USB stick for Stockhausen.

When he got back to Germany, Stockhausen analysed the data only to find that each of the data curves had been measured using a different experimental set-up – none of them was reproducible, a basic premise of any experiment. He emailed McCarthy to tell him this and, knowing Stockhausen's fondness for a mathematical equation, McCarthy sent him one of his own devising. According to Stockhausen, 'It took only minutes to find his error ... and I mailed him back showing where I spotted an error. He promised to send me a corrected version soon. That [April 2010] was the last time I had any contact with Sean.'

He had always known Steorn would fail to prove their claim. But he had now, finally, satisfied himself on what he regarded as the real question: how had Steorn convinced themselves in the first place? It was simple human fallibility, in his view.

> If Steorn would have been a fraud from the beginning, why did they seek scientific advice, help and set up the jury process? It doesn't make sense. But they also lied when confronted with some of their boldest claims. So, I think that they really believed in their magnetic anomaly which showed up only in the static torque tests. I can even understand how Sean's logic about delayed magnetisation can lead from the original Orbo design to the E-Orbo device

and later to a solid-state version. I think that incompetence played also a major role and contributed to their confusion. Nevertheless, they had no problems with lying when facing inconvenient truths which didn't fit their 'facts'. Maybe it was a type of face saving or denial to save this house of cards for their company?'

———————

After the Waterways demonstration, Steorn investors found themselves unmoored. They were not only struggling with their own money problems, but also getting little information from the management about what was happening inside the company.

It had been five years since most of them had first invested, during which time Steorn had probably relied on the investors to provide cash and prayers rather than wanting them to be closely involved. Certainly, the company didn't expect them to be making any demands.

In March 2010, a few weeks after the Waterways demonstration ended, Mike Daly of Steorn wrote to the investors to give them a rare update. The demonstration had been 'successful in terms of attracting the right quality and number of third-party developers, who are ultimately our core market'. The company had been 'privately testing Orbo with selected third-party developers and a number of jury members' – though they didn't name them. Moreover, he told them, 'these tests have been successfully concluded and the parties that have been privately testing are now actively working on the development of Orbo'.

More than that, Steorn was flagging up another substantial change of direction. Having begun with a purely mechanical Orbo, they had switched to an electromagnetic version. Now, the letter stated, Steorn was switching to yet another version: solid state.

During the demonstration and subsequent private test sessions, our engineers have developed a solid-state version of Orbo – i.e., a version that requires no moving parts. This is a significant development because it substantially reduces the cost and effort for third-party developers

to work on Orbo and also provides a faster path to product for these
developers.

Moreover, anyone interested in buying a licence from Steorn's website
could do so and begin their own experimental work at home in a kind
of amateur developers' club the company had set up through its website.
Steorn would work on 'converting these pre-applications into paying
customers in parallel' and it was 'also starting to direct sales to development
groups'.

On the face of it, it was an odd decision to start selling intellectual
property and essentially crowd-fund the product development, but Steorn
was desperate for progress, and it had a large online audience of skilled
and semi-skilled enthusiasts who could help generate plenty of test data
and ideas. This audience would pay for the opportunity, which, as the
Steorn letter implied, was perhaps the most beneficial part. Professional
and hobbyist engineers could expect to pay €419 to join. For this sum, the
engineers would get a kit containing instructions on how to build their
own Orbo device, which they could tinker with and refine, feeding their
findings back to Steorn – a revenue-generating, outsourced research and
development mechanism.

And what revenues it promised to generate. If 500 people signed up –
and often on the message boards it seemed like there were easily that
number of people hankering after insight into the company – it would
generate more than €200,000.

With that and the apparent speed of development, it was perhaps not
surprising that Daly's letter closed with the assertion: 'We are confident that
the company will attain profitability this year.'

As with many Steorn initiatives, however, the outsourcing plan didn't
work as smoothly as that. By November 2010, Mike Daly was writing again
to apologise for the delay and to discuss two more developments. The
first was that 'the development stage of Orbo technology is now complete

and the evaluation and development system is now available online to qualified engineers'.

The second was that the company was gaining traction within academia. Daly added that 'three universities have requested the evaluation and development system in order to test and report on the technology'.

The long-term goal remained the same: cracking the world of mobile consumer electronics. To that end, the company's internal research and development team was focusing on the possibility of products for the heater industry, which Daly said was 'the quickest route to wide adoption of a commercial product while also serving the purpose of acting as a game changer for the energy industry'.

Steorn was in talks with a company headquartered in the Middle East, Daly wrote, which had led to that company's British subsidiary appointing two

> highly qualified consultants to review our technology. They have visited Steorn where they spent the day testing and to date they have supplied a report to the company including suggested additional testing[;] the company is currently reviewing this proposal and we will keep you informed of developments on this front.

The coming year, 2011, would be focused on the structure of the company so as 'to enable rapid growth and the commercialisation of the technology via product sales and joint ventures with suitable companies'.

All this was a preamble for the next communication. The following month, December 2010, Daly raised the most pertinent issue: money.

> Following on from the recent update, I wish to inform you of our position with regard to cash flow resulting from efforts to close the balance of the second round of funding.
>
> The current market conditions have restricted our ability to close the outstanding balance with respect to the second round of 20 million euro. As a result, cash flow has become a critical issue and the company faces an uphill struggle to secure the necessary resources that will allow it to reach commercialisation and profit.

Our commitment to this venture remains firm, the technology has huge potential and this is evidenced by people within Steorn that have placed over €120,000 in the company to help the cash flow situation.

There was good news, however. A system the company was working on was

attracting interest from engineers that have requested private demonstrations and we have a pipeline of engineers that wish to review, test and document this technology.

Commercially we are at contract stage with an Irish company in relation to the design and build of a water heater product, and we have stated discussions with a UK based company also.

We strongly believe that next year will see an Orbo-based product on the market, this will ensure both revenues and provide the ultimate form of technology validation.

In addition to the above commitment we now need to secure interim funding of four hundred thousand euro.

The share issue would work like this: the directors, Mike Daly and Shaun McCarthy, would hand over some of their shares, which would be offered for sale at €400 a share, with a special incentive for existing shareholders to keep up their stakes in the company. So, an existing shareholder who bought 10 shares for the original price of €16,428.50 would now be entitled to purchase a further 20 shares for €8,000, a heavy discount. The letter continued:

The directors believe this is the soundest and fairest mechanism for providing the funding the company needs until … revenue is flowing and further equity can be raised by completing the second round.

They were close to striking deals with companies to license the technology, they said, as well as to 'joint ventures with companies that have market reach and manufacturing capability'.

They were working on a business plan for commercialising the technology as well, and they were preparing a new management structure, including the appointment of a new chief executive. It was the first indication that McCarthy had soured on the top job, preferring to be working with soldering irons and magnets than with grumpy shareholders. It was also a tacit admission that the company had recognised that substantial change might calm shareholders who had money to invest but were reluctant to give it to substantially the same company in the fear that it would produce substantially the same result.

That new management structure and new chief executive would 'take the company through the commercialisation and expansion phases', the letter stated.

> We hope that the shareholders will support Steorn in its transition from a technology development company to revenue generation and profitability by taking up their full entitlement under the open offer.

On the same day the letter was sent, Daly sent a follow-up email to clarify a few items, evidently having received confused phone calls and emails from shareholders. Unsurprisingly, the questions all seemed to relate to the suggestion of a new chief executive. In his email, Daly wrote that Steorn had been in contact with

> two individuals to fill the roles of chairman and chief executive officer. While it would be inappropriate to name them, I can say that [they] are well known and respected in the Irish business circle and also internationally. They have the ability and history of opening new markets worldwide, vast business contacts, and a strong commercial history.

And more good things were to come in that email.

> We have signed a heads of agreement with an Irish company to produce a water heater product; we aim to have the full contract in place by year end, [and] this will see us design and develop a Orbo based product for the market identified and supported by our partner company.
>
> In addition, early-stage discussions are being held with a UK company for a similar product.

The number of shares being offered (1000) represent less than 1% of the total number of shares currently in issue and are being offered at a discount to existing shareholders only; discussions with potential new investors to close the balance of the second round are at the original offer price.

It was the first mention of a product that differed from what had hitherto been the Steorn core business of developing the anomaly into a battery. And it wouldn't be the last.

13. MISSION DRIFT

Shaun McCarthy: The Rise of HephaHeat

There were two things happening. With the motor, we were talking to scientists who were curious and they were telling us to do calorimetry [heat testing] because that's the ultimate way to test energy. It was something we hadn't done to that point. With the E-Orbo – the spinning wheel, the battery – calorimetry would provide an awful lot of high-grade test data. In many ways, even before the Waterways demonstration [in Dublin] had ended [in early 2010], we had started to build a calorimetry room.

The idea of calorimetry is simple: you stick something in a room that has all the other energy sources, both incoming and outgoing, blocked. So, you can't get in telephone signals; it's thermally stable, so it's insulated to fuck. You can't even have electricity cables running into it. So it's in essence a black box.

So, we converted one of the rooms in East Wall into a calorimetry room. That's a big job, so there was a bunch of guys working on that. We figured that would answer the magical question, because the whole point of calorimetry is looking at thermal shit and measuring how much of the energy was coming off in heat.

When you're looking at any type of energy generation – traditional or Orbo – heat is your enemy. If you've a car engine and you put petrol into it, the energy you lose to heat is a loss: it's not doing what it should be doing, which is moving the car forward. Heat is always something you're trying to avoid in terms of energy interactions.

If you're talking about building moving things or mobile phones or anything in electronics, heat is something you're actively trying to avoid, and a lot of the excess energy we were throwing off was heat.

So, heat is your enemy – unless, of course, you're *trying* to generate heat. And that's when, somewhere, a bell must've gone off: 'Ooh, storing heat! Lovely.'

That was the genesis of HephaHeat – the realisation that, hang on a minute: maybe there's a route here in parallel where we just sell the heat.

So, the propeller-heads [engineers] were like, 'How do you prove you're generating excess heat?' So, you have to store it. You want to store it somewhere, so we came up with a fairly simple way of storing the excess heat. The systems were really, really simple. You have a calorimeter, you're putting in a measured amount of electrical energy, and you measure the amount of heat that produces, and the answer comes back: yes, the amount of heat you produce is greater than the amount of energy you put in.

In the process, you then need to do something to store that.

HephaHeat was an energy-storage and energy-release project. It wasn't an Orbo project. So, the actual heating was traditional engineering. It was the storage and release of the energy that was a complete throw-off of all that calorimetry crap we were at.

So, if you consider this: you have an immersion tank in your house because if you want to run a bath of hot water, you can't draw enough energy fast enough from your electrical output to do that. So, you have to store energy in a big water tank, and you're heating it up over a couple of hours before you run your bath. That's simply because you can't draw energy fast enough or release it fast enough from the electrical circuit. But what we could do with the storage thing was extract the energy that had been stored at an unbelievable rate – a *ridiculous* rate!

All this meant that Steorn was now developing two types of technology, splitting its time and efforts into the core claim of energy from nothing and this rapid water-heating discovery. To develop both, Steorn would need even more money, so they redoubled their fundraising efforts. In 2011, rather than rely on emails and on Pat Corbett's abilities, they drew up a shareholders memorandum – a new fundraising prospectus, that is – to hawk the company's wares, outline its plans for the coming years, set out the money it would need and make predictions about the return on investment.

Compared with the bound, glossy, beautifully illustrated prospectus they had been distributed in 2006, the 2011 version was positively low-tech. Any of the original investors would have immediately seen the difference. It was printed on standard A4 sheets from a basic office printer; it was bound with black plastic rings and seemed to have been hole-punched by hand; and the page numbers had been scribbled at the bottom from a master version of the document before being photocopied.

This decline was a physical representation not just of the company's fortunes, but of Ireland's fortunes – and most likely of the fortunes of the investors into whose hands it had been thrust. There was no longer any pretending that Steorn was an ambitious young start-up with a new technology and a chance to change the world: this was an effort to save the company from extinction.

As such, the section of the prospectus that dealt with risk factors was of particular note. In it, the company warned that

> prospective investors are strongly advised to consult an authorised indepen-dent financial advisor who specialises in making investments of this kind prior to making any investment decisions. The investment in Steorn should be regarded as a highly speculative investment [to be] made only by those with the necessary expertise to evaluate the investment. In addition to the usual risks associated with an investment in a business with an unproven revenue stream, the following principal risk factors should be considered carefully by those making an investment in Steorn.

Those risk factors included the following:

- *Retention of key personnel:* This was a factor because 'the departure from Steorn of any of the executive directors or certain senior employees could in the short term materially adversely affects Steorn'. The prospectus noted that while the company 'will make every effort to ensure the retention of such key personnel, [this] cannot be guaranteed'.
- *Competition and new technology:* Precisely which other companies were devising Steorn-like technologies, the prospectus did not reveal.
- *Patent applications:* This related to Steorn's patents not being specifically for any fully articulated over-unity device (the US Patent Office would not entertain such applications) but for component elements of their demonstration models. The patent applications were therefore running risks either of being worthless or of being struck out as attempts to patent perpetual motion.
- *Sales:* That is, the inability to generate any.
- *Further funding:* 'It may be necessary for Steorn to raise additional capital in excess of the funds to be raised by this placing to enable it to further expand by way of acquisition or to complete its business plans.'
- *Liquidity:* Perhaps most relevant to shareholders, especially since the crash, was that unlike shares listed on the stock market, Steorn shares would

be hard to offload should they run into difficulty. Like most privately held shares, they could be sold only if there was a willing buyer. Because Steorn's shares 'are neither listed nor afford a trading facility … there can be no assurance that a trading market in the shares will develop' and prospective investors 'may bear the financial risks of holding their shares for an indefinite period'. The prospectus was warning that once you'd put your money into Steorn, you couldn't expect it back any time soon.

Anyone looking at Steorn's financial accounts at that moment – particularly if they had been following the Steorn story – could have judged the merit of this investment from a financial standpoint simply by glancing at the balance sheet. By the time the 2011 prospectus was circulated, any existing or prospective investors would have been quite interested to look at the 2010 accounts, which showed that at the end of 2010, the company had raised €17 million from its shareholders but was sitting on losses of €17.2 million. Its assets were worth a tiny fraction of that: €41,071 in tangible assets such as scientific equipment; €372,458 owed to it by creditors (mostly tax credits it believed it was owed); and €47,618 in cash (down from €293,248 the year before). All this was dwarfed by what it owed to others – €593,514 to unnamed creditors – and it had been loaned €146,339 by shareholders and €21,378 by directors.

Investors who saw those accounts would also have seen advice from the company's auditors, Phelan and Prescott.

> In forming our opinion, which is not qualified, we have considered the adequacy of the financial disclosures made in note 1 to the abridged financial statements … [This note indicated] the existence of a material uncertainty which may cast significant doubt about the company's ability to continue as a going concern.

The note in question read:

> The company is dependent on the commercially successful outcome of its research and development activities in order to generate future income. [If] the company is unsuccessful, the going concern principal may cease to apply

with consequent impact on the future viability of its activities. The company
is dependent upon support from shareholders for its continued existence.
Additional share capital was subscribed after the balance sheet date which
allowed the company to continue operating up to the report date. [If] future
shareholder support is not available, the company will have to cease to trade.

The 'going concern' stuff was boilerplate: virtually every new start-up
must state this fact during its early days when it's yet to sell a scrap of its
product and when it's relying on its shareholders to provide all its funding.
However, it would have been a concern for any investor looking at the
balance sheet because Steorn was now more than a decade old, which is long
in the tooth to still be relying on investors to put in fresh money.

But of far more significance in those 2010 financial accounts was that
new sentence in the report by authors Phelan and Prescott – a sentence not
in any previous year's set of published accounts: 'Additional share capital
was subscribed after the balance sheet date which allowed the company to
continue operating up to the report date.' This meant that Steorn was living
hand to mouth.

No shareholder saw this report by Phelan and Prescott in the 2010
accounts, however. As the accounts filed with the Companies Registration
Office show, those accounts weren't formally signed off until 27 February
2012 and they weren't available to the public until the following month,
long after the 2011 prospectus was issued.

What those accounts also showed was that Steorn was no longer
controlled solely by Shaun McCarthy and Mike Daly.

Shaun McCarthy: From CEO to Employee

What had happened is we had realised that all this money had been raised on
what was, in retrospect, a ridiculous valuation. That was retrospective. At the time
we thought it was fair, but hindsight proves that not to be the case.

Obviously, we were going nowhere and we needed money. Otherwise we
were fucked. So, a group of shareholders got together and said that they would
continue to fund it on the basis of them getting a better chunk of the equity –
which wasn't an issue for us – and board representation.

It ended up with the board consisting of the promoters – me and Mike [Daly] – and four or five shareholder representatives.

Effectively, the company became very weighted towards shareholder views of what to do. That wasn't a bad thing. In terms of rebalancing the equity, that wasn't an issue at all. We had a crazy valuation, and it needed to be addressed.

Myself and Mike agreed in principle that we had too much of the equity and then went to lawyers about it. So, whether it happened via dilution or a direct transfer I can't remember. But in principle, anyone who was a shareholder prior to 2004 in effect gave up equity. Those who had paid fuck all, or who had put in sweat equity [non-financial investment], were getting diluted, and if you put money in at that time you were actually increasing your share respectively in the company.

At the time it was slightly difficult to achieve because we had some shareholders who were trying to do the right thing but wouldn't listen to what the legal advice was telling us, as in, it's one thing to tell the lads you need to give up your shares and spread them out to the rest of the shareholders. In principle, we'd absolutely zero issue. However, without creating a massive tax bill, it became a slightly fractious matter in execution.

You could consider that in such an equity swap there's a problem with the control of the company, but for me that was never an issue because I had an innate confidence to convince the shareholders to do the right thing.

Anyway, my view was that Steorn was one of those things that, if it had worked, the amount of equity you owned wasn't relevant because you were holding the winning lottery ticket. So, I wasn't too tied up in that.

To be honest, I'd actually signed away any money I would ever make from it to a charitable trust. There ya go. I'm a believer that obnoxious amounts of money make people obnoxious, and I'm obnoxious enough to start without adding to it. So, I had agreed with James Meenan, who was a shareholder and also at Merrill Lynch, to do this thing that, if I ever made any serious wedge out of this, just to take it away and give it to whatever good cause he thought needed it. He did tell me I was completely raving mad, but we all knew that.

People thought – and still think – that [Steorn] is a scam, and I'm quite accepting of how this looks from a thousand yards. That's something I've never argued with. However, I can only say what my motivations were. My motivations were not solely money. Obviously, I wanted to make a few quid out of it … but I wasn't doing it to defraud people: I wasn't doing it just for a salary – I could've earned it in the Far East through less high-profile ways. I was doing it because I honestly thought we stood a chance of winning.

And now, having raised money pretty easily through the Celtic Tiger, we had to raise it the hard way.

The mechanism was to create the Steorn Orbo Trust and rebalance our position. People who had the sweat equity – me and Mike and a few others – got too much of a sweet deal in the view of the fundraising shareholders. And, again, there's nothing you can disagree with in that. If the money was coming from the same pool of people – and you could argue it's good money after bad – then, as part of that, there was a redress about the equity that everybody got rebalanced.

That included the people who decided not to partake in the emergency funding or whatever the hell you want to call it. It wasn't that we were telling people that if they got in now, they'd get a really sweet deal. A lot of people who didn't have the money to follow their money – or who didn't *want* to follow their money – still got their equity rebalanced.

That was just about fairness. We had gone out, in retrospect, on a stupid valuation. Of course, it wouldn't have been stupid if it had worked, but it wasn't working, so it was stupid. Obviously, what everyone wanted us to do was just win, but that was the thinking behind it.

It was just about saying, look, in retrospect, we'd come up with the valuation using stuff we don't really claim to understand, which is discounted cash flows and all these VC [venture capital] type valuations. But we didn't pull the number out of our asses: it was a valuation model used by VCs, but ultimately it reflected us succeeding, and if we succeeded, the numbers were off the Richter scale.

But we were far beyond on any time projections we had ever projected and we'd fallen on our faces a few times. So, while it's poor comfort to be increasing someone's stake in the company that had fallen on its face, it was all that we could do from that perspective.

It turned out to be fucking pointless in the end. Or to date, I should say.

14. STEORN'S TROIKA

By 2010, Steorn had raised more than €17 million, and those investors who had stumped up money during the Celtic Tiger, and particularly after the financial crash, were no longer prepared to sit back and observe from a distance; they wanted to be involved.

One of those investors was the Waterford businessman Eamonn McKenna, who had built up an empire in the south-east. His career began in 1993 with the company Store-All Logistics, which he founded with his business partner, Liam Dalton. It started with two very large customers: the baby-food manufacturer Cow & Gate and the Waterford dairy co-operative.

McKenna followed that company with a crane and scaffolding business, Sky Scaffold and Access, which he set up with his brother Eugene in the late 1990s. During the boom, one of his companies, Imperial Developments, got the contract to build a massive four-storey office development at Waterford Port.

McKenna's businesses were large and lucrative. In 2007 he and his wife, Eileen, sold their stake in a tool and equipment hire business, Waterford Hire Services, for €6.5 million to the British company Speedy Hire.

As Shaun McCarthy would later discover, McKenna was not a shrinking violet. If he needed to, he could throw himself into any fight and do so with relish. He even ended up in prominent legal spats with his own brothers. (The cases were settled out of court.)

In fact, McKenna was part of a group of investors who had approached McCarthy and Mike Daly about the radical restructuring of the company. Steorn first needed to restructure the share register, which had developed legally but untidily over the previous six years. What McKenna's group proposed in early 2011 was a fresh fundraising round that would initially tap existing investors to avoid the appearance of their shareholdings being watered down by new money coming in. The share register would be structured in a kind of trust, to be headed by McKenna, James Murphy, Pat Corbett and a Meath businessman called J.J. Sullivan.

That trust, to be known as the Steorn Orbo Trust, would hold the money on behalf of the investors and dole it out only as they saw fit. The trustees, they explained to investors, 'would provide the company with a letter of comfort setting out our intention to advance monies to the company but without creating any legal obligation to do so'.

The shares for the trust would be taken from the existing issued share capital, specifically from 22,000 shares transferred by Daly and McCarthy, and sold for €50 per share – which would raise about €1.1 million if fully subscribed.

It was, at least on paper, a high price to pay. To sell those shares, they'd had to slash the price – €50 was a hell of a discount from the €1,642 that investors had paid per share only six years before. There was also the incentive that if the company ever made a profit, the shareholders could get their €50 back or maintain their holding and get an extra three shares for every four they owned. As it was set out to those investors, if they invested €1,000 they'd get 20 new shares, and they'd either get that sum back when the company made money or get an extra 15 shares free.

But the most significant part of the deal was that Daly and McCarthy were no longer in control of the company. While the Steorn Orbo Trust was technically not the controlling shareholder of the company – that was still Daly and McCarthy, who held the majority of shares – the two men had given explicit commitments not to exercise their controlling shares in the main company. The decisions would all be made by a vote of the board, and the board was stacked against them. Because the board controlled the purse strings, it controlled Steorn.

Today, Eamonn McKenna no longer wants to talk about the company: 'Steorn is in the past. I only deal with the present and plan for the future.' His attitude is understandable. He sank millions into the company and encouraged others in good faith to sink millions more. For a number of years, McKenna was a true believer in Steorn and in what it claimed it would be able to do, but during the austerity years that belief would waver and his meetings with the Steorn management would become increasingly tempestuous.

But first, there was to be one more – perhaps calming, tempering – personality to be added to the board. Alan Wallace had heard that the trust was being set up, so in January 2011 he wrote to McCarthy to ask for clarification on what was happening in the company in relation to the shares and on this deal between McCarthy, Daly and the investors Eamonn McKenna, James Murphy and J.J. Sullivan.

As a shareholder himself, Wallace wanted to know the structure of the new issuance of shares and he wanted to learn more about the Saudi Arabian firm with which Steorn had signed the heads of agreement to develop a mobile phone charger. (Though the deal was definitely signed and certain financial targets agreed to, nothing was ever produced.) He asked if the new money would be used to fund the development of the 15-kilowatt water heater Steorn was developing.

Clearly, Wallace was tired of getting his information at second hand and was offering himself up as a shareholder member of the new board of Steorn. His credentials, he believed, were impeccable. He had been the managing director of Beechill Growers. Now retired seven years, while in that position he had marketed the company, struck deals and developed customer bases in the US and Europe. (Implicit, accidentally or otherwise, in his request was Steorn's failure to build customer bases in any markets at all.) Also, as a retired businessman of some success, he was in the fortunate position of not needing to be paid for his time.

But most of all, Wallace was still fervently supportive of Steorn, as he wrote to McCarthy. He had been to London for the lowest moment in Steorn's history and had stuck with the company for years after that. He 'never wavered in [his] belief that ultimately Steorn would be a success in its dreams/aspirations' and he had often urged other shareholders to do the same. In his letter to McCarthy, Wallace wrote that he had

A) the unflagging interest in what Steorn is attempting to do; B) the time to devote to my duties as a director of the company; C) the steadiness and experience of making decisions calmly; D) the experience gathered over many years of chairing meetings where I stood up and calmly talked straight to the people at that meeting and thusly gaining their respect.

The letter evidently impressed McCarthy, and Wallace became the final shareholder member on the board.

Shaun McCarthy: Training the Board

There was a certain amount of tetchiness on the board in those early days, and Eamonn McKenna in particular would have been representative of how a lot of people felt. So, yeah, some of the board meetings had temperatures beyond the air-conditioning setting, and there were raised voices and so on. But ultimately, the way it worked out was that any expenditure of more than €20,000 had to be approved by the board, and ultimately nothing we ever suggested was rejected.

We continued to do pretty much what we were going to do; we just had to justify it on a month-by-month basis, and there's nothing wrong with that. Sure, the chief executive is the chief executive because he executes on this; but we were a company in crisis in terms of the finances. We needed money – and was it a pain in the ass sometimes!

At the time, I was going through a divorce. Trust me, driving down to wherever the hell we used to do these things out in bogger land every month was not necessarily the top of my agenda, but a lot of these people on the board would've been talking to a lot of other shareholders and passing on the information of what was happening at the board meetings. While it didn't make them feel happy about the situation the company was in, it did make them understand that they had an awful lot more insight into what we were doing – and that they had a veto on that.

I don't think they ever brought forward an idea, but they looked at the things we were doing – including the creation of HephaHeat – and they got a say in that.

Again, I had a personal relationship with all these people, so I don't think you could compare it to the troika [of the European Commission, the European Central Bank and the IMF]. Outside of the board meetings, we'd have a laugh and a joke – that kind of thing. It was – how do I put this? – a necessary evil, but 'evil' is the wrong term because we'd fucked up, and if we hadn't fucked up, this wouldn't have happened. So, it wasn't a bad thing, necessarily.

Anyway, it took us six months to train them [the board] in, but the effort was worth it. That sounds incredibly condescending, but none of them had been involved in tech business before. So, if we were going to buy a thermal camera or whatever, they had to build an understanding around it. It was just going to take some time to train these boys.

There was plenty to be tetchy about, not least Steorn's financial situation. In an email soon after the board was formed, Shaun McCarthy wrote to some of the main shareholders to point out that he'd had to write to staff members to keep them up to date on the fundraising. He noted in the message that he had told staff that 'the deal that we struck with our investors involves them providing funds through the end of this year (note that we will also be looking at new sources that will fund the company beyond this period, mixed with revenue from sales)'. Part of that deal, he had told the staff, was that Shaun and Mike had appointed five representatives on the board of directors and that the first of the monthly board meetings had gone well. He described the board as 'genuinely only interested in moving the company forward; we agreed the cash burn for the year and the board will be meeting again in the middle of the month'.

This was a fine effort to calm the troops, but McCarthy's forwarding note to the board was rather more pointed.

> Gents, see below the mail I just sent out to staff. Obviously, everyone in here is a bit nervous with respect to getting paid this month. Not a significant issue at the moment, but certainly one that we need to get on top of.

Mike Daly replied in support, pointing out that no one had been paid in January, traditionally a month of penury and penny-pinching after the splurge of Christmas. Daly also noted that 'at the end of February the staff are due two months wages. So, we can imagine the difficulty they are experiencing.'

Eamonn McKenna, who had pumped in millions of his own money and who was now in effect running the company, replied archly.

> Just to be totally clear, 17m was burned in the last five years and it's now very difficult to raise only 1.1 million so times are not going to be like they were for any of us.

As McCarthy would later acknowledge, McKenna had probably put the most money in, and because of the size of his business empire he had been forced to do the most juggling during the crash. By now in his sixties, Steorn had his full attention.

Hitherto, McCarthy had full confidence in his own ability to manage the investors, even the most irate ones, through the force of his charisma. It was simply a matter of taking shareholders out for a pint and a laugh afterwards, maybe with an extra dollop of technical language and a glimpse of a possible Orbo-powered future.

For McKenna, though, that wasn't enough. He had lost a lot of money, as had plenty of others, and many of them were becoming very vocal about it. Pat Corbett had his hands full with fundraising, which had become more than a full-time job, so McCarthy and his fellow board members went out more often and more proactively to talk to shareholders, to smooth ruffled feathers and to ensure that there could be no suggestion that the investors didn't know what was happening with their money.

They were simply attempting to stop the outflow of money and achieve some kind of stability so as to raise more money and proceed with the main plan of achieving some form of validation to allow them to licence their technology to much bigger companies. McCarthy knew there was nothing he could say to change the facts: they had lost money, and unless they stumped up more it almost guaranteed that their losses would be crystallised.

———————

The mood hadn't been good in the summer of 2010, and there was clear tension between McCarthy and McKenna in particular. They had a discussion in June 2010 about 'issues with regard to the spending of allocated monies from the trust', McCarthy urging that 'we as a board are all on the same side and that we have to learn from past mistakes and ensure that these things do not happen again'. At least during that meeting, McKenna agreed 'and pointed out that we draw a line in the sand and leave the past in the past. Billy [Irwin, chairman of the board] confirmed that our focus has got to be on Steorn being in a position to survive and thrive.' But those tensions were still close to the surface.

That line didn't hold for long. In a meeting in July, McKenna once again became frustrated about a relatively innocuous matter during a discussion of Steorn's latest efforts to get heating companies to take an interest in the E-Orbo as a component in heating products. Shaun and Mike had approached the British company Midland Combustion, the Australian company Zip (which made water heaters for domestic kitchens and an instant-boiling device called Hydroboil) and the giant German heating manufacturer BDR Thermea, which would lead to prototypes being built for Zip and BDR Thermea.

They had also given the board an update on an engineer's report that was compiled for sending to several companies, including the Monaghan forklift maker Combilift, which had been founded by two engineers, Robert Moffett and Martin McVicar, entrepreneurs with long and distinguished engineering pedigrees. Moffett had been the driving force behind Moffett Engineering, which had developed the Moffett Mounty, a truck-mounted forklift. McVicar, meanwhile, had joined the company on work experience one summer and so impressed them that he was the company's chief engineer before he had even turned 20. Combilift's Robert Moffet had come down to meet the company because he had heard about the spin-out into heating devices. He was partly interested in having the company build some sort of industrial heater prototype as well as the possibility of an investment in Steorn. Though the investment would never happen, the two companies talked for a couple of years on a potential device.

However, the minutes note that the meeting had to be adjourned 'when Eamonn got upset that his efforts with [the US energy company Con Edison] was not [number] three on agenda in front of number four on agenda. Con Edison was [number] 4 on agenda. The chairman wanted to withdraw for 15 minutes but Eamonn left the room.'

A later email set out the context. McKenna had a personal contact in Con Edison who had 'expressed an interest in looking at our technology', and McKenna felt that Steorn should be showing far more interest in a potential link-up with one of the biggest electrical utilities in the world.

It wasn't an unreasonable suggestion, but McCarthy wasn't entirely keen on Con Edison. Its development arm was focused on large-scale construction projects, not on developing products for the consumer market. McCarthy, the email shows, granted that it would be useful to have such a company

> test our technology and provide positive feedback [and that] this would certainly have an impact on organisations who sell products to them, and so the relationship is worth developing from that standpoint. [But] I do need to caution … that right now we have a lot on our plate and so supporting a test with these guys is … not going to happen in the next few months, unless we … delay the projects that we are currently working on.

It was agreed that Steorn send a non-disclosure agreement to Con Edison, but once again, the fractiousness had spilled over, prompting McCarthy to write an open letter to the board members.

> Following last night's board meeting, Pat, Mike and I feel that we need to write this letter to table some serious issues with the operation of the board, and hence the company itself.
>
> The first issue is an old one. Despite continued assurances from all board members (and indeed the issue being record in various board minutes) there is a continued insistence by a number of board members to focus on what they see as the failings of the company in the past. The management … have paid a very heavy price for the delays that the company has experienced and the board must focus on the current positive progress and the future of the company.
>
> The second issue is far more serious. The executive directors … report monthly on the progress and challenges that the company has experienced, [and] the reports are made in an honest and open fashion. On numerous occasions the reports provided by the management are called into question with respect to their factual accuracy, and indeed [in] some cases more serious allegations are being made. If we take the example of last night's meeting, the following accusations have been made by [some] board members about the executive management of the company:

- Misappropriation of funds
- [The suggestion that] 17 million euro is missing
- There is no evidence of the meetings of two of the directors with any companies in the UK.

The above list is representative of the types of accusations that the executive directors face on a monthly basis. This represents a complete lack of trust of the executive directors … by other board members.

Continually holding meetings on the basis that the reports of the management … are not believed, or viewed with extreme suspicion, is untenable … [The] company has for the past few months made significant market, technical, and validation progress. The board environment that exists because of these constant accusations and lack of trust is counterproductive and has a negative impact on the operation of the company.

We believe that we have reached a point … where this core issue needs to be discussed by the board as a matter of urgency and a solution found. We believe that the next board meeting … must address and resolve this problem so that the board may start to function as a board and the company can focus on the opportunities it has in hand.

Even the more mild-mannered shareholders were now feeling the pinch. In the middle of the summer of 2010, Alan Wallace wrote to Shaun McCarthy to express some reservations. These are couched in typically restrained language, but they are no less forthright than Eamonn McKenna's outbursts.

I [believed] that Steorn would have met shareholders by the end of June 2010. At then you told me you needed to go on holiday until mid-July 2010. Fair enough.

I have been getting various phone calls from shareholders who … are getting wound up. I have done my best to pacify them.

However I now have reached the stage where I need to meet you and have a straight talk – not in magnetic language, which largely goes over my head, but in plain talk as to where Steorn is … and what we can – with a bit of luck – expect to happen this autumn.

I still believe that Steorn will ultimately win out on the solid-state version of Orbo. I refer you to Dr [Sean] Rice's video where he stated that the big hurdle was to convert computer simulations to practical products and that whoever did that had the Holy Grail.

In the present climate, Steorn … will have to bring the most practical product to market and not depend on another company to do this – as was planned originally. This will take extra money to make this happen.

Pat [Corbett] has just rung me to say a small group of shareholders are to meet you on Tuesday 3rd August 2010, prior to 3–4 shareholder meetings later in August. This is very good and I look forward to meeting you [then].

… I look forward to the day you present the first product to the world. Finally then you and Steorn will get the credit you deserve for sticking it out when the going got tough.

By early 2011 the company had raised more than €17 million, almost all of which had been spent on trying to develop something that could be licensed to some big company, with licensing revenues flowing naturally from that. Instead, the money had evaporated, with no demonstration successfully showing the technology and no product of its own to show.

The original targeted investment of €20 million had, as noted in a circular to investors, been based on 'an optimistic timeframe for market entry'. The money was slow in coming, though, and the investors on the trust decided it was time to take even more drastic action because the time frames they were working with would – according to painful experience – likely be longer than they had planned for. The board pulled together a document stating that

as of the start of June 2011, TSOT [the Steorn Orbo Trust] is circa €23,000 behind in the funds committed to the company as part of the funding agreement and the company understands that TSOT will not be in a position to complete the agreement reached with the company in early 2011.

There was money out there, they were sure, since the company had 'identified €1 million of qualified and interested investors with specific next steps to close in place', with a 'further €1 million of less qualified prospects' lined up for potential investments. The company had also identified potential research grants under the EU's Seventh Framework Programme for Research for the period 2007–2013.

In June 2011, there was another unhelpful reminder of just how difficult it would be to raise funding from any other source than private investment. A letter from the board's chairman, Billy Irwin, notified investors that the attempt to access EU research funding had failed. In fact, 'Steorn was not selected to pass to stage 2 of the … grant application process. The assessment score on our proposal was 2.26 from a total of 8.'

McCarthy would later explain away the problem, with typical panache and us-against-them rhetoric.

> We were a commercial research organisation and … the lead investigator was a commercial scientist. [For] an organisation such as ours to qualify we would have needed a host university or a cross border cooperation partner.

He reminded them that the risk of not meeting the criteria had been flagged before the application was made and added that there were other EU funding programmes. None would ever materialise, however.

Understandably, the board was worried. Once again, it fell to Eamonn McKenna to articulate those concerns and propose a solution. A few months before the failed EU grant application, he had asked how the company would proceed if they couldn't raise the proposed €1.1 million. He suggested a few alternatives, one of which was that the shareholders should club together to each employ a member of staff for a year.

The board also tried some radical new ideas. After one email that outlined how the company was struggling, the board members concluded that the financial situation was perilous. They also concluded that as well as trying to raise money, it would be prudent to cut back on spending.

The board suggested that the staff be 'reduced to four key personnel', the remaining staff to be laid off on a short-term basis until sales were generated. They would then be re-employed according to the company's needs. Steorn, the board said, should also concentrate its energies on the water heater as 'the most effective way to demonstrate the technology to potential customers'.

McKenna and the board then proposed that the company should accelerate the process of generating money from the contracts it was slowly negotiating. In one meeting, McKenna suggested that Steorn should 'raise an invoice to Combilift on the basis that the company has delivered what it undertook to do. [Steorn] should also put a detailed proposal as requested to Combilift.'

With money dwindling, the board said it needed to prepare a contingency plan, work out a policy to deal with creditors, establish a list of all 'current employees and detail their respective roles', make financial statements for previous years 'available to all board members' and 'agree and implement a proper communication protocol from within the company for all officers of the company'.

The board's plan wasn't entirely welcomed by McCarthy, however, and he wrote a few days later to set out his responses. First, he didn't think layoffs would work. 'There are significant costs associated with such a reduction in headcount. Indeed it would increase the short term cash requirements of the business.' He then set out legal advice he had received 'with respect to the company's legal position when considering layoffs'.

More than that, though, there was an operational question over slashing staff numbers so dramatically. How, he asked, could the company operate with only four employees? There was also a dark warning.

> We also have strong reasons to believe that none of the key technical staff would continue to work in a company of only four people ... [and] we believe that this would mean that no new investment in the company would be forthcoming, since in reality there would not be a company to invest in.

As for controlling expenditure, McCarthy believed that

> appropriate financial controls exist within the company and the company cur-
> rently operates to a budget set by the board. In the event of the availability of new
> funds, the company will continue to operate to a budget defined by the board.

He added that the management team was already 'preparing a contingency plan for board review. The plan will be available for July's board meeting', and a system for dealing with creditors already existed. On the question of an invoice to Combilift, he kicked to touch.

> The agreement with Combilift calls for a period of up to four weeks of test-
> ing prior to any invoice being raised. [Steorn] met with Combilift this week
> and has agreed to agree a formal method of test between the two companies
> so that the contract may progress.

For McCarthy, the board's proposal to move from the office in East Wall Road was like setting fire to money. The company had invested hundreds of thousands – if not millions – in setting up the calorimetry room there, and while the idea of moving the office to a cheaper part of the country seemed like a good one on paper, it ignored the fact that the rent in Dublin was relatively low and that they would have to spend even more than they could ever save on setting up the calorimetry room in Waterford or Kilkenny or elsewhere in the country.

For McCarthy, too, any staff members currently employed would almost certainly have left the company had they proposed a move out of Dublin. The plan was silently killed.

Even so, by early 2012, the recession had really begun to take hold. The new situation is reflected in a letter sent to the board by shareholder Peter Ruysen, an English daffodil grower and friend of Alan Wallace's. It outlined a position that was unique to him but that was almost certainly felt by a large group of Steorn's shareholders.

Since the meeting of shareholders at the end of March [2012] ... I was a little disappointed not to receive a written update on the business progress etc. This would be of use to those with anxious bank managers, and surely would allay any of their worries about loan repayments.

With the value of Steorn and the large reputable companies to whom you are discussing business ventures, this would make good reading and also inform those shareholders who did not make the meeting of the current progress and keep them happy too. Realising that some of your colleagues have invested many years ago, I would feel this is rather important.

Seeing something in black and white is rather better than verbal, which can soon be misconstrued.

The board would decide against issuing an update in writing, but it was now clear that the shareholders were getting antsy, due in part to the company's change in direction and its mission drift from free energy derived from magnets to using excess heat to develop domestic boiler systems.

For Billy Irwin, the board chairman, that was likely to continue so long as there was no contract signed that could show that Steorn was making progress. Minutes of board meetings from 2011 and 2012 show that the discussions noted in Ruysen's letter were mostly with big-name companies. Along with conversations with Midland Combustion, Zip and BDR Thermea, the conversation with Combilift, and in particular Robert Moffett, seemed to be showing promise. Minutes of various board meetings described the meetings as 'very positive' and as having 'discussed a wide array of potential products'. The meetings heard that McCarthy had 'told Robert that he needed to focus on a particular product and ... establish what engineering support is needed for the development of this product'.

Moffett's visit generated great excitement among board members and led to wide-eyed discussions about which companies to approach next, perhaps Glen Dimplex or smaller companies.

Then there was the relationship being built with Jim Grant of Grant Engineering, who had made contact with them in relation to a possible investment but who now saw the advantage in their heating products in creating a wood-drying system for wood-chip boilers. So, Steorn set about producing an ignition system for a wood-chip boiler using hot air. After all, if their machine could heat water, it could also heat air. Grant Engineering may have been a small Irish player, but the benefits of having the system working in a verifiable, for-sale product were massive.

They weren't all positive. Early on, McCarthy had reported back to the Steorn board on his approach to Dyson, recorded in a terse note. McCarthy 'confirmed Dyson had been approached but they have no interest in our technology'.

Such contacts were giving Steorn increased hope that, even allowing for the rebuff from Dyson, it could target maybe half a dozen contracts with confidence. Each could produce its own revenue streams – and recoup all that lost credibility.

Steorn had by now turned its back on media coverage. From having been the centre of a storm of attention, using McCarthy's native genius for drawing publicity, the company suddenly became almost allergic to press coverage. In the weeks leading up to the annual general meeting in 2012, McCarthy warned – as the board meeting minutes record – that

> we need to be very careful about the attendees to ensure no bloggers are in attendance. The inner workings of the company will be discussed on the day and we need to ensure that only registered shareholders attend.

Billy Irwin explained that Pat Corbett would be on the door, interrogating entrants to ensure they were shareholders and not journalists trying to blag their way in.

However, developments were leaking nonetheless. In July 2012, soon after the AGM, the *Sunday Times* reported that Steorn had 'signed collaboration agreements with two large multinational manufacturers. The agreements cover the design work required to incorporate Steorn's HephaHeat technology into products that use steam and water.' It was, as the article pointed out, the first time that consumer-product manufacturers had considered using Steorn technology.

In the *Sunday Times*, McCarthy said the 'royalty fees from these agreements could be bringing in up to €50 million a year by 2017 if these deals progress beyond the design stage'. Steorn was at that time having difficulties with a copper wire that was melting and shorting, but McCarthy gave plenty of assurances – in July 2012, according to board minutes, Mira had been 'blown away with [Steorn's] steam showers' – but nothing was coming of it yet.

The news of consumer-product developments was repeated a few months later after a visit to Steorn by Sterling Allan, a free-energy blogger who had grown up a Mormon and later railed against the church before turning his attention to perpetual motion, cold fusion and over-unity, subjects he wrote about on his blog, PESN (Pure Energy Systems Now). Throughout 2012, Allan had been on a tour of free-energy companies and had stopped in to Steorn's office in Dublin. It was, to the free-energy online community, the first they'd heard of Steorn in any detail. Allan would write that he had expected Steorn to have fizzled out, but instead found a company striking the same anti-establishment pose as ever. He took a photo of himself beside a quotation Steorn had used prominently ('People who say it cannot be done should not interrupt those who are doing it') and reported – as the *Sunday Times* had – that Steorn had

> signed exclusive contracts with two of the largest electric hot water heater companies in the world. These two contracts each provide 25 million a euro/year to Steorn and that is prior to the royalties that will come from sales. That contract amount is considered modest compared to the licence valued …
>
> Steorn has graduated from the fringe to the major league. They have gone where any free-energy technology dreams to go. They are going commercial, big-time, to where many millions of units will be manufactured and distrib-uted, by companies who each hold at least 30 per cent of the global market in that sector …

> [One of the companies is] a name that pretty much any American would recognise. Under conditions of confidentiality, McCarthy let me take a peek at the contract with the European company, with signatures, dates, terms, etc. It's real alright.

(Rather shockingly, in 2016 Allan was arrested in the United States for, among other crimes, abusing infants between 2003 and 2009. He would be sentenced to 15 years to life).

In 2012, in light of the media attention the company was now getting, including Sterling Allan's blogging about what contracts were being considered, some at Steorn were unhappy that, having been lectured at by Shaun McCarthy on the importance of keeping company matters confidential, there seemed to be a different rule for him. In the 'any other business' section of one meeting after the contract developments were reported, the matter was raised, and Billy Irwin 'undertook to discuss a formalised flow of information with Shaun and this was to be included in the agenda for next meeting'.

This didn't sit well with McCarthy, however, as the minutes of a later board meeting would record.

> [McCarthy] confirmed that he receives numerous requests for interviews each week and that 90 per cent of these interviews are never published. He is not given the heads-up as to when and if the interview is published. He commented that we set out in 2006 to build a relationship with the press. If we decided not to engage with the media, this could lead to negative feed-back … Sterling [Allan] is important in that he operates on the fringes of the energy industry looking at exotic energy companies.

By the end of 2012, Steorn could finally name those companies that it was striking preliminary contracts with, and it became apparent that Sterling Allan and the *Sunday Times* had both been accurate in their reports.

Steorn, the shareholders would discover, was now working in partnership with BDR Thermea, one of the biggest companies in the home-heating-device market in Europe. It was also working with another major European shower-maker, Kohler, and had met representatives of that company in England. There, 'our device outperformed all of the leading seven products in the US steam shower market'. McCarthy had met Kohler's head of engineering in Europe, who presented to Kohler's team in the US. The Steorn board heard that Kohler

> may pay Steorn an upfront fee in 2013 which will give them exclusivity in the US market. Kohler's US management has agreed to pay Steorn a patent royalty fee of €15 per unit. They have also expressed an interest in our under-sink tap heater and instant-boiling water system for the US market. Two engineers from Kohler will begin working with Steorn, effective from early January 2013. Kohler has given Steorn access to all information in relation to the market. [Kohler's lawyers] have assessed our non-granted patents and are very satisfied with their robustness. Kohler is a private multi-billion dollar market driven company and its business model is 'to buy'.

All this could reasonably give the board members hope that Steorn's shareholders might be bought out for a substantial sum in the future. It didn't seem outlandish to hope that, whatever the size of a possible deal, they might at least get their money back. They had even been told that Kohler's founder, Herb Kohler, had been made aware of the talks and was 'enthusiastic about the technology'.

In a circular to all shareholders at the end of the year, the mood was lifted even further, with news that substantial progress had been made in developing 'our core technology into water heating applications' and also that the meetings with the likes of BDR Thermea and Kohler had produced

> very positive response from key players within the industry … During the year, we signed a license agreement with a leading European water heating company and our engineers are currently working with their engineers on design for manufacturing and testing for EU regulatory approval. We will

provide an update next year on when we expect to see this product in the marketplace. We are also working closely with a significant US player in the domestic water heating market and believe that we will have a license agreement in place by the end of Q1 2013.

In summary, the circular said, Steorn was 'taking real and significant steps towards becoming a major player in the domestic water heating market in both the EU and the US'. However, because of the vagaries of the home-heating market, that progress would be slow, and investors were cautioned against expectations of swift returns.

That note of caution seemed to be contradicted by an ebullient report produced by Dr Gerard Murphy of the Department of Science and Health at Carlow Institute of Technology, which described Steorn's heating technology as

> not an invention as such but a fundamental principle that can be applied to a whole range of inventions. It is on a par with discovering electricity and the biggest challenge to manage all the various uses to which the technology can be put.

The document seemed to have been written with a view to rallying Steorn investors, pointing out that the biggest obstacle to Steorn achieving its goals was its financials.

> It would not be able to bring these extremely promising technologies to market without some external financial assistance.

According to Gerard Murphy – a brother of one of Steorn's major investors, John A. Murphy – investors who put money into the Steorn Orbo Trust 'to bridge the gap between promising technologies and potential income' (the long-term potential of which technologies was 'limitless') deserved 'enormous credit for helping to keep the technology alive and for allowing Steorn the breathing space to bring this version of Orbo almost to the marketplace and … turn this dream into a reality'.

In that, at least, Gerard Murphy was accurate. Steorn was ending 2012 in a stable position, the company's circular stated.

> The financial support of the trust for the last two years has allowed the company the time to start to take a market position and we are now beginning to attract new investors. The company will continue to raise funds during 2013 until our original target of €20 million is reached.

In any case, whether by accident or design, the news had generated some goodwill among shareholders, and – in a development likely surprising to Eamonn McKenna and to anyone who had observed the company's repeated failures to get blood from a stone in the early years of a biting recession – it turned out that raising the initial €1.1 million happened a lot sooner than anyone had predicted.

Throughout the year, the company had issued a number of circulars to shareholders. In one, they noted that they had got

> a very positive response to their fundraising efforts. We are conscious of and appreciate shareholders' commitment to Steorn. It is possible that at the end of our fundraising efforts, we may be oversubscribed.

Whether that was a psychological gambit to exaggerate the existing demand, forcing people who might have been sitting on the fence to follow through with their investments, or merely a statement of a genuine possibility of oversubscription, the coming years would see an extraordinary level of fundraising by Steorn – and in particular by Pat Corbett.

15. RAISING MORE MONEY

S teorn's fundraising efforts still relied heavily on one man, as they had during the boom, but the presentational materials were substantially less slick.

To the amateurish prospectus Steorn had given to shareholders in 2011, the company now added an information document to explain – to those who needed a refresher – what Steorn was and what it was proposing to do with investors' money.

The company, this document stated, 'was founded in 2000 and has developed leading edge intellectual property in a variety of areas including the surveillance and anti-counterfeit markets for various organisations ranging from Europol to Microsoft'. So far, so benign. What followed, however, was a series of questions and volunteered answers that seemed, with each subsequent answer, to grow more outlandish.

The first question: What is Orbo?

Orbo is a controversial and revolutionary energy technology based on magnetism. The technology produces more energy than it consumes. Orbo is currently being introduced to the water and oil heating markets and the company has plans to introduce into the mobile phone and laptop markets [within] the next three to four years.

The controversy surrounding Orbo is because the laws of physics state that what it does is impossible. From the moment that the company discovered the effect behind Orbo we have focused on engagement with the scientific community, and while validation from key scientists was achieved, they would in no way allow the use of that validation to go public. As a result, the company went public with the technology in August 2006 in a very high-profile manner ... Due to the controversy surrounding the technology, the bulk of the coverage was negative in nature[;] this however was expected and indeed planned for and is part of a careful and long-term brand-building exercise for Orbo.

What is Steorn looking for?

Steorn is in the process of raising a final investment round of 2.8 million; this will bring the total investment in the company to 20 million. The funds will be used to support the company during the period of time that it takes to reach profitability.

In return for this, the investor will receive shares in the company. Shareholders can see a return … in a number of ways, via payment of a dividend from future trading profit the company makes; from the sale of the company; or via the sale of their shares.

When was the company valued?

The company valuation was done end of April 2011 … and is premised on the company's entry into the heating market.

Who valued the company?

The company is valued using industry standard valuation models. The valuation is performed based on the company's revenue projections.

Why has the valuation not been changed by the global economic downturn?

While the market may have declined somewhat in value, the valuation … is based on a risk-reward model. As time has progressed, the risks associated with the investment have decreased.

What will the €2.8 million be used for?

The company's business model means that substantial revenue [is] only generated when our customers sell products with our technology embedded (a royalty fee). Hence it takes time from the signing of a contract between Steorn and a customer before revenues flow. During this period the company continues to pursue new customers and support existing ones. This is the prime use of the funds, i.e., the funds are to act as working capital.

Why is the internet saying that your technology is a fraud? What about this independent jury?

In general, the internet is not a forum for rational debate on any matter. The controversial nature of Orbo technology makes the company a prime candidate for the internet rumour and discussion mill. Indeed, this 'chatter' about the company ... is something that the company has provoked and encouraged deliberately as part of its overall marketing campaign.

What happened with your demonstration in London?

The company decided ... to demonstrate the technology in London in 2007 in order to place pressure on the jury process, [which] was simply moving nowhere fast. The strategy was high-risk, and ultimately the company was unable to demonstrate the technology due to the adverse conditions (excessive heat) at the demonstration location. The company has subsequently run a three-month public demonstration [in Dublin] of the Orbo technology.

The scientific jury recruited by Steorn, hand-picked by Steorn and shown the Orbo technology by Steorn stated that Orbo did not work. What happened?

The actual statement by the jury was that it had not seen evidence of energy production. However, this was later clarified to say that it had not seen *sufficient* evidence of energy production. The jury did acknowledge that [their] experiments ... did produce data supporting the production of energy ... [However,] they did not feel that the evidence provided was sufficient to support the scale of the claim. An internal jury report is available under NDA.

And then came the question they all wanted to have answered: What are the potential returns?

Based on projections the first dividend of €10.94 will be paid by 2013 ... with no increase in issued capital the dividend would be €509.54 – valuing the company at €1.064 billion and with a share value of €7846.88.

This was an extraordinary document for anyone who had followed Steorn's story, but the response to it would prove even more so, given the economic climate. Ireland was yet to finish its first year within the troika's bailout plan, which was imposing biting austerity budgets with tax increases and cuts in public spending. Emigration was soaring and unemployment was nearly 16 per cent, more than twice what it had been just three years before. National debt had been rated at junk status by the international ratings company Moody's, which was advising major investment firms not to put their money in Ireland. A debate was raging over whether Ireland would need a second bailout, even though €150 billion had been pumped into the banking system alone. There were protests all over the country about the cuts, and this was only the beginning of a decade of pain.

Yet despite this economic carnage, and despite the outlandish claims made in the Steorn Q&A, the company and Pat Corbett somehow continued to collect money.

Minutes of Steorn board meetings between 2011 and 2013 show just how bloody-minded and effective Pat Corbett was during this period.

In one meeting in April 2011, some board members expressed concern that Corbett might not be able to achieve the €2.8 million in fundraising the company believed it needed. The response was clear: Corbett said he could do it and in fact had 'already spoken to a number of potential investors who would be paying €1642.85 per share'.

In each monthly board meeting for nearly three years, Corbett would report on the amount he had raised and what his ongoing target was. By May 2011 he had raised €436,000, and there was €2.88 million left to reach the target of €20 million. The following month, Eamonn McKenna handed him cheques totalling €160,000. By the end of 2011, Corbett was nearly at €1 million.

Corbett stepped up the fundraising in 2012, telling the board in its May meeting that he had collected €131,160. He then went through his list of target investors, identifying those who were on the fence and those who could be convinced if, say, a contract was signed with a major heating company. Then he explained that he was 'presently speaking to two groups who have confirmed that funds would be available but would be looking for a discount'.

Through the summer of 2012, Corbett collected over €500,000 more, with 'commitments for about €100,000 from a group of Kilkenny investors' on the signing of any contracts with customers. By Christmas 2012, the company was €856,000 off the target €20 million.

There was no let-up through 2013, with €35,000 in March, €142,216 in April and €141,054 in September. By the beginning of 2014, the company was a mere €377,310 off the target.

In the spring of 2014, Corbett wrote to investors to tell them the 'details of our EIIS [Employment and Investment Incentive Scheme] tax shelter for 2014, which may be of interest to you'. In fact, it was not a tax shelter at all. That was an unfortunate slip of the finger by Corbett, since the EIIS is a legitimate scheme that gives the investor a tax rebate if the investment leads to the creation of jobs. What mattered is that it was yet another legitimate mechanism Steorn and Corbett were exploiting to keep Steorn funded.

Indeed, the money was flying in the door. Steorn's published accounts for December 2008 – the first Christmas of Ireland's austerity generation – had shown that the company was sitting on €15.3 million in funds raised, and it had spent just over €12.4 million of that. Virtually any company in the country would have envied a nearly €3 million cushion against the coming decade, and they certainly would have salivated at the prospect of being able, like Steorn, to raise even more.

Steorn's financial reports for the five years after the crash – the five most brutal years of cut-back budgets and business collapses Ireland had seen – showed that that the figure of €15.3 million in 2008 had risen to €20.5 million by 2014.

A small but not insignificant chunk of this sum – in the hundreds of thousands in that period – was from new investors. So just who was putting money into Steorn after the years of derision and slagging?

Angela – who has asked that her real name not be used – was running
a small communications firm in Dublin when she was approached by Pat
Corbett. Though she considered Shaun McCarthy obnoxious and arrogant,
she immediately took to Corbett, who won her over with what she regarded
as his sincerity and friendliness. A single parent, she had a young son who
was due to start school in a few years, and Corbett suggested in his pitch
that by the time her one-year-old son was ready for secondary school, she'd
have made enough money from Steorn to send him to an expensive private
school.

Corbett had a good energy and didn't strike Angela as a shyster; he
seemed to have an authentic belief in the company and its claims. For
someone like Angela, struggling to run a business and raise a family in the
middle of a recession, it was an alluring pitch.

Then there was the HephaHeat side of the business. Angela knew
that Steorn had signed contracts with a large manufacturer and that it
was involved in high-level discussions with companies in Britain. The
investors who came through, she noticed, weren't annoyed yet, despite the
prominence that the company had courted and its embarrassing failures. All
this created an environment in which Angela felt confident investing 'every
fucking penny I own'.

One man put money into Steorn because he wanted to support a friend.
He got tax relief through the EIIS system but still lost €7,000. His friend had
put in close to €400,000. The man felt an obligation to his friend, but he
also wanted the company to succeed. It had reached him by word of mouth
within an ever-widening circle, and he relied on his friend's good advice to
make the investment.

He, too, was impressed by Corbett's sales abilities and capacity to sell a
story in the face of overwhelmingly bad news headlines. Indeed, he had told
Corbett he would come in because he wanted to see a demonstration of the
technology before he invested. He gave Corbett a week's notice.

The day they arrived at office, however, there was minor chaos there,
with sections of the place quarantined for some reason, so they couldn't
take the man to the demonstration area.

Another woman, who was more elderly, was similarly drawn to Corbett. She knew he was a *plámáser*, being a man who made his way through flattery and ingratiation, but she also detected a sincerity underpinning the sales patter. She had been introduced to Corbett by a friend after she had come into a small amount of money.

By then, Steorn had announced a deal with a company that sold e-cigarettes. Steorn claimed that its battery could be used in such devices, and this woman was convinced that the contract reflected a real and imminently profitable business. As well as the e-cigarettes, there were steam cleaners and talk of a kettle that would boil water within 60 seconds. Steorn just needed some more money to get a prototype over the line and be able to market it.

The woman was given heart by attending a meeting at which she saw a range of credible and serious business owners. They couldn't be making stupid decisions, she reflected, not with their experience and success. She didn't feel gullible. After all, most modern technology seemed faintly magical to her, so she put in €15,000.

Corbett struck her as a charming, efficient and intelligent man with answers to every question. Moreover, he described the technology in terms that didn't seem outlandish or far-fetched. So, when he got to the part of his sales pitch in which he said that her investment could double or treble or multiply by 20, it sounded reasonable.

16. SPINNING OUT HEPHAHEAT

Shaun McCarthy: Going Door to Door

Remember, our reputation in the engineering world wasn't so fucking hot, yeah?

But the thing about having our reputations [is that] people would always want to meet you. It was the classic door-opener so they could giggle at you. So, we went in and we looked at it and said, 'Our storage technology is so much better than a traditional immersion heater. Forget the Orbo bit: it's so much better than a traditional immersion tank that it's frightening.'

We spoke to a few companies and came to a view then that we would try and pursue them, simply this spin-off bit – the energy storage and release technology which became HephaHeat.

So, we had developed Orbo into an over-efficient heating element, and we developed a heat-storage system that we needed to develop to wrap around that. We found that we didn't need to fight the over-unity battle (and neither did we have the stomach to fight [it] with these big cylinder manufacturers), because we could just sell the storage idea.

The whole strategy here was [that] we never wanted to end up building phones or immersion tanks or any of this crap. We wanted a prover – a system that proved that our concept worked. As part of the process, we threw off a couple of technologies, some of which ended up as lab equipment and some of which ended up as heating stuff. But fundamentally, what we were at was never different: it was always 'Before we can knock on doors with the core tech, we need to prove it.'

We had confidence in how this heating system worked, so we identified someone, rang them, and it was like, 'Howaya!' There was no sophistication to it whatsoever. We'd say, 'We'd like to come and visit you and discuss this water-heating technology we've developed.'

To be honest, water heating is the easiest market for guys with ideas to approach, because no engineer with a brain or any modicum of ambition is going to go into the water-heating industry. The technology hasn't changed in a hundred years. There's nothing new. So, when you have something new, you were approaching a market that's open to new ideas.

The biggest driver at that time was that the EU was introducing energy ratings on water tanks. So, when you look at your washing machine that's rated A through D, the EU was beginning to say, 'Well, we should put that on water tanks.' And every water-tank manufacturer in Europe, and the world, knows theirs is a Z. The whole industry is just terribly energy inefficient. We were lucky that there were programmes in these large corporates that were going, 'Before we stick our energy rating on the side of this tank, we bloody well need to find something that isn't embarrassing.' And they're not the kind of industry where some young kid is knocking on the door every day trying to sell the dream; they're not Intel.

So, they were very easy to talk to. … They were very interested because we were offering them test data, and they could see they had a need for it or a need for something that did what it did. The biggest challenge they would've faced was that these are primarily manufacturing businesses, so what they do, in effect, is roll sheets of metal, stainless steel or copper, and what we were proposing is a completely different type of manufacturing process. It's not something they could switch on to immediately or something that would have changed the heartbeat of their business; but still, they were more than wise enough to look at this and go, well, 'We know how to measure the heat of water; we know how to measure flow; we know that what these guys are saying is something that is of immense interest to us.' So, it was a relatively simple process to get them interested.

———————

By mid-2013, it had become apparent that Steorn couldn't keep riding two horses: it had to choose between the work on magnetism, which was mostly research and development, and the work on heating. So, the board decided to split the heating work into a new company to be named after the heating project: HephaHeat.

In November 2013 shareholders were informed by letter that HephaHeat had been formed after ratification at the previous annual general meeting. Every shareholder in Steorn, they were told, would get a directly proportional number of shares in the new company.

Those who didn't know what HephaHeat was were given a handy explainer. The system worked by charging a metallic thermal store to a high temperature (500 to 900° C). By using a material such as steel, which has approximately the same volumetric heat capacity as water, substantially more thermal energy may be retained than in a similar tanked volume of water.

When hot water is required, the cold water input is split into two separate branches. One is allowed to flow into the thermal store, with the flow rate controlled by a standard valve. When this branch flows through the thermal store it is instantaneously converted into steam which is then mixed (via a steam injector) into the second branch of cold water.

This mix of steam to cold water allows the output water temperature to be controlled.

HephaHeat, they were told, would immediately set about raising money to fund this enormous heavy-engineering project. It was aiming initially to raise €400,000 at €50 per share, and the offer was being made only to existing shareholders. However, 'this offer … expires at the end of December of this year [2013] and any shortfall in funding at that time will be raised from outside our existing shareholder base'.

On paper, it was a far more alluring offer than Steorn. For starters, HephaHeat was taking the only potentially revenue-generating ideas with it, which was outlined in a letter. 'Our prime technical focus has been working on the materials and production methods used to manufacture HephaHeat products' – contracts for which products, as board meetings for the previous three years had shown, were the prime inspiration for a great many investors who had put yet more money into Steorn. The letter continued:

> This work is necessary so the production costs of our systems are reasonable and that our products are robust and reliable. This process is nearing an end … and to date we have demonstrated that manufactured versions of our products can withstand ten years of normal use. The next step in this process is the safety and regulatory certifications that will be required prior to any formal introduction of commercial or consumer products.
>
> On the commercial front we are … in various stages of engagement with four leading blue-chip companies, this in addition to the contract that is … in

hand. As pointed out at the meeting on September 3, we do expect that one of
these blue-chip companies will have a product on the market before the end
of 2014. The nature of the market we are in is inherently slow, but the recep-
tion of these organisations to the technology and our business model remains
highly positive. It is also important that we understand that the companies that
are adopting our technology have to completely change the manufacturing
processes [they] use to produce their product lines, hence we retain realistic
expectations of product introduction by these companies and the associated
revenues to us.

This letter, written by Shaun McCarthy, is notable for its measured tone,
its setting of realistic expectations and the small amount of money it said
the company was aiming to raise. Moreover, unlike the Steorn letters of
previous years, the validation here was uncontested. While scientists and
engineers had in previous McCarthy missives been either anonymous or
heavily disputed, there was no doubt that the company had held lengthy
discussions with the likes of Kohler and BDR Thermea. Contracts had
been signed, money handed over and prototype models built. It is possible
that the product would never come to market, but Steorn and HephaHeat
had never been closer to striking the kind of licensing deal they had long
identified as their likely main source of income.

From a wild pipe dream about free energy got from magnets, somehow,
virtually by accident, Steorn had produced a viable business model.

Mike Daly had been placed in charge of HephaHeat as chief executive
and had moved some of his engineering staff from the Steorn heating
project to HephaHeat to continue their work. For Daly, HephaHeat was a
double-edged sword. To him, an engineering job based on heating water was
incredibly dull compared with the controversy and adrenaline of challenging
the foundations of physics. Except, of course, there was money in it.

By the time Daly had taken over the newly formed company, he had
met with BDR and signed a contract for research and development work.

He had also held meetings with the Australian company Zip (which made domestic water heaters and boiling-water taps), Grant Heating (an Irish boiler-manufacturing company), Kingspan (an insulation manufacturer) and Ireland's biggest domestic-heating appliance maker, Glen Dimplex.

So far the conversations had been fruitful and Daly was recognising that even if HephaHeat wasn't using free-energy batteries, there was now a chance to build a business that would make money for Steorn and give it breathing space to continue working in the background on Orbo, which was now being developed into a third iteration.

For that reason, Daly agreed to be seconded to HephaHeat, which took the upper floor in Steorn's building in the East Wall business park in Dublin. It would later take a unit across the campus to develop its heavy-engineering and manufacturing side.

HephaHeat had simplified the proposed boiler as part of those discussions with manufacturers. The boiler was now just a very small steel block that would remain heated and draw water across it, thus heating it, allowing for almost instant hot water for showering or for heating radiators throughout the house. What HephaHeat was pitching to these manufacturers was genuinely novel: instead of a 300-litre tank that needed the bulk of an hour to heat a volume of water, it used a much smaller 10-kilogram block, which could do the same job.

While the other conversations – with the likes of Zip, Kingspan, Grant Boilers and Glen Dimplex – didn't proceed past a few meetings, HephaHeat had signed a contract with BDR during the Steorn days, and it was now working on iterations as required by BDR. And while Daly had initially bridled at moving to a water-heating project, he began to realise that it was a relief to be away from the notoriety of Steorn. The years of news coverage had begun to try his patience. One year, he would later recall, he had helped his son with a school science project, and when the time came for the project to be presented to the other students, one of his son's friends strolled up to Daly and casually said, 'Oh, I would've thought your son would be doing a project with magnets.' Daly smiled, maybe grinding his teeth a little when the student turned away, but he knew that the joke had landed on target.

It had been an odd eight years for Daly, during which his appearances as one of the owners of an anti-fraud company, which regularly turned up in the more respectable newspapers, had got him invited to his fair share of Celtic Tiger dinner parties. However, those invitations had dried up after the *Economist* ad and the London demonstration, so much so that it seemed to him that some people were going out of their way to avoid acknowledging his existence, at least until an opportunity arose to make a sly dig.

Not everyone can be Shaun McCarthy, taking opprobrium in his stride and almost wearing it as a badge of honour. Daly was therefore relieved to be out of the spotlight. He would later joke that he'd had to eat some humble pie before going to HephaHeat, but that being back to traditional engineering work was refreshing.

And before long, the dull business of boiling water would start to look like a far better bet than free-energy batteries.

17. THE LAST ROLL OF THE DICE

Shaun McCarthy: Solid-State Orbo

So, there were three versions of Orbo. There was the old, pure magnetism version. Then there was the electromagnetic version, which was a spinning wheel with a battery attached. Then there was what we call 'solid state': something with no moving parts.

We had developed that and began to look at that during and after the Waterways [demonstration in Dublin in 2009/2010]. In fact, we stayed an extra month in the Waterways [building] simply because myself and the developers who were stuck up [there] had freedom where we could actually work on this shit.

Solid state is more like what you could consider a traditional battery. There's no spinning wheel; there's no moving parts. It's literally just a traditional battery. You stick something across it, and it provides voltage and current.

Once we understood that all we had to do is have magnetic interactions happening over different time frames – and that took us a long time to figure out – all of a sudden it gave us the ability to engineer different physical formats.

Also, in terms of demonstrability, the permanent magnet [the first Orbo] was a pain in the ass. You needed the precision of a watchmaker, and it might run 10 per cent of the time. The electromagnet one was great, but everyone just goes, 'Ooh, look, there's a battery moving it, you dick.'

So, the solid state was going to be far more demonstratable to a type of audience. Therefore, remembering our objective was always just to prove it works, a physical implementation that more easily proved it worked was gold dust in what we were about, if that makes any sense.

By early 2014, former Davy corporate finance boss Tom Byrne had, like most shareholders, concluded that Steorn was a dud, being unlikely to produce a return for its investors. His initial hope for the company – that it would be a consultancy firm that would slowly build its revenues and eventually be bought out, producing a small but measurable return on his original investment – had been upended by that infamous ad in the *Economist* in 2006. Even his outside hope that some battery technology could be produced now seemed very unlikely to be realised.

In the early years, he thought the increased valuation of the company could only be a good thing: the more money other people paid for their shares, the more money his were worth. But time eroded that hope. Quite apart from the impossibility of what Steorn was claiming, the ballooning share register diminished his percentage stake over time.

It placed Byrne among a small group of shareholders known as the 'pre-2004s': the people who had funded Steorn before it became a free-energy company. Byrne knew the later investors had paid a higher price for their shares, but he also believed that although he had paid less, he had paid that money earlier. It was therefore riskier, so he didn't deserve to be watered down as much as he had been. He also had questions about the governance at the company, given that the shares had been watered down without Steorn properly advising him of it.

Byrne's hopes had dimmed by the time of the Waterways demonstration that began at Christmas 2009. He attended with his son, who had been dismissive of the whole thing, hoping his father hadn't invested too much in the company. When Byrne comforted him that he hadn't put in too much, in fact very little, his son jokingly replied, 'Even that's too much.'

For several years, even though Steorn continued to raise money and the staff continued to work, circumstance seemed to have placed a very clear value on Byrne's investment. He knew how the investment was perceived publicly – his friends joked with him gently about it – and even though he remained as positive as he could, their scepticism was irresistible.

Then, in early 2014, he heard about the progress being made in HephaHeat and learned that Steorn was ready to be spun out into a new company and was having meaningful conversations with some household names.

Byrne knew a little about radiators, as he'd been involved with Zehnder, a Swiss heating company. He knew that if HephaHeat really had the next big thing in home heating, it could be very valuable indeed. He also knew that, in any spin-out, the shareholder base would likely be mirrored exactly, and he didn't want his stake in the new company – which was now far more likely to produce a financial return than Steorn – to be watered down.

He therefore arranged to meet Shaun McCarthy and a solicitor at the Burlington Hotel in Dublin in spring 2014 to thrash out a deal that would see Byrne and another early investor, Barry Nangle, being presented with new shares so as to bring them up to a fair proportion of the company.

––––––––––––

Perhaps surprisingly, another pre-2004 investor kicking up some trouble about the share register was McCarthy himself, who had decided that after more than a decade of blood, sweat and tears, he wasn't quite getting the rewards he deserved.

In May 2014 he wrote to Steorn's chairman, Billy Irwin, to give the substance of his complaint.

> I am writing this letter to you … with respect to my own position and con-tinued involvement in the company.
>
> I started the company 15 years ago and I have been the chief executive and a director of the company since that time. As a founding shareholder I held 25 per cent of the [company's] issued shares. My own share … has diluted via external investment and [from] holding shares in trust for key employees over … the past 15 years. The dilution process is entirely normal, and shares granted by me to key staff (under trust) became necessary for retention when the company had to reduce salaries.
>
> If I exclude the deal that the company reached with the Steorn Orbo trust, my shareholding would have been in line with the expected result for any founder of a technology business, i.e. circa 10 per cent.
>
> However, as you are aware, the Steorn Orbo trust had a circa 50 per cent dilution effect on my personal shareholding in the company. While I still believe that this level of dilution was excessive, it is something that I have personally accepted as a consequence of the delays in the progression from a pure R&D company to a commercial operation.

I again need to stress that in this matter the early investors in the business are absolutely correct, and I have nothing but great appreciation for the calm, non-legal [manner] in which they have sought remedy. They have agreed to settle the matter for circa 70 per cent of the equity that they are entitled to. However, the net result of settling this matter is to leave me with virtually no shareholding at all in the company.

The salary that I am paid by the company has only ever made sense in balance with a significant shareholding in the business. The removal of my shareholding due to the actions of others has created a situation for me … that has become untenable.

At today's share price, the Steorn Orbo trust deal has cost me in excess of €20 million and many multiples of this into the future. The deal and cleaning up the deal has left me, after 15 years, as a low paid employee of the company. While I have never been motivated by money, I do need to consider my own and my kids' financial wellbeing today and in the future. Hence I must request that the board consider my current and future compensation as a matter of some urgency. I would like to make the following proposal:

- Base compensation of €240,000 per year with immediate effect.
- A bonus payment of 5% of net profit of the business going forward, and surviving for 5 years after my departure from the business.

The above proposal would grant me approximately 70% of the salary that I could earn on the open market and also provides me with an effective 3% shareholding in the business.

I must stress that this letter, and the above proposal, is under no circumstances to be viewed as some form of ultimatum. After 15 years I trust that no one doubts my dedication to the company, or my absolute desire to see [it] reach the huge potential that it [can] reach.

This … is simply an attempt to reach a level of fair compensation for the losses that I have suffered, the time I have invested, and the time and effort that I will have to invest into the future.

I request that this letter be placed before the board at the next meeting. Obviously I will not attend the meeting while the matter is considered. I must also note that other employees in the company are long overdue a compensation review and I strongly advise that we deal with this matter with some urgency.

What is significant in all this is not McCarthy's agitating for more money or more shares – after all, who could begrudge him either, especially since he was, like most people, suffering during the austerity years – but the inference that he considered Steorn valuable and was upset that he had lost a chunk of that value over the years.

If – as he was frequently portrayed – McCarthy was a fraudster who wanted only to raise money from gullible farmers and shuttle it to a bank account in a Caribbean tax haven, he would not have demanded more shares in the company on the basis of a valuation that would prove to be hopelessly unfounded. McCarthy, a gambling fan who typically drops such metaphors into his speech, was looking for more chips at the roulette wheel; but someone looks for these only if they think they're backed by real money. Otherwise, they're just pieces of coloured plastic.

What it showed, if nothing else, was that even after all these years, McCarthy still firmly believed not just that the company could do what he had long promised, but that it *would* do so.

In the end, Steorn hammered out a deal with McCarthy on shares, allowing it, the following year, to start a build-up to what would prove to be Steorn's last roll of the dice.

Shaun McCarthy: The Decision to Launch a Product

There were always people pushing us for product, and it's something we entertained, but we also concluded that, look, the chances of us developing a product with the skills, time frame and budget we have was small. I know €25 million sounds like a lot of money, but look at the amount it takes to develop a phone and put it in the market. €25 million is not even going to get you past the drawing board. But in the end, we had no choice.

What could we do? Science is saying, 'You're a bunch of tossers.' No one gives a shit about engineering. We were left nowhere. No one cared about a working demo; they didn't think it worked. So, we were wondering where to go with this thing.

Through all the noise and the messing that went on with Steorn, there was only ever one thing that mattered: how to get this thing accepted by a reasonable number of people. Ultimately, you end up nowhere other than it has to be in something that somebody can purchase.

Of course, it was a massive risk. If we could have done it with any surety, we would've done it day one. We had no choice. There was nothing to run through our head, no big decision to make. This was the only option. It wasn't even a purely financial decision. It wasn't that we were running out of money. It was also about our reputations and the perception of the company.

If we re-engaged with science – not that we'd ever disengaged – we'd still be here in 30 years. So, we did look at doing demos; we looked at putting a phone-charging station in a public area, say Grafton Street or whatever, and just leave it there. Build a big charging station, and people stagger out of McDonald's after the pub and charge their phone. But so many people are just going to go, 'Look, there's 20 car batteries in the shagging thing.' Or maybe it will take forever. Or maybe it's solar powered. Or whatever.

To make it work, we started looking at low-power applications, so those good old-fashioned phones, like your Nokia 6310 or whatever it was back in the day. You could keep one of those going for 10, 12 days. The reason for that is not because the battery technology is so great – in fact, it sucked compared with today's battery technology – but because it just used fuck-all power.

I never had any doubts about the durability of the [Orbo's] inherent technology in its solid-state format. That shit still works to this day. I can pull batteries from the little drawer beside me, and they're still outputting power years later. You can't run ordinary household devices off it; it just doesn't produce that level of power output. We'd have to build very big batteries to do that, and that wasn't our point. We're not manufacturing experts, we're not product development experts: we were just in this to prove a point.

So, can I run anything useful off the battery that's sitting in the drawer beside me? No, but their objective when it started this off wasn't in powering some product; it was just to say that we have continuous anomalous power output, so our technology is worth something. It was worth somebody who knows something about this area licensing this and carrying the heavy load into sinking it into your microwave or whatever the hell products it might end up in.

The reason we hadn't shot for the stars before is there is a world of difference between that and putting a product into the market, which is something we'd avoided and avoided from day one, because we're just not the right people to do it.

So, the risk was large, but you can't just look at the risk. I'm a big fan of probabilities, and you have to look at the consequences of doing nothing, which were that we would've ended up in the same place, only faster.

You could look at the risk of the play and say, 'That was high risk,' but the risk of not doing it ended in the same result.

———

By the autumn of 2015, Steorn and Shaun McCarthy had been out of the spotlight for a very long time indeed. That had suited McCarthy for the most part, allowing the company to quietly raise money and avoid the kind of scrutiny – and public errors – that made shareholders uneasy. But McCarthy knew that they were running out of money and that, for the first time, the company was finding it difficult to raise fresh investment. The existing shareholders had been exhausted – both financially and in their reserves of patience – so they decided to take the risky step of launching two consumer products, to be launched in December 2015.

The first was a large charging power cell called the O-Cube, which was a deep-red colour and shaped like the skull from a skull and crossbones. In place of two holes for the eyes, it had the plus and minus symbols of a battery.

The O-Phone, the other product, was a small phone with basic functions, similar to the old Nokia 6310 that McCarthy referred to. The O-Phone was €480 and worked using a trickle charge, meaning that it would die but eventually charge itself again. The O-Cube, meanwhile, was a whopping €1,200. Both operated on the principle that the Orbo technology, as McCarthy had stated, only produced a low volume of power output – not enough to run anything useful. However, the company concluded, maybe that constant low-volume trickle charge could, say, recharge a very simple phone while its battery was being discharged through ordinary use.

Steorn made the announcement in a webinar broadcast on its website. This was preceded by a well-produced video that served as both a preliminary to the announcement and a catch-up for anyone who hadn't been following Steorn closely.

So, in October 2015, Pat Corbett and Shaun McCarthy had sat down in a Dublin pub for a chat. Their conversation was to be recorded and included in this company update, also to serve as an advertisement for the next big leap forward for Steorn. After a short bit on the company's history and Corbett's and McCarthy's friendship over the years, McCarthy cut to the chase.

'Okay, Pat, so you have hustled 20-odd million and went to private investors around Ireland, and that started 12 years ago, yeah? In 12 years, the company has failed, and failed again, and failed again. And Pat Corbett has raised money again, raised money again and raised money again. What the fuck?'

Corbett, after a long pause, answered, 'Em, see, that's the word, "failure", y'see. Look, you know, we haven't ...' He had evidently been caught flat-footed by McCarthy's abundant self-deprecation, and the ultra-positive, Tony Quinn-trained Corbett – even after 12 years – still didn't quite know how to handle the arch cynic McCarthy.

Before he could spin the question into a positive, McCarthy cut him short with another dose of the kind of criticism the company had been subjected to over the years. 'Failed. Failed with the jury, failed with the London demo, failed ever to show anything convincing to anybody; failed to put a product in the market. Twelve years of failure, [and] Pat's driving around the country taking money from people.'

It forced Corbett to concede the point, at least partially. 'Yeah, as it was, if you look at it like that – if you're looking at it from the outside in, Shaun – that's what it is. It's failure, you know.' He added, 'Right now ... [and] ... over the three years, there is a huge level of fear and nervousness among the shareholders.'

So, McCarthy asked him, how does Pat Corbett know this technology works?

'Pat Corbett has always known that it works.'

McCarthy refused to let him away with that. 'No, no. How does Pat Corbett know the powercube [the O-Cube battery] will work?'

There was another long pause from Corbett, who hedged and obfuscated. 'The only reason Pat can say, based on ...'

McCarthy knew how this looked on video. To a simple question about confidence in the technology, Corbett had stalled, a rabbit in the headlights. So, McCarthy stepped in to make a joke of it. 'A great pause! That's ... Fucking aye, that's the money shot ... Go on. ...'

Corbett, continuing to refer to himself in the third person, gathered himself somewhat before answering. 'Pat has had one of the original powercubes that he had going around in his car for a month. That shouldn't happen, [but] that did work.'

'So, where's the money gone?' McCarthy asked him, taking up the role of antagonistic interrogator that he knew, from bitter experience, would be on the other side of the screen, waiting.

Corbett was ready. 'It's 12 years, so, like, if you said to run a business over 12 years that cost money – like, we've spent a lot of money on equipment; we've spent a lot of money on papers; we've spent a lot of money on staff.'

Those weren't the only costs, the two men made clear. There was also the price in reputation they'd have to pay if these new products didn't work as advertised. So, what would that mean?

In the event of failure, McCarthy asked him, 'Where's Pat Corbett? Where's Pat Corbett when he looks at his fucking two kids and his wife and he goes, "I just wasted 12 years of my life, destroyed my reputation." Where's Pat then?'

We all have our own ways of handling conflict and adversity. McCarthy's is to meet it head on, aggressively and defiantly; Corbett's is to ignore it and focus on the positive. Failure was clearly a graveyard he'd been whistling past for more than a decade, because he paused again before answering. 'Em, it's not something I've actually thought about.'

'I'm asking you, though,' McCarthy pressed.

'Yeah, that's the most important thing in my life, is how my wife looks at me and how my two kids look at me.'

'And if it goes tits up?'

Corbett was by now visibly uncomfortable, and even more visibly emotional – in fact, he was on the verge of tears. His face crumpled and it became clear to the viewer, and to McCarthy, that he had been pushed too far. Instead of whistling past it, Corbett had been forced to look right into the graveyard to see the headstone and what was written on it.

Too late, McCarthy tried to change course. 'Leave it,' he said, 'don't [try to answer].'

'No, no, this is relevant,' Corbett replied huskily. 'We're not leaving it. That emotion is for my wife and kids.' After another pause to gather himself, he answered, 'It's nothing to do with this gone tits up, okay?' he said before inhaling again. 'Now, I can't tell you in a way that you will understand that this thing is not going to go belly up. I can't tell anybody, like.

'Henry Ford said, "I want the V8." They said it couldn't be done. Steorn – you know, creating a battery to recharge itself – can't be done. But actually, I know! And that's what it is, Shaun: I know!

'The very thing about all of these years … and let's forget about Shaun McCarthy for a second and forget about Mike Daly for a second. … In all of the years that basically I've been with Steorn, every single scientist or technologist that came in to us – do you know the first thing I do? I build a relationship with them. That's it. You remember the two boys who came in [who] represented the company from the Middle East, let's say, and they said, "But this works!" Well, of course it does. What did you think we'd do? Bring you across [just] for the day off?

'There's a question here: does this work? Yes, it does work. The question is: can we turn this into something?'

From a point near tears, and feeling emotionally overwhelmed, Corbett had composed himself, gathered his thoughts, separated the emotion for his family from the emotion related to the company and given a bravura performance that extolled the company and its validity, in classic Steorn fashion, by reference to unnamed technologists who confirmed that the product worked.

Then, subtly, to shift the point from a fundamental one of whether the laws of physics can be broken to a more nuanced one, he had reframed the question so as to be relevant to the product launch. In short, can their 'discovery' be turned into something usable. It was a far lower, and potentially more profitable, hurdle.

McCarthy's next question was manna from heaven for Corbett. 'Is there more fight left in you? Twelve fucking years is a long time. Any more fight left in Pat Corbett?'

In response, Corbett fixed McCarthy with a look of determination. 'Listen, my fight hasn't begun yet. I haven't started yet. … This'll be the first hurdle. Look, man, the fight hasn't started yet.'

The Steorn products launched in December 2015, and in a Facebook post that month, shareholders and fans were told that sales numbers for the

O-Phone and the O-Cube were 'exceeding our expectations at this time and
the company remains focused on increasing these sales figures on a month
by month basis during the course of 2016'.

Shareholders could be forgiven for being excited. The pain of the past
six years seemed to have faded. HephaHeat was striking contracts with
well-known brands, and Steorn was finally selling recognisable products
that not only worked – they were told – but were selling at a rate that
exceeded the company's expectations. At last, the shareholders could look
their neighbours and friends in the eye and brag about their own vision and
foresight – not to mention their handsome investment returns.

The Steorn investor Alan Wallace, buoyed by these developments,
decided in February 2016 to grant an interview to his local paper,
the *Tullamore Tribune*, to express his enthusiasm for the corner the
company had turned. Wallace was introduced as a 'Tullamore farmer and
businessman … involved in a venture which could revolutionise global
energy production'. Wallace described the Steorn batteries that were going
on sale and expanded on the broader implications of the technology.

> You'll be able to get into an electric car, drive to the north of Scotland, come
> back down through Belfast, go down to Cork, to Galway, back to Dublin
> and during the life of that car you will never have to plug it in. It will have a
> self-charging battery.

Wallace then grew bullish.

> We're going to hurt badly the battery companies; we're going to hurt the oil
> companies; we're going to hurt governments who get taxes from oil; and this
> is because what we have is a disruptive technology in that sense.

He could be forgiven for such an enthusiastic view of the technology.
After all, he was only reflecting the equally bullish messages he was getting
from the company.

In one board meeting, the shareholders had been given a circular that listed key points about the product launch. It noted that

> the incredible challenge that Steorn undertook, by definition, was never going to be easy. Inevitably mistakes have been made as the company treads new scientific ground without any guidance from precedent. These have, in many cases, been compounded by external parties' reluctance to view the work in an objective and solely scientific manner. However, throughout, not one scientific evaluation has countered Steorn's claim on sustainable energy.

But now, the circular insisted, 'the technology works – internal validation work is complete and Steorn are producing reliable and robust batteries'. That was buttressed by the evidence of 'long term testing with [a] global chip manufacturer' and 'field testing for public validation'.

In another document, Steorn stated that it expected to break even in 2016 and become profitable by 2018. By 2019 it would be making €9.7 million. By 2020, €21.5 million.

So, Wallace was hardly breaking with the party line by doing a small interview for his local paper. Yet when he got back from his holidays – he'd been away when the *Tullamore Tribune* went to print – he was phoned up and chewed out by Pat Corbett for giving the interview. That's when Wallace began to get worried.

What he didn't know was that despite the low-key guerrilla marketing campaign, which saw prototypes of the devices running in well-known Dublin pubs, and despite a little-known Dublin model blogging about her use of the O-Phone, the launch was not going well at all.

Shaun McCarthy: Failure, Again

If we got a 100,000 orders [for the new products], we'd never have filled them. First of all, you've got to look at the ultimate objective. If we get 100 people who take a chance on buying these shagging things, and 50 of them are still working in three months, that's a victory. That is such a massive victory for us in the context of what we're trying to do, which is simply to prove it enough that some big company decides to have a look at this and to start having real commercial conversations.

So, how did it go?

It was stunning. We were blown away by the success.

Oh, wait, no. That was in my dreams. It went shit.

Firstly, nobody had any interest. We had probably overestimated the amount of attention we would get. Secondly, there weren't enough interested parties. And thirdly, it didn't work. You wrap those three together, and you can describe it as nothing other than an entire clusterfuck.

We had all kinds of problems, to the point that – just to show you how complicated this is in terms of doing simple things – we were using a company that was beside us in our industrial estate who did shipping and logistics and who we shared a lunch room with. So, we went, 'Look, we get an order, somebody literally walks next door and gives it to you.' It's not exactly just-in-time manufacturing. And they began running away from us because they started getting a whole flood of people writing to them saying, 'You're involved in a fraud.'

The people who were convinced we were a fraud, enough of them were so hostile towards us that anyone who was in any way related to us got this unbelievable abuse.

So, there's that bit. But that wasn't the actual reason. The reason was the phones themselves. We had a bunch of them out on test, and one of them in particular was getting dangerous. We had one that was down with James Murphy in Cork, and he rang me up and was measuring it, and I said, 'Dude, you have to put this in the ditch. Just get this out of your hands. It's going to burn the place down.'

So, yeah, it was all done badly.

There was one with a guy called Frank Acland, who had been a long time in this little internet forum we had run. He got one of the O-Cubes, got a couple of charges out of it, and it stopped working. I spent quite a lot of time with him trying to figure out what went wrong remotely, and he had some test equipment. To this day, I'm still in touch with him about it.

But once James's one went batshit, we literally stopped shipping them. I'd say less than 10 actually shipped – a mixture of the cubes and the phones.

There's no point in me trying to sugarcoat it. I'd just had it.

It was an ending. I know that sounds uncaring, but I'd given everything to this, but everything just obviously wasn't enough. I had no doubts in my mind, with the risks we were taking with the cube and the phone.

It was a relief. That's the God's honest truth. It was an ending. It was either going to end well – which was what we wanted – or it was going to end badly; but it was going to end.

I'm not proud to admit it, but that's the truth. I was happy. Fuck it: if you want the answer, I'm in my fifties, and I ain't enjoying life under this thing, the way it's going now.

I can only speak to my own side in this, but I knew we were going under. I'm not an accountant, but you don't have to be an accountant to know this company is going to crash.

18. THE GREAT COUP D'ÉTAT

The attempted launch of the new Steorn products in December 2015 had been a failure; everyone knew that. It really should not have come as a surprise that Shaun McCarthy, who had been looking for his own replacement for several years, would find himself the subject of a coup.

While he may have finally embraced the idea that the company was on its last legs, at least for the sake of appearances he decided to go for another rights issue in order to raise money. He also needed to face a couple of hard facts: after the failures of the past decade, the investors needed to be served a head on a plate, and the head needed to be McCarthy's.

So, he offered to stand down as chief executive and proposed that his friend Killian McGrath, an investor in Steorn and founder and chief executive of the e-cigarette company Liquid Solutions, which makes Wicked e-Juice, should step into his place. (Rumours had suggested that Steorn had made batteries for vaping devices made by Liquid Solutions, though this plan was never put into operation.) McCarthy would continue to work as chief operations officer and work on addressing the issues with the O-Cube by looking at types of phone chargers that would be easier for them to deliver.

This situation was set out in an email circulated to shareholders in late June 2016. Written by James Murphy of the Steorn Orbo Trust, it was a lengthy apologia for the debacles that had precipitated the changes in management.

Dear Investor,

We are writing to inform you that we have decided to implement some significant changes in the management structure and management staff of the company. These changes are designed to ensure that Steorn successfully brings its technology to the market by utilising the skill base that is available to the company from you our investors. As part of these changes Shaun will be stepping into the role of Chief Operations Officer in order to focus exclusively on advancing our core technology and production processes.

We are pleased to announce the appointment of Killian McGrath as Interim Chief Executive Officer to oversee the management of our business in this next phase of our development. Killian's extensive experience in founding and growing the leading Irish e-cigarette company, Liquid Solutions, will be invaluable. Killian is a long standing investor in Steorn and is also a customer of the company. We look forward to working with him as we set the strategic direction for the company.

We are also pleased to announce that [the shareholder] James Meenan has agreed to take responsibility for the management of communications between you, our investors, and the company. James is a longstanding investor in Steorn, and has a strong track record in investor management with blue-chip companies. For the past seven years, James has been running a business that focuses on investor protection. It is important to stress that both of these appointees have agreed to provide their time, effort and expertise at no cost to the company. Their only objective is to ensure the success of Steorn.

In order to further detail the current position and future roadmap for Steorn we have attached a presentation for your attention. [It] has been developed both internally and with extensive input from a variety of shareholders.

We are confident that Steorn has never been in a stronger position in many ways than it enjoys today. We believe that these management and process changes strengthen the company, and places us in the best position to capitalise on our market opportunities. Both Killian and James will be in contact with you [during] the next couple of weeks.

Together with the email was an extensive prospectus that set out what the company needed to do to win back shareholders' trust, to push the technology forward and to raise yet more money. In typical Steorn fashion, it did it in an overtly self-deprecating manner, first setting out the Bad:

1. The company is withdrawing from the sale of o-Cube & o-Phone products for the time being.

2. The company has, again, failed to meet the expectations that we have set with investors and we have, again, failed to effectively communicate with our investors.

3. The company is out of funds and needs to urgently put in place additional funds, or wind-up.

For those not utterly depressed by the Bad, it then provided the Good:

1. The company is currently manufacturing robust and reliable self-charging batteries that have been tested both internally and externally.

2. The company has put in place a new technology release & test process that will prevent preannouncement based on future predictions of power density.

3. Based on extensive market research the company has identified the wireless networking & camera market as the best techno/commercial fit for the production release of our battery.

4. The company has been engaged with a leading microchip manufacturer and has successfully completed phase one of a test programme.

5. The company has appointed an Interim CEO from its investor base.

6. The company has put in place an investor-controlled channel of investor communications to ensure that expectations are managed to a realistic level.

7. The company is beginning to utilise the skills and experience of the investor base, including additions and changes to the internal management team.

Understandably, shareholders were underwhelmed by yet another set of excuses and rationalisations about power density in batteries and the robustness of Steorn's technology and also by explanations that the failure had come about only because Steorn had '[rushed] high power density versions of our battery technology into production'. After all, this was the same explanation – rushing – they had been given for the failure of the Kinetica demonstration in London seven years before.

Moreover, the shareholders were witnessing yet another pivot to a different idea, this time closed-circuit cameras. Instead of trying to fix what was wrong, Steorn was once again ripping up the plan and embarking on a new one.

Steorn seemed to anticipate the grumbling and included in the presentation a section headed 'Steorn Does Not Ignore Its Investors'. In it, shareholders were told that

> while it is true to say that Steorn is not very effective at communicating with its investors, this has not been due to any lack of desire, or understanding of our responsibilities to do so. Indeed nearly 9% of the company's budget (based on management time and travel and living expenses) has been spent on communicating with existing investors. Various methods of communication have been tried, from meetings, letters, social media etc. Regardless of this, the communication has by and large existed only between one Steorn employee (Pat Corbett) and the vast majority of investors. In order to resolve this issue, the company is putting in place an existing shareholder [James Meenan] with a background of professional shareholder communication, and representation of investor interests in place as the prime channel of communication. In addition, the company is putting in place 'working groups' of willing shareholders to look at, and work with the company on all aspects of its business.

Shareholders might also have been unimpressed by the claim that 'our battery technology is being tested by one of the top five microchip manufacturers', whose 'engineers have done initial testing on one of our production batteries, found positive results that they have presented internally to the [chief technology officer's] office and received the go ahead for the next phase of testing'.

The company in question was never named, but shareholders were told that this mystery company 'expects to continue to test the technology over the course of the next 12 months', with a coming demonstration in that company's chief technological officer's office.

Steorn attributed this development to its 'branding and marketing' approach. It acknowledged that this had been an 'uncomfortable strategy' – a tacit admission that being a Steorn investor had exposed many people to scorn and derision – but the company insisted that 'the perceived downside that we will "scare away" blue-chip companies is disproven by the facts of the situation … As a pure marketing exercise, its return on investment has been high.'

Even so, Steorn had to acknowledge that it had been

> a prospect that has been oversold to its investors. The 'overselling' of Steorn has been based on a naive optimism on time frames for tasks to be completed. This is clearly a failure of the management team of the company. Once oversold, the company has continued to set objectives to regain investor confidence that have again been naively optimistic. We have created a vicious circle, and in doing so have set ourselves up for repeated failure. We have made forward looking prediction on the status of the technology, built launch plans around this prediction, and rushed development processes to match a perceived need. This 'drive' has been hugely counterproductive with respect to the rate at which progress is actually made. We have recognised this mistake. We have made management changes to ensure that the company retains a more realistic approach to its future plans. The board will continually assess the effectiveness of the management of the company and make changes as necessary.

Unsurprisingly, this did not convince all the investors. One in particular was entirely unconvinced: Pat Corbett, who evidently had decided that enough was enough.

Corbett no longer speaks about Steorn, so the account of his attempt to overthrow McCarthy and take over the company is deficient, at least when it comes to Corbett's reasoning for the move. Nonetheless, it can be presumed that he was tired of bad decision after bad decision, each of which gobbled up money and reputation without producing a single positive result for the company. This view is something McCarthy would hardly be in a position to dispute. In fact, he wholeheartedly agrees. At least, he does now.

Shaun McCarthy: Fight for Control

I'm going to caveat all of this by saying Pat was genuinely doing what he thought was right. You genuinely couldn't argue with the need for a new CEO at this stage after many years of unrivalled failure. To be honest, if we had some CEO who popped up [in those years], I would've been the most relieved motherfucker on the planet.

We were looking for a new CEO. I would've been happy to lower the burden from my shoulders.

What I found out subsequently is that there's some sort of legal way to do this – that you can get X number of shareholders to sign up to something; and what happened was Pat had quietly gone around to any shareholders who he knew wouldn't speak to me. He gathered them up, and then it turned out that he didn't actually have enough.

He then called an emergency board meeting, which I refused to walk in to. And this is the silliness of this: they tried to put it to a vote, but I pointed out that the board meeting hadn't been properly convened, which it wasn't. So, it wasn't a board meeting, simply because of the way it was convened. Which was acting the maggot by me.

Then we had a properly convened board meeting where I managed to speak to some of the other board members, and the motion for Pat to take over was rejected.

I hadn't fired a shot at this stage. I was quite taken aback. This shit all happened out of nowhere for me. I went, 'Whoa, what is this shit!' We sat beside each other, me and Pat. Our offices were beside each other, and obviously we were talking to each other every day. So, I guess I felt a bit naive and stupid.

After that, his position was untenable. There's no two ways about it. If you're in the trenches and there's some fucker who's trying to bayonet you, it's you or him. This is not a prayer meeting we're attending: we're in a fight, and the fundamental requirement of a company that's battling is that the business isn't dissolving from the inside. So, yeah, he had to go. End of, whatever the consequences. You could equally say I should've gone, but there was no one there – for whatever ridiculous lack of skills I have – who could replace me.

According to what Pat Corbett's wife, Lisa Carroll, would later tell a group of shareholders in one particularly angry meeting, Corbett got a text message from Steorn on 22 June 2016 informing him that he had been fired for gross misconduct.

The message didn't elaborate on the matter, and Corbett read it only at 10:30 the following morning. The message was followed by a phone call from a board member telling him that the decision had been ratified by the board and that his work phone would be shut off in 10 minutes.

The fallout was immediate and very public. While Corbett went around to supportive shareholders airing his grievances, McCarthy was publishing a blog post on his personal website. The post, entitled 'On Betrayal', explained that he had met Corbett when he approached McCarthy looking for help with Marcus Fearon's music career. McCarthy then recalled that he had grown to like Corbett and 'fell under the Corbett spell'. In spite of hearing warnings from others, McCarthy thought that Corbett had a 'power about him' that is 'difficult to deny'. He then described him as a 'force of nature', adding that 'a guy with that much ability to convince people can be dangerous'.

Corbett's ability to raise money, McCarthy wrote, 'had been fundamental in the direction that Steorn took with Orbo almost from the day of its discovery'. McCarthy's logic appeared to be that if the large sums of money that Steorn had raised had been responsible for misdirecting the company, the man who had raised that money was equally guilty. 'Over 12 years every step the company took was a Pat step.'

McCarthy added that 'while on paper I don't really get to complain about this, because I was at the end of the day his boss, I am anyway going to moan a bit about the man'. But he would go further than that, accusing Corbett of having 'distorted views of people inside and outside [Steorn]' and of having tried three times to take control of the company.

Though McCarthy never named the investors that Corbett was alleged to have lined up, he made it clear that he was not impressed by their credentials. 'The problem with this betrayal was that it did not just affect me,' he said. 'If Pat had got his way then Orbo would never make it outside of the lab and Steorn would be run by some guys who break ankles and kneecaps first, and debate later.'

But in his blog post, McCarthy wanted to display his resolve for the fight too. Those opposing McCarthy would

> need to kill me to get their hands on Orbo. Pat is no longer in Steorn, the
> company is 10 times what it was, doing great things at last. Doing what we

should have been doing 10 years ago. Pat and his 'hard money' backers have
not given up – but they will need to kill me to get their hands on Orbo, Steorn, or any part of it. I took 12 years to learn the lesson, but it's well learnt.

It was heady stuff, so much so that McCarthy took the blog post offline,
possibly because it was defamatory. He would later describe it as the
product of a bad divorce. But there was plenty of calculation in it too.

Shaun McCarthy: The Dirty War

I'm a conniving bastard. That blog post I wrote was when Pat was still, despite
everything, trying to move the shareholders against me. 'Anger' would be
the wrong word. It was like: 'Do you want to know something, dude? My
background may not be CEO material, but your background is just never going
to suit this. You're still pushing to be elected CEO from outside.'

So, that blog post was just me saying, 'Look, I've known this shit for years.
I knew it when I met you. In fact, it's the very reason I met you – and you keep
playing these silly games, so I'm fucking releasing the hounds.'

It may have read angrily, but it was quite purposeful. It was to say, 'Sorry,
mate. Back the fuck off.'

Lots of people were extraordinarily unhappy with it. It just wasn't cricket.
And look, Pat had a huge amount of support amongst the shareholders. A lot of
the shareholders were going, 'What did you do to Pat? Poor Pat!' There were an
awful lot of people whose whole experience of Steorn was Pat. So, to them, when
Pat was let go, it was very difficult to engage with.

So, we did what we do: we went out and stood up in front of them, and we
faced up. This is what happened; it ain't rolling back. People leave companies; it's
not the end of the world.

I went out and tried to smooth feathers as much as I could, but it was
awkward, not least having to face his wife in several meetings, which was really
uncomfortable, because I really do like Lisa [Carroll]. She's a lovely woman.

So, I ended up getting shouted down by Lisa in several meetings, which is not a
great fucking thing, I can tell you. It wasn't on my 'Shit I'd Like on My Bucket List'.

There was a group of them [shareholders] who didn't accept it, and they tried
to gather up votes for a changing of the board or me or whatever; and ultimately,
they just couldn't get the necessary votes.

Corbett's inability to fire the fatal shot didn't mean that McCarthy was in the clear: the investors, unsettled not only by the failures of the past decade but now by the appearance of a bloodbath in the boardroom, were getting restless.

On 26 July 2016, in the Maldron Hotel in Port Laoise, the shareholders held the first of what would prove to be a stormy series of meetings, flecked with anger about the failure of the product launch, Pat Corbett's sacking and the dawning realisation that their money was now never coming back.

The former Fine Gael TD John V. Farrelly, who was a shareholder in Steorn as well as an auctioneer and political lobbyist, chaired the meeting in Port Laoise, which had about 50 attendees, including the well-known businessman Paschal Naylor (he had founded the successful IT company Arkphire), Robert and Anne Seale, Eamonn McKenna and Pat Corbett's wife, Lisa Carroll.

Tensions were high. Officially, the meeting had been called to discuss the company's position, to present the facts, to talk about funding options and to 'put forward positive actions to move forward and carry our suggestions forward to meetings being held next week'; but the truth was that it was a group counselling session for victims of financial trauma.

Many of the investors assembled that night had experienced what might have seemed like worse days in the past decade (such as the embarrassment of Steorn's failed London demonstration, the collapse of their own finances and the collapse of the global economy), so the more positive among them could easily have rationalised the latest turn of events as merely a bumpy start to the launch of an innovative product. After all, no one had yet said that the launch had failed.

Moreover, all previous problems at Steorn had been solved by the liberal application of fresh funding, which had put investors in a position where the company was now apparently on the verge of striking a series of lucrative contracts – at least on the HephaHeat side of things.

So, even though the Steorn difficulties and the HephaHeat spin-out were not what investors had been sold in 2004, it would have been easy for them to conclude that they were closer now than ever to finally making some money from this thing. But the difference this time was that there was a great deal more sublimated frustration in the room than anyone had anticipated – something that soon spilled over.

Lisa Carroll, understandably, was one of the angriest people in the room. Her husband, Pat Corbett, she said, had been trying only to effect change in Steorn. To her, a new product mentioned in conjunction with the funding round – a closed-circuit camera – was 'pure crap'. Steorn was 'floundering around from product to product but nothing was ever finalised, and he [Corbett] was not happy about that.' Maybe the way he went about that wasn't the right one, she conceded, but at least he was trying to do something.

Corbett had been victimised in all this, she said, which meant he couldn't even appear on the night to give an account of himself – to 'stand up and take whatever it is you have got to give him yourself' – because Steorn's decision to sack him had tied him up in legal negotiations over a settlement.

Shareholder Jim O'Leary was frustrated at the lack of transparency and accountability for the money that had already been spent. How, he asked, could they be asked for more now?

'I don't know,' replied another shareholder, Eoghan O'Sullivan. '[To pay the] June wages, I talked to some people discussing buying a share just to keep the company going. It bought us four weeks to try and sort something out.' O'Sullivan went on, 'I would find it very hard to put €10,000 into the company … because we still have the same chiefs looking after the same pot of money – and they weren't very good at it before.' This was just a fire brigade measure, he said – a desperate effort to douse an inferno.

He was frustrated by the failure of Corbett and McCarthy to arrange the extraordinary general meeting they'd been calling for – and he understood only too well why they hadn't turned up that night. 'It's just going to be a bashing match. If you bring Shaun McCarthy down and a few other boys from Steorn, we will all want to tear strips from them.'

Jerry Fitzgerald agreed: there were massive blanks in communication. He'd travelled up from Cork for the meeting, and it was 'an absolute disgrace that the people who took my money are not accountable for it. I want to tear strips off them now. We are all here asking about funding. That's the number one question: no one knows where our money is gone.'

John V. Farrelly tried to urge the shareholders to stay positive, reminding them that management would be present at meetings the following week, but David Willoughby was in no mood for such talk. 'There's been a cash burn of wages of €50,000 a month – that's €600,000 a year. We are 12 years into this and I know we have rent and equipment, but over the period of €6 or €7 million in salaries – where is all the rest of the money gone? It's a disgrace.'

'The company nearly went bankrupt in 2010 or 2011,' Alan Wallace said, and had been rescued by the Orbo Trust and the board formed to manage the company. 'At that stage, €17 million had been spent – we do not know exactly how ... While the board was in place, staff numbers were cut in half, wages cut, part time working pension cut by 40 per cent, annual spend of €2.5 million reduced to a little over €500,000 per year.' Wallace wanted to make it clear that the problem wasn't financial, but tactical. 'We are where we are because the launch didn't work last Christmas. How a product was brought to market without field testing, I will never understand. I sent emails on this and got short shrift from Shaun. If the products had worked last Christmas, we would not be here tonight and we would already have got money from the company. Who you want to blame for this is your decision.'

Austin Ahern was similarly angry. 'I would not recommend [investing in] Steorn to my worst enemy, let alone a friend.'

Hope died hard with some investors, though. One, Deirdre Cash, told her fellow investors that Killian McGrath had promised to meet any shortfall in the wages in the form of a loan, having already put up money for wages in April.

Some investors believed that there was still value to be had in selling their shares. Damien O'Connell, for example, wanted to know what the shares were valued at.

Eoghan Sullivan told him there were 3,500 shares, which was roughly 1.3 per cent of the company, valued at €3.5 million. 'Has anyone thought of selling less than 25 per cent to the company or to another energy production company like Duracell or BP or Exxon?'

Farrelly seemed to think it was an idea too. 'I represent about nine investors who can't be here tonight,' he told the room. 'The short discussion

I had with them would have asked that very question: have we looked at the possibility of teaming up with another energy company to move this forward?

Damien O'Connell believed it could constitute a pay-out for the long-suffering shareholders. If a bigger energy company put in €50 million, €30 or €40 million could go towards research and development, and €10 million would go towards a dividend for the shareholders.

Austin Ahern, however, was sombre, pointing out that such an idea had often been mooted – and was rejected at every turn. He didn't point out – and probably didn't need to – that if they were struggling to raise barely more than €1 million, €50 million was unlikely. 'Any institutional investor is probably going to look for 15–20 per cent equity,' he said. 'And they are probably going to look for two to three directors on the board – and they'd be well entitled to.' No, Ahern concluded, the saving of Steorn lay in their own hands. 'If we are going to salvage something from the wreckage, we have got to get the right structure in place at board level. Start with the structure, as it is completely wrong currently. We have one man [McCarthy] railroading decisions, [and] there are other people who are better placed to explain how voting rights are working at board level.'

This brought the shareholders to a delicate question: if a new company could be formed – perhaps a public limited company rather than Steorn's current private limited company structure (a change that would make it easier to list on the stock exchange) – could they leave McCarthy in a position of executive power?

Even though McCarthy had stepped down as chief executive after Corbett's attempted coup, there was a perception among the assembled investors that he was still calling the shots. This perception was solidified when Eoghan O'Sullivan said, 'When I was trying to settle things between Pat and Steorn, it was Shaun I was dealing with, not Killian.' There was real fear, however unfounded, that McCarthy would run away with the patents or fail to hand over the battery for validation.

As with any large gathering of angry people, it was loud, it was emotional, it was incoherent and undirected, and, quite often, it was just plain inaccurate.

But it offered several crucial insights into the company and its shareholders, chief among them being their unwavering belief that the technology was still valid. For all the lost money and frustration over strategic decisions, the belief that Steorn had found a way to create energy from nothing had, for a large group of Steorn investors, never been in question.

At the end of the meeting in Port Laoise, the investors agreed on a basic platform of ideas and questions with which to proceed. For the first time, the shareholders held the whip hand, and since they believed fervently in the technological discovery, they felt it was incumbent on them to tell the management what to do.

They compiled a list of questions for Shaun McCarthy and Mike Daly to answer. The list included questions about the structure of any new board; about new testing processes for the Steorn technology; about several major corporate governance issues, not least the issuing of individual share certificates for every shareholder; about a settlement with Pat Corbett; and about an extraordinary general meeting.

As emails from the time show, this list would become the foundation for a series of meetings of shareholders around the country and for protracted negotiations with the management team in East Wall Road. At meetings in Dublin, Navan, Waterford and Cork, shareholders discussed and thrashed out the issues of greatest importance to them.

And yet, the documents from that time show that, 12 years and €23 million after the first 'discovery', after academic validation by a 'Dublin institute', after the jury process, the Kinetica disaster, the Waterways demonstrations, a series of field trials of its battery chargers in several Dublin pubs and the launch of a range of commercial products, Steorn was somehow still talking about that one big score that would prove to the world that the product wasn't simply a misinterpreted reading from a badly designed experiment.

Despite arguments about the number of shareholders on the board and about the corporate structure, it was clear that the investors and management all believed they could get over this hump and move forward.

'A global chip manufacturer has completed phase 1 testing and optimistically has recently begun phase 2 testing,' shareholders were told in one communication. Another message showed that there was broad agreement that just a little more money – between €400,000 and €600,000, in the short term – could get the company through this difficult stretch.

The next thing they needed? 'A public validation, and work has started to produce an events charging station.' This would consist of 'a mass of Steorn batteries built into a mobile unit … fitted with a number of charging connections for mobile phones to be quickly boost charged at public events such as for instance the ploughing championships.'

The device, which would would cost €420,000 to develop, would be presented at the National Ploughing Championships. Doing this would 'give unequivocal and very welcome proof of concept to all the nay-sayers once it has been field-trialled. Then we move towards licensing and an eventual return on investment.'

Needless to say, this never came to pass. According to one account, the company had run out of money within a few weeks of the proposal to build this device and the sheriff was ringing the doorbell with a warrant to close Steorn on behalf of the Revenue Commissioners. At that point, a number of investors had clubbed together to offer around €400,000, which would have mostly gone to pay off the Revenue Commissioners and the bulk of the rest to pay staff redundancies and certain unspecified settlements with former staff, leaving Steorn with just €60,000. It cost, according to this account, roughly €85,000 a month to run the company.

These efforts, however valiant, would simply not be enough. The company was now months away from being placed into liquidation.

––––––––––

On 25 October 2016, a few months after the meeting in Port Laoise, an email arrived in the inboxes of several hundred Steorners. Its subject was 'Important Announcement from Steorn Ltd'.

> The board … wish to advise you that, regrettably, it has been left with no option but to file for voluntary liquidation. As you will be aware, there have been sustained and determined efforts by the company over the last number of months to raise additional investment. The research and development

work on building power output units that would give accreditation to Steorn's technology has progressed further in that period, but unfortunately the funds required to sustain the necessary work to completion have not been forthcoming.

The board has, very reluctantly, taken the decision to appoint a liquidator. It had been believed until very recently that such a drastic action would not be necessary. Unfortunately, this belief did not materialise.

The board would like to place on record its gratitude to all those who invested in, and supported, the company's efforts in pursuing its ambitious objectives. It would also like to place on record its gratitude to all those who have worked with Steorn over the years for their ambition, skill, dedication and hard work.

While acknowledging [that] this announcement represents a hugely disappointing and bitter blow to both groups, the commercial reality is, unfortunately, unavoidable.

In December 2016, RTÉ broadcast a programme about Steorn in its flagship current affairs programme, *Prime Time*. Presented by Robert Shortt, it gave a brief history of the company and interrogated its claims. Much of it was standard Steorn material, but RTÉ went to Paul O'Leary, an engineer at Waterford Institute of Technology, to ask him to evaluate the company's patents. His finding was that the patents

refer to magnetic fields and working with magnetic fields to cause some effects. However, it is not clear in the patents how they would benefit a limitless supply for energy. This is missing both from the protective claims and also from the context surrounding the patents.

In this case, if they were going to be effective, it wasn't clear how they were going to be effective.

Yet many of Steorn's shareholders still seemed to believe that the patents were worth more than anyone was letting on.

19. DEFEAT FROM THE JAWS OF VICTORY

I n late June 2016, the same week that Pat Corbett was attempting to overthrow Shaun McCarthy, the celebrity chef Kevin Dundon took to the stage at a well-known food festival, the Taste of Dublin.

Dundon ran the kitchen at Dunbrody Country House Hotel, presented several of his own cooking shows, wrote the obligatory cookbooks for Christmas, was named 'signature chef' at an Irish gastropub in Walt Disney World in Florida, and boasted of having cooked for a queen, an Irish president and an American president. In a world of almost ubiquitous 'celebrity' chefs, Dundon was one of the most high-profile in Ireland.

He was taking to the stage in Dublin to demonstrate a sous vide cooker, which uses hot water to slowly cook and tenderise food at low temperatures. The cooker was designed to work in conjunction with a mobile phone made by Sony. Users of the phone could control the cooker with an app, flicking the cooker on while on the train home from work so that they could come in to a delicious cooked meal.

The cooker was made by Soho Appliances and it was due to be launched on the market by October 2016, with a price around €450. It was costly, especially for those in the midst of a financial crisis, but a cooker that could be controlled remotely was an attractive concept.

What few knew then was that the company behind the Soho Appliances brand was HephaHeat, and the people due to benefit most from the sale of these 'internet of things' cookers would be the beleaguered Steorn shareholders. Not only that, HephaHeat had a raft of products in various stages of design and production. As well as their contracts with BDR for the water heater – which had been renegotiated slightly to better favour HephaHeat – and the Soho products, HephaHeat was working on a product called SteamBoxx, a steam cleaner, and on a kettle that could boil water in less than a minute. The company was also still in contact with Kohler as well as Sony in relation to other products.

Daly had raised less than €1 million, along with a €30,000 feasibility grant from Enterprise Ireland. It was a fraction of Steorn's €20 million and a fraction of the time, yet within three years HephaHeat had placed itself on the verge of creating multiple products. Steorn, meanwhile, was yet to develop even one working prototype. HephaHeat had been a remarkable feat of economy and ingenuity, and Mike Daly could quite reasonably sit back and contemplate a job well done.

———————

When Steorn was going under in late 2016, Mike Daly and HephaHeat were quietly inching forward. As civil war was taking place in the Steorn boardroom, Kevin Dundon was making his presentation, using HephaHeat products, to visitors at the Taste of Dublin festival. The progress at HephaHeat was real and measurable, as it had recently set out in an email to shareholders.

> Since March 2014 there has been a period of continuous transformation for your company. Mike and his team have been working on developing, testing and trialling products with a view to commercialising same.

Those products included:

1) Steamboxx, our steam cleaning products currently in field trials in several national food outlets.
2) Soho Sous Vide, in association with a nationally renowned chef [Kevin Dundon].
3) Soho beverage system.

> Because of our company size we are challenged by scarce capital and human resources and we are presently, as a Board, taking steps to address these constraints. We are actively considering co-branding and joint venture opportunities to maximise the potential of our products.

The shareholders were told that the Soho Kettle was complete and would be launching in autumn, together with the Soho Sous Vide. The SteamBoxx cleaners had been placed in Supermac's fast-food restaurants around Ireland for testing. And the company was still in the midst of fruitful research work with BDR Thermea.

HephaHeat was being run by Mike Daly, Jim Grant and Roger Hatfield, and they were making progress. They hadn't got any more money from Enterprise Ireland after the initial €30,000 feasibility grant, and they hadn't been admitted into EI's High Performance Unit, an accelerator programme for promising start-ups. Nonetheless, there was just enough money available to get them through particular projects.

They had started off with €393,621 in the bank and had spent €274,984 – a lean operation, when salaries and material costs are factored in. It was, perhaps, an unconscious decision not to do things as Steorn had done them during the Celtic Tiger, when people were handing them cheques and slapping them on the back – almost, as Daly would later recall, thanking them for allowing them to invest.

Instead of raising money all in one big lump, HephaHeat had raised small sums as it needed them and linked them tightly to specific milestones. If it didn't reach the milestones with that sum, it wouldn't get any more. So far it had always reached those milestones, and the documents lodged with the Companies Registration Office show just how many fundraisers it had had in those three or so years.

By the time Steorn went bust, HephaHeat had raised €990,000 from Pat Corbett (though, as was typical of Corbett's money, it was never clear if it was his or someone else's) and €300,000 from Eamonn McKenna, Folke Rohrssen, James Murphy, J.J. Sullivan and Pat Corbett. It had also raised money from several new investors, including two Wexford businessmen, David Pym and David Murphy, and a Meath businessman, Kieran Meegan.

HephaHeat had also spent frugally. By the end of 2016, of the €986,102 they had raised, they would spend only €860,111. The relatively frugal approach had served the company well, but the email they'd sent out to investors wasn't merely a cheerful update: it was a cash call. Firstly, the Soho

Kettle was ready and a manufacturer had been found in China, but this would require money. Secondly, the company had struck a deal with BDR to deliver a prototype and now it needed money to build it. The prototype was due in early 2017 and BDR had made a down payment to partially fund building it. All of which meant that Daly and his team were into a critical phase of the company's development and they would need to go back to the shareholders to raise more money.

Their timing in doing so could hardly have been worse: the HephaHeat email was arriving in shareholders' inboxes just as they were learning of Steorn's liquidation, and it was not a receptive audience. Daly, though he had since left Steorn, became a lightning rod for their anger and resentment.

Daly knew that the shareholders were in shock and would view him as a proxy for Shaun McCarthy or Pat Corbett – depending on which way they had swung in the civil war for Steorn – but he also knew that HephaHeat had precious little by way of cash reserves. That hundred grand could be stretched only so far.

It was a bitter irony: the main criticism of Steorn was that it raised too much and felt obliged to spend it in increasingly imprudent ways; HephaHeat had done the opposite, raising money incrementally and communicating regularly with shareholders, only for the new company to be punished for Steorn's profligacy anyway.

Daly arranged his own series of meetings with shareholders around the country and found that he was merely stepping into Steorn's footprints. Instead of fruitful conversations about fundraising targets and progress milestones, he was subjected to shouting, accusations and recriminations from a large rump of angry investors.

While there were plenty of people who supported HephaHeat, it soon became clear to Daly that a certain amount of vengeance was about to be meted out to whoever was left within the shareholders' sights. Steorn might be gone and Shaun McCarthy gone to ground, but HephaHeat and Daly were still around, and by way of retribution for 12 years and €23 million of investment between Steorn and HephaHeat, someone was going to have to pay. What the shareholders wanted was a management clear-out, removing any trace of Steorn and installing themselves as bosses. They wanted a revolution.

Daly understood that people were angry and wanted him to step down. He told himself that it didn't matter that people had been grown-ups when they invested in the company; that they had been told it was high risk but potentially high reward, with the emphasis on high risk; that they had been told that this technology was controversial because it claimed it could break the laws of physics; that a lot of Irish companies don't work out; and that an even larger number of Irish technology companies don't work out. Daly, although knowing that they were entitled to their anger, couldn't understand the conspiracy theories or why people told him that they simply *knew* he and Shaun McCarthy and Pat Corbett had split the money three ways and that the only thing they had yet to figure out was why they weren't all living on their own islands.

Every HephaHeat fundraising meeting, it seemed to Daly, swiftly veered off into rants about Steorn – with a focus on the whereabouts of the Steorn patents. Daly knew he had to let people vent, but the need to raise funds seemed to be sliding down the priority list. If Daly was looking for quick money to finish the projects, he wasn't going to get it.

By November 2016, the shareholders had decided that Daly should be demoted to acting CEO. He took it with equanimity, agreeing to step down and, reading between the lines, understanding that he would later step down again to an operational or technological role. It struck him as a reasonable move. Even allowing for the heightened emotion of the situation, perhaps a non-engineer – someone with marketing or specific industry knowledge – could step in and take the company forward in a way he couldn't. He wasn't about to let his ego get in the way of the company's progress, and he could console himself by looking at a job well done. Also, even if he wasn't a director, he was still a shareholder.

So, he concluded, change might well be a good thing. But then he saw exactly what changes they were proposing. In November, the new shareholders – led by John V. Farrelly – announced that they would be reconstituting the board and adding three sub-committees: finance;

intellectual property and legal; and marketing. Each committee would have four people and 'be formed with a lead person ultimately responsible for the work of the committee and the reporting of the committees' work and findings to the board for consideration'. Three committees of four people – together with Farrelly, Jim Grant and Roger Hatfield – meant that a company with three employees – Daly and two fellow engineers – now had fifteen people running it.

It struck Daly as ludicrous, but more worryingly, they were still waiting for the €100,000 the shareholders had promised. Though they had received commitments for the money, it hadn't yet been produced. The email that called for volunteers to the board had added, 'Please be assured that funds committed will be held in a separate account and will be returned in the event that the company fails to reach a €100,000 minimum target.'

By December 2016 they still hadn't got there. On 5 December an email from Roger Hatfield notified shareholders that they had received the commitments for money but that the funds hadn't yet been sent. 'We would ask that anyone who has committed funds but has not sent the funds to please do so today,' he wrote. 'We need to complete the funding process by receiving the funds already committed.'

Two days later, shareholders were told that 'commitments for over €100,000 had been received with some €66,000 either in the bank or en route. Funds will not be released until the target €100,000 has been received.'

They were also told that Daly and Hatfield had resigned as directors after a meeting of the 'newly appointed directors and the three shareholder committees for HephaHeat'.

———————

Daly, though now removed as HephaHeat CEO and resigned as a director, remained an employee; he would have to run any decisions past an expanded board that was still feeling its way into the operations of the company.

He was initially told that the company would have to freeze wages for the three staff members. He angrily told the board that this would kill the company. The board paid the wages, but by now great uncertainty had started to creep into the company. They got through Christmas, but Daly seemed to find himself continually at odds with the board over money.

John V. Farrelly brought in a venture capital investment adviser from Philadelphia and asked Daly to make a presentation. He did, presuming that this was for the €100,000 they were still trying to raise. Instead, the adviser recommended that the company be restructured and that €1.5 million be raised. It struck Daly as absurd that a company with no CEO, more board members than employees and no sign of the €100,000 they were supposed to be raising could talk about figures like €1.5 million.

After one particularly frosty meeting with the board in February 2017 – a meeting led by Farrelly – Daly tendered his resignation. It had been less than two months since the board had taken over.

Daly told BDR Thermea that HephaHeat was under new management and then used the next few weeks of his notice period to finish the test system – assisted in no small part by the money BDR had sent the company up front – before leaving on 7 March 2017.

———————

In late March 2017, John V. Farrelly wrote to shareholders to give them an update on the company's progress. The new board, he wrote, had met 'over 12 times since their appointment' and the three board committees had been 'very active'.

HephaHeat had received more than €110,000 in funding commitments, so it had been 'decided to continue operations', including 'making necessary payments to the staff, rent, insurance and to maintain the [intellectual property]'.

They were concentrating on delivering an 'upgraded unit' to BDR that would 'release a further payment from them' of €13,000. They were also hoping to 'open the door' to further negotiations with BDR.

The original staff of HephaHeat had all now left, so the work was being done by 'experienced engineers under short term contracts'. This, Farrelly told them, had 'resulted in some delays but will provide third-party validation of the technology. The company hopes to have a working prototype suitable for delivery to BDR Thermea by the end of April [or] early May [2017]'.

The board had also concluded that the fast-boil kettle and the sous vide cooker that Kevin Dundon had presented in Dublin were, for financial reasons, 'prohibitive at this stage and would be addressed once more resources were in place'. They were still trying to decide what to do about the SteamBoxx cleaning products.

Finally, in relation to its finances, Farrelly wrote, the company was keeping its fingers crossed for the €13,000 from BDR as well as for a €58,000 research and development tax credit, and 'regular meetings are being held with potential investors'. The company 'urgently needs to draw down on the balance of commitments made by shareholders last December in order to maintain momentum'.

It seemed as if the company was hanging its hopes on acquiring the Steorn patents. In his memo to shareholders, Farrelly wrote that HephaHeat had

> reviewed the situation with the patent lawyers PR Kelly who were assist-ing the company in reviewing the existing IP [intellectual property]. Once resources allow, they can assist in making further patent applications in the company's own name. Following meetings with [the accountancy firm] Grant Thornton and other potential investors, it was clear that, before fur-ther material investment could be found, the company needed to secure de-finitively its rights to the IP.

Meanwhile, HephaHeat had 'recorded its ownership interest in the IP with the liquidator of Steorn who acknowledged the company's position. The formal acquisition will take a number of weeks.' Once the patents had been secured, Farrelly wrote,

> a new identity and capital structure will be devised for presentation to shareholders at an EGM in May or June this year [2017]. This will recognise the relative rights of shareholders who have subscribed cash

into HephaHeat and those whose shareholding mirrors their original investments into Steorn prior to June 2014 and be as fairly constructed as possible.

Whatever that meant in practice, the goal was to get more investment, perhaps even from Enterprise Ireland.

———————

By July 2017, however, HephaHeat was still looking for money. An email sent in late July by Roger Hatfield informed investors that the company had been delayed in sending its usual updates by third parties, including 'our actual and potential customers, the Steorn liquidator and his agent, and the Revenue Commissioners, all of whom have delayed us in one way or another'. It was clear from Hatfield's email that the prototype for BDR still had not been delivered, even though

> the viability of the technology has been independently validated by a local technology firm which has agreed to provide the engineering work to complete the testing and delivery of the prototype to BDR at a modest cost to us. Our legal interest in the IP underlying our technology, originally licensed from Steorn, has been forcefully expressed and we have made an offer to the liquidator at modest cost.

The shareholders were voting with their wallets, however, and the money was still not coming in in sufficient volumes.

> To continue this progress all seven members of your board and committee members have each recently subscribed a further 500 to enable operations to continue and we urgently request that those who offered to subscribe to our round last Christmas continue their support by each subscribing at least a further 500 now to enable us to meet our targets.

To date, Hatfield wrote, the company had received €76,600 from the original commitments of €110,000.

To let the opportunity for a return slip by for the sake of very modest resources by completing our target investment of over €100,000 would we feel
be a terrible shame.

Unlike Steorn, which died in a firestorm of recriminations and anger,
HephaHeat – its smaller and quieter offshoot – seemed to fade away, starved
of attention and finance.

The investors who said they'd invest never did, while the investors who
invested on the promise that it would be returned never got theirs back.
HephaHeat published a final set of accounts that showed that, by the end of
December 2017, it had raised €1,007,949 and spent €942,841. It was owed
€155,735 by its debtors (mostly tax credits); it owed its creditors €89,773
(mostly money owed to other companies); and it had €450 in cash.

Nobody knows exactly when the company shut its doors, but according
to some accounts, when they left Unit 10 in the Docklands Innovation Park
on East Wall Road – the last remnant of the Steorn saga – the owner of the
park cleared out the premises and threw everything in a skip outside. A few
days later, it was collected – three years and nearly €950,000 in hard work
and engineering – and dumped.

20. THE END

David Van Dessel, a partner with the accountancy firm Deloitte, was appointed liquidator of Steorn in February 2017. A liquidator's job is to interrogate the accounts of the company, weigh up the value of its assets, estimate what it owes its creditors and distribute the former to the latter. If the liquidator comes across something untoward, they have the right to forward a report to the proper authorities for further investigation.

Van Dessel did the usual things a liquidator would do, such as determine just what the employees – now former employees – were owed in salary and try to get them paid. In that endeavour, he got €64,718 from the Department of Social Protection and paid it over to the workers.

He also managed to get some money that might not have initially appeared to be there, including a refund of €24.92 from Bank of Ireland against bank account charges, as well as on its overall bank charges of €212.53. He also discovered that the company was owed €296,915 in special tax credits designed to stimulate innovative research in Irish business.

In May 2017, Van Dessel put Steorn's assets up for sale at the Cookstown Industrial Estate in Tallaght, Dublin, through Cooney's Industrial Valuers. There were the predictable items, like oscilloscopes for displaying electronic test results, an energy transducer, a gaussmeter, a robotic arm for a display model and slightly more than a dozen battery cases for the failed O-Cube.

Then there were some less predictable items: a limited-edition framed and glazed Picasso lithograph, a coffin and a full-sized replica suit of armour, incorporating a 'candle shelf within the pierced metal torso complete with shield and axe'.

Liquidators reports filed with the Companies Registration Office show that Van Dessel took in €12,624 from the auction of Steorn's assets, and the auction itself had cost €2,293.

To date, after the sale of assets and the payment of creditors, Steorn has a sum total of €76,787.80 left in its account. Enough, incidentally, to have

funded HephaHeat in its final push to deliver that heating unit to BDR
Thermea.

What of the patents? The accounts for the company show that Van
Dessel had engaged Metis Partners, a specialist patent and intellectual
property firm, for €5,000 to arrange the sale of the patents. The deal,
apparently, never went through.

For those who had watched Steorn closely, this was the moment when –
had the company been a scam, and had money been spirited away to a tax
haven or to a bank account without showing legitimate paperwork – Van
Dessel would have discovered it. But he didn't find anything. Having gone
through the books and the records, examining payments in and out, he
found that every penny was accounted for. Insofar as anything at Steorn was
normal, their spending was normal. Despite the anger at the shareholders'
meetings, the money went where Steorn said it went.

———————

In November 2016, just after the Steorn liquidation had been announced
but before David Van Dessel was appointed I met Shaun McCarthy in that
coffee shop near Trinity College, Dublin. He was a broken man. His usual
machine-gun-speed, chuckle-peppered rhetorical style had evaporated,
and he spoke slowly and ruefully about the collapse of Steorn. Everyone
had lost money on Steorn, including McCarthy, who had put a quarter of a
million euro into the company. But no one had lost their reputation the way
McCarthy had.

A year after that, I met him again in his new office in an industrial
estate on the west side of Dublin. He was back to his old self, ebullient, self-
deprecating, smoking heavily and attempting to blow the smoke out the
window with the aid of a household fan.

To online poker – which he still played for additional money – he had
added an interest in cryptocurrencies. He had set up a business in this new
premises, which was filled to the brim with rows of hard drives running
constantly, generating the computational power to back up large volumes of
cryptocurrencies.

He called the new company Suthain, an Irish word meaning 'eternal' – something that would never die, like a battery, or a dream.

Shaun McCarthy: Lessons

I've probably taken on board an awful lot about how we should've approached the project [of Steorn]. And so, when the day came that the office shut down – it was a Friday – we were back working on the battery on the Monday.

In what capacity? Entirely myself, a few of the guys, and entirely privately. We spoke to most of the shareholders and said, 'Look, if this shit goes under and we make anything of this, you'll get whatever shares in a new company that we found. But we're not doing this business of coming out and reporting to you every three months. We're not doing this with any publicity. But we sure ain't giving up. This is going to take a long time.' That was something that we didn't realise at the beginning, and we came to realise it at the end. This isn't something – unfortunately – that's going to happen any time fast.

Or, at least, it shouldn't have been funded the way it was. I take responsibility, but it was only with the benefit of hindsight that we realised this is more of a philanthropist kind of investment. Saying, 'Look, give us a shot; give us 20 years to have a go at this, because, on the off-chance that we pull it off, the positive consequences are going to be so great' – instead of 'Get into this; we're going to conquer the mobile phone market: we're all going to go home in limos, blah, blah, blah,' which creates this type of requirement to move forward and be seen to move forward, which was fundamental in a lot of the things we did that turned out to be wrong.

Except for the last thing – the O-Phone and O-Cube – which I certainly knew was a last roll of the dice, or the last chip in the casino – everything before that we did thinking that we'd a really good chance of pulling it off.

But I've since come to the conclusion that we approached this completely wrong from the beginning.

Which is a horrible, horrible, horrible thing, because a lot of people lost a lot of money.